The Case against War

The Essential Legal Inquiries, Opinions and Judgments Concerning War in Iraq

Edited by George Farebrother
and Nicholas Kollerstrom

SPOKESMAN
for the
Institute for Law and Peace
and the
Legal Inquiry Steering Group

The Institute for Law and Peace may be contacted via its website
(www.inlap.freeuk.com)

First Published in 2003
Second revised edition published in 2004 by Spokesman
Russell House, Bulwell Lane
Nottingham
NG6 0BT
England
Phone 0115 970 8318.   Fax 0115 942 0433
e-mail elfeuro@compuserve.com
www.spokesmanbooks.com

ISBN 0 85124 692 3

A CIP Catalogue is available from the British Library

Printed by the Russell Press Ltd (phone 0115 978 4505)

CONTENTS

FOREWORD
by Lord Murray
(Former Lord Advocate of Scotland and High Court Judge)

The "Case, against the War" is the absorbing contemporary record of a valiant
- if predictably unavailing - endeavour of people-power to bring to account
the U.K. Government's conduct as a matter of law in its proposed support of
the U.S. in its intention to use force to compel Iraq to change its ways. The
calm logic and rigour of legal reasoning of the highest calibre is brought to
bear in presenting the case for and against the legality at international law of
the impending intervention, purportedly in support of the authority of the
U.N. Security Council. The bare bones are laid forth without spin, or
comment, giving this legal material austere authority.

The focus from High Court judge to BBC documentary is exclusively on
international law. This is a strength and perhaps also a weakness for
international law is only one dimension of a problem which encompasses
morality and political justification as well as legality. These aspects are fully
canvassed along with law in the House of Lords' debate on the legality of the
proposed Iraq war on 17 March 2003 (H.o.L. Hansard. vol.646, cols.68-96
and 106-124*) which was a debate of the highest quality but without a vote.
The present legal discussion with its judgements is a fitting complement.

On this occasion the attempt to stop a resort to force, of highly dubious
legality, did not succeed. Unhappily other occasions may well arise; and, of
course, the U.K.- and U.S. - may yet be called to account before a competent
international court or tribunal for their incursion into Iraq. It is too early to
conclude that twentieth century efforts to outlaw war in the Treaty of Paris
1928 and the U.N.Charter 1945 have ended in failure on the threshold of the
twenty-first century. Instead we must redouble our efforts to build for the
peoples of the world a just and secure international order in which war can be
effectively outlawed without allowing oppression and injustice to flourish.

PREFACE

By Dr Mark Levene, Department of History
Southampton University
& Dr Nick Kollerstrom STS Department at University College, London.

"We're being told a lot about the doctrine of pre-emptive strikes... Given that our defence secretary Geoff Hoon explicitly threatened to use 'our' nuclear weapons system, Trident, against the Iraqi civilians in the defence committee of the House of Commons on 20 March would it not be essential in a democracy, given the fundamental commitment we have to the rule of law.... for a UK citizen to challenge that decision if it was in breach of international humanitarian law? As a lawyer, I say it is."

Phil Shiner, 'the Future of Democracy,' Imperial College, November 2, 2002

This dossier is a weighty legal document, full of intricate, and detailed considerations as one might expect from learned lawyers and QCs' examining a complex issue of law. But it grew out of a very simple issue that should matter to everyone who lives in Britain and which we can all grasp. We hear a great deal, especially from government, about the value of our much-vaunted British democracy and how our democratic parliamentary-based system of governance is founded on the rule of law. We are all supposedly participants in this system and the notion of good citizenship has even become part of our school curriculum.

So, how is it that when a decision as fundamental as going to war is taken, law, Parliament, citizenship and democracy all seem to be thrown out of the window? The government has repeatedly stated since the events of 11th September 2001 that any military action it undertook would be in compliance with international law. However, there was no judicial review in the High Court with regard to its participation in the war in Afghanistan, nor was one ever offered with regard to further proposed military action against Iraq. Equally, there was no parliamentary vote until the troops were actually deployed.

In high parlance, this is what is known as a democratic deficit. For those at the grass-roots who would wish to establish a democratic credit, some mechanism has to be found to challenge the government's impunity and not least its face-value assumption that pre-emptive military action against Iraq was lawful.

In the summer of 2002 an ad-hoc group of legal experts and peace activists came together to form *The Legal Inquiry Steering Group* (LISG), believing that the issue should not go untried. A key component of this group was Peacerights, the Birmingham-based legal service that specifically deals with issues of international human rights and humanitarian law. It is primarily through the actions of Peacerights that this corpus of legal arguments has been developed. The High Court of Justice in The Strand, London, refused to accept CND's argument - presented here in Part II - by declining to express an opinion on whether it would be legal for Britain to initiate war. As a matter of International law, the judges argued it was not within their remit. Then Britain's Attorney-General, Lord Peter Goldsmith, expressed the view that three UN Security-Council resolutions taken together warranted a legal justification for the war. This work argues against that view.

These 2002 UK debates synchronised with the setting up of the UN-sponsored International Criminal Court in The Hague. The ICC reaffirmed the Nuremberg Principles of 1948 concerning the personal moral responsibility of politicians and soldiers, and the concept of crimes against humanity: "The International Criminal Court will be able to prosecute individuals charged with genocide, crimes against humanity and war crimes. There is no immunity against the jurisdiction of the Court"[1].

However, the ICC is not presently empowered to deal with the crime of aggression, as expressed in the 6th Nuremberg Principle: a 'Crime against Peace' is the 'Planning, preparation, initiation, or waging of a war of aggression or a war in violation of international treaties, agreements or assurances.' The attack upon Iraq is a clear instance of transgression of this 6th Nuremberg principle. The letters sent by Public Interest Lawyers (see Appendix) to the Prime Minister and Defence Secretary give one hope for the recognition of international law principles by politicians in the future.

Tam Dalyell, Father of the House of Commons, has said of the Prime Minister: "I believe that since Mr Blair is going ahead with his support for a US attack without unambiguous UN authorisation, he should be branded as a war criminal and sent to The Hague ... Blair is a man who has disdain for both the house and international law" (27.3.03 The Guardian). The Coalition partners, that is most specifically those who planned, organised and executed this war, cannot and must not be allowed to remain above the law, or to assume that they can act with such impunity again. Peace, and indeed the continuance of civilised life as we know it could now well hinge upon the culprits being brought to justice.

The UK now has a higher proportion of its citizens behind bars than any other nation in Western Europe, according to Home Office figures for 2003 (139 per 100,000, c.f. 85 France and 686 for America) - an achievement of the present government. Persistent government criminality in waging its wars of aggression could be a major factor that has brought about this situation: how, after all, can citizens be expected to obey domestic law, if the Government is seen to flout international law? America, with seven times more of its citizens behind bars that the European average, has been leading the way with its disdain for the international laws of war. But, for free and open societies to endure, they surely need a serious and shared respect for the Geneva conventions - and, Nuremberg Principles.

[1] *Glen Rangwala, The Promise of Justice - first Steps towards an International Criminal Court, 2002, (INLAP publication).*

SUMMARY OF CITIZENS' LEGAL ACTIONS

A Citizens' Legal Inquiry into the Legality of use of force against Iraq on October 11 2002 at Gray's Inn, London was chaired by Professor Colin Warbrick, Professor of Law at Durham University. Rabinder Singh QC of Matrix Chambers argued the case for illegality, and Julian Knowles, also of Matrix, put the case of the UK Government. Professor Warbrick concluded that the use of armed force against Iraq, in the absence of a clear UN Security Council mandate, would be in breach of international law. The Legal Inquiry Steering Group raised £8,000 from ordinary activists to help pay for the Legal Inquiry.

A Legal Challenge to the Government took place on 19 November 2002 when lawyers for the Campaign for Nuclear Disarmament (CND) sent a letter to the Prime Minister, Defence Secretary Geoff Hoon and Foreign Secretary Jack Straw. This warned that they would face a legal challenge unless they gave a written guarantee within 7 days that the UK would not use armed force against Iraq without a further United Nations Security Council Resolution. There was no satisfactory response and on 28 November the High Court was asked for a judicial review to decide the matter. However, the court did not allow the case to come to trial. On 17 December Lord Justice Simon Brown ruled that in order to decide whether war would be unlawful, the courts would have to interpret UN Resolution 1441. Normally, he said, "English courts will not rule upon the true meaning and effect of international instruments which apply only at the level of international law."

A Shadow Judicial Review by the BBC programme "Today". This took place on 19 December at the Inner Temple, London and investigated whether British involvement in any war against Iraq, without further specific UN endorsement, would be legal under international law. The programme makers expressly acknowledged that it was directly inspired by LISG-initiated Citizens' Legal Inquiry at Grays Inn. Professor Nicholas Grief, Head of the School of Finance & Law at Bournemouth University, argued that a war under these conditions would be illegal. Professor Anthony Aust, Deputy Director of the British Institute of International and Comparative Law, and formerly Deputy Legal Adviser of the Foreign and Commonwealth Office, made the case that a strike could be legal. Professor Vaughan Lowe, Fellow of All Souls College, and a barrister practising from Essex Court Chambers, acting as judge, was persuaded by Professor Grief's argument and BBC listeners had a rare opportunity to hear a legal analysis of the Iraq crisis.

Further Opinions

On 23 January and 3 March 2003 Rabinder Singh QC & Charlotte Kilroy provided CND with further opinions on the potential use of armed force by the UK against Iraq relating to Resolutions 678 and 1441. With the outbreak of hostilities imminent the Attorney General issued a written Parliamentary answer to outline his view on the legality of military action. The following day this was contested by a letter from lawyers acting for CND.

On 6 June 2003 Rabinder Singh & Charlotte Kilroy provided an opinion for CND and Peacerights on the implications of the absence to date of the discovery of weapons of mass destruction in Iraq since its invasion on 20 March 2003 and strongly recommended a judicial inquiry to examine the issue. On 23 July 2003 they provided a further opinion on the legality of the occupation of Iraq by UK armed forces.

A War Crimes Project. Legal actions prior to March 2003 concerned the legality of initiating war. With the outbreak of war a new question arose - the legality of how it was actually conducted. On 22 January 2003 Public Interest Lawyers wrote to the Prime Minister, the Foreign Secretary and the Secretary of State for Defence informing them that their conduct of any attack on Iraq would be carefully monitored.

As there was no satisfactory reply to these letters Peacerights held a war crimes inquiry in London on 8-9 November 2003. A panel of eight eminent lawyers, mainly British but including representatives from France, Canada and Ireland, heard evidence from eyewitnesses and experts on aspects of the military operation against Iraq in 2003.

Their report cited the use by the British military of cluster bombs in civilian areas and said that Britain was complicit in the actions of the US military, including the killing of international journalists. The panel answered yes to the question "Is there sufficient cause and evidence for the International Criminal Court prosecutor to investigate members of the UK government for breaches of the Rome Statute of the International Criminal Court (ICC) in relation to crimes against humanity and/or war crimes committed during the Iraq conflict and occupation 2003?"

A copy of the findings was sent to the ICC, which is based in the Hague, and to the Attorney General, Lord Goldsmith. The ICC Prosecutor is bound to consider whether to initiate a formal investigation and, in the light of the eminence of the Professors and the clear nature of the concerns, is likely to do so. If he does he must report to the Pre-Trial Chamber of the ICC who make the decision whether to prosecute.

Phil Shiner of Peacerights said: "International law does not recognise victor's justice and both sides to the Iraq war must be fully accountable. Many respected groups and lawyers have expressed serious concerns about the apparently unnecessary and unjustified civilian casualties, particularly because of the use of cluster bombs in urban areas. It is critically important for those who lost their lives, and for future generations facing future wars, that the leaders of governments waging war are fully accountable for war crimes committed. There must now be a full and proper investigation and serious consideration given to prosecuting those with ultimate responsibility."

PART I

A CITIZENS' INQUIRY CONCERNING THE LEGALITY OF A
PROSPECTIVE USE OF FORCE BY THE UNITED KINGDOM AGAINST
IRAQ (11 OCTOBER 2002)

1.   THE CASE AGAINST WAR: 8 OCTOBER 2002:RABINDER SINGH QC & JANET KENTRIDGE

****

Inquiry into the Legality of the Use of Force by the United Kingdom against Iraq

Skeleton Argument on behalf of Peacerights

Introduction

1.   This inquiry concerns the legality of the use of force by the United Kingdom against Iraq. Peacerights will invite the Inquiry to reach the following conclusion:

'The Inquiry concludes that it would be unlawful for the United Kingdom to launch or take part in a military attack on Iraq under present circumstances without the express authorisation of a United Nations resolution.'

2.   In essence, Peacerights contends that:

   (1)   the right of self-defence would not justify the use of force against Iraq by the United Kingdom;

   (2)   Iraq's alleged failure to comply with all or any of the existing 23 UN Security Council resolutions would not justify the use of force by the United Kingdom; and

   (3)   a further UN Security Council resolution would be required clearly to authorise such use of force.

3.   These contentions are based, in summary, on the following arguments:

   (1)   The use of force against Iraq would not be justified under international law unless:

      (a)   Iraq mounted a direct attack on the United Kingdom or one of its allies and that ally requested the United Kingdom's assistance; or

        (b)   an attack by Iraq on the United Kingdom or one of its allies was imminent and could be averted in no way other than by the use of force; or

        (c)   the United Nations Security Council authorised the use of force in clear terms.

(2)   Iraq has not attacked the United Kingdom or one of its allies, and no evidence is currently available to the public that any attack is imminent.

(3)   Existing Security Council resolutions do not authorise the use of force against Iraq. Such force would require further clear authorisation from the Security Council.

(4)   The United Kingdom is therefore not entitled, in international law, to use force against Iraq.

Factual Background

4.   The factual background can be outlined briefly. The United States is publicly considering the use of force against Iraq. This use of force would appear to have the aims of (1) destroying such stores of nuclear, chemical, biological and other weapons of mass destruction as Iraq may have; and (2) bringing about a "regime change." The United States appears to consider such action to be justified on the basis of the right to carry out a pre-emptive strike in self-defence, the right to respond in self-defence against an armed attack, (in this case the attacks on 11 September 2001), and/or on the basis of current resolutions of the United Nations Security Council.

5.   The United Kingdom Government is at present considering whether to support any such action by itself joining in the use of force against Iraq. According to Government statements, no decision has yet been taken. The Prime Minister, on 24 September 2002, released a dossier which is said to set out the evidence against Iraq and the arguments in favour of military intervention. In outline, the dossier is said to demonstrate that Iraq has at present:

        (1)   the capability to produce chemical agents mustard gas, sarin, cyclosarin and VX and biological agents anthrax, botulinum toxin, aflatoxin and ricin;

        (2)   up to 20 al-Hussein missiles, with 650km range, the warheads of which carry chemical and biological agents;

        (3)   at least 50 al-Samoud liquid propellant missiles, the range of which is sought to be extended to 200km;

        (4)   the capacity to deploy some chemical and biological weapons within 45 minutes;

(5)   mobile laboratories for producing biological warfare agents;

(6)   expertise and data to make nuclear weapons.

In addition, Iraq is at present said to be seeking:

(1)   nuclear weapons;

(2)   longer range ballistic missiles with a reach of 1000km. A new engine testing stand has been built for this purpose;

(3)   "Front companies in third countries" are seeking propellant chemicals for ballistic missiles, in breach of the UN embargo, as well as uranium from Africa;

(4)   to modify L-29 remote piloted jet trainer aircraft to deliver chemical and biological agents over a large area.

6.   Iraq has persistently failed to co-operate with the UN weapons inspection programme, violating a large number of resolutions of the UN Security Council, so that the weapons inspection team was eventually withdrawn.[1] However, it has recently engaged in negotiations with UN inspection agencies on the terms and conditions upon which the inspection programme could be resumed. After two days of talks with UN inspection agencies held in Vienna, Iraq agreed on 1st October to jettison restrictions on inspections of a large number of sensitive sites. The agreement on practical arrangements did not, however, deal with access to Saddam Hussein's eight presidential compounds. This has led the United States to oppose the return of inspectors to Iraq without a new resolution which fortifies the UN inspections regime and the steps which may be taken upon failure to comply.

7.   Significantly, the United States, supported by the United Kingdom, continues to make strenuous efforts to persuade the UN Security Council to adopt a strongly worded resolution. The terms of the proposed resolution which they have placed before the Security Council, and the significance of this proposal, are considered further below.

The Use of Force in International Law

8.   The United Nations Charter provides the framework for the use of force in international law. Almost all States are parties to this Charter, including Iraq, the United Kingdom and the United States. The Charter emphasises that peace is the fundamental aim of the Charter, and is to be preserved if at all possible. The preamble expresses a determination 'to save succeeding generations from the scourge of war', 'to practise tolerance and live together in peace with one another as good neighbours', 'to unite our strength to maintain international peace and security', and to ensure 'that armed force shall not be used, save in the common interest.'

9. Article 1 of the Charter sets out the United Nations' purposes, the first of which is:

    'To maintain international peace and security; and to that end: to take effective collective measures for the prevention and removal of threats to the peace, and for the suppression of acts of aggression or other breaches of the peace, and to bring about by peaceful means, and in conformity with the principles of justice and international law, adjustment or settlement of international disputes or situations which might lead to a breach of the peace.'

10. The other provisions of the Charter must be interpreted in accordance with this aim: see the 1969 Vienna Convention on the Law of Treaties, Article 31, which provides that a treaty must be interpreted in accordance with its objects and purposes, including its preamble.

11. The Charter goes on to set out two fundamental principles:

    '2(3) All Members shall settle their international disputes by peaceful means in such a manner that international peace and security, and justice, are not endangered.

    2(4) All Members shall refrain in their international relations from the threat or use of force against the territorial integrity or political independence of any state, or any other manner inconsistent with the Purposes of the United Nations.'

12. Article 2(4) has been described by the International Court of Justice (ICJ) as a peremptory norm of international law, from which States cannot derogate (*Nicaragua v United States*, [1986] ICJ Reports 14, at para 190). The effect of Articles 2(3) and 2(4) is that the use of force can *only* be justified as expressly provided under the Charter, and only in situations where it is consistent with the UN's purposes.[2]

13. The Charter authorises the use of force in the situations set out in Chapter VII. Article 42 states that, if peaceful means have not succeeded in obtaining adherence to Security Council decisions, it 'may take such action by air, sea or land forces as may be necessary to maintain or restore international peace and security.' In effect, this means that States require a UN Security Council resolution in order to use force against another State (subject to Article 51: see below). Force is only justified where there are no peaceful means available for resolving the dispute. We stress that, in our view, where Members believe that another State has breached a resolution of the Security Council, they do not have a unilateral right under Article 42 to use force to secure adherence to it or to punish that State: what action should be taken is a matter for the Security Council.

14. Article 51 of the Charter reserves States' rights to self-defence. This right is additional to the provisions of Article 42. A State does not require a Security Council resolution in order to defend itself by force but even the right of self-defence is subject to action by the Security Council, as is clear from the terms of Article 51:

> 'Nothing in the present Charter shall impair the inherent right of individual or collective self-defence if an armed attack occurs against a member of the United Nations, until the Security Council has taken measures necessary to maintain international peace and security. Measures taken by Members in the exercise of this right of self-defence shall be immediately reported to the Security Council and shall not in any way affect the authority and responsibility of the Security Council under the present Charter to take at any time such action as it deems necessary in order to maintain or restore international peace and security.'

15. As exceptions to the fundamental principle of the prohibition on the use of force, Articles 42 and 51 must be interpreted narrowly.

16. According to the Charter, therefore, there are only two situations in which one State can lawfully use force against another:

   (7) In individual or collective self-defence (a right under customary international law, which is expressly preserved by Article 51 of the Charter).

   (8) Pursuant to a UN Security Council resolution.

Self-Defence

17. This skeleton argument deals with the legality of the use of force by the United Kingdom. It does not traverse the argument concerning the legality of the use of force against Iraq by the United States.

18. The United Kingdom has not been the subject of any direct attack which could even arguably be linked with Iraq. It is clear that the right of self-defence *in response* to an armed attack does not arise. The only possible justification is as an *anticipatory* form of self-defence against a future threat. It is our submission that, to the extent that such a right is known to international law, it exists only in a very narrow and defined set of circumstances which do not apply to the United Kingdom at present.

Anticipatory self-defence in international law

19. Article 51 of the Charter is silent about whether 'self-defence' includes the pre-emptive use of force, in addition to the use of force in response to an attack. In order to answer the question, other conventional sources of international law must be used, including state practice and the works

of learned writers on international law. This follows the approach set out in Article 38(1) of the Statute of the International Court of Justice, which provides that:

> 'The Court, whose function is to decide in accordance with international law such disputes as are submitted to it, shall apply:
>
> (a) international conventions, whether general or particular establishing rules expressly recognised by the contesting states;
>
> (b) international custom, as evidence of a general practice accepted as law;
>
> (c) the general principles of law recognised by civilised nations;
>
> (d) subject to the provisions of Article 59, judicial decisions and the teachings of the most highly qualified publicists of the various nations, as subsidiary means for the determination of rules of law.'

20. State practice is ambiguous, but tends to suggest that the anticipatory use of force is not generally considered lawful, or only in very pressing circumstances. There are numerous examples of States claiming to have used force in anticipatory self-defence, and being condemned by the international community. Examples of state practice are given by Professor Antonio Cassese, former President of the International Criminal Tribunal for the Former Yugoslavia, in *International Law*, (Oxford, 2001) at 309-31. One particularly relevant example is the international reaction to an Israeli bombing attack on an Iraqi nuclear reactor:

> When the Israeli attack on the Iraqi nuclear reactor was discussed in the [Security Council], the USA was the only State which (implicitly) indicated that it shared the Israeli concept of self-defence. In addition, although it voted for the SC resolution condemning Israel (resolution 487/1991), it pointed out after the vote that its attitude was only motivated by other considerations, namely Israel's failure to exhaust peaceful means for the resolution of the dispute. All other members of the SC expressed their disagreement with the Israeli view, by unreservedly voting in favour of operative paragraph 1 of the resolution, whereby '[the SC] strongly condemns the military attack by Israel in clear violation of the Charter of the UN and the norms of international conduct.' Egypt and Mexico expressly refuted the doctrine of anticipatory self-defence. It is

apparent from the statements of these States that they were deeply concerned that the interpretation they opposed might lead to abuse. In contrast, Britain, while condemning 'without equivocation' the Israeli attack as 'a grave breach of international law', noted that the attack was not an act of self-defence. Nor [could] it be justified as a forcible measure of self-protection.'' (p310).

21. Cassese concludes that, '[i]f one undertakes a perusal of State practice in the light of Article 31 of the Vienna Convention on the Law of Treaties, it becomes apparent that such practice does not evince agreement among States regarding the interpretation or the application of Article 51 with regard to anticipatory self-defence.' (*International Law* (Oxford, 2001) at p309).

22. Oppenheim states that:

> 'while anticipatory action in self-defence is normally unlawful, it is not necessarily unlawful in all circumstances, the matter depending on the facts of the situation including in particular the seriousness of the threat and the degree to which pre-emptive action is really necessary and is the only way of avoiding that serious threat; the requirements of necessity and proportionality are probably even more pressing in relation to anticipatory self-defence than they are in other circumstances.' (R Jennings QC and A Watts QC (eds), Oppenheim's International Law: Ninth Edition 1991 pp41-42)[3]

23. Detter states that, 'it must be emphasised that anticipatory force falls under the prohibition of force in Article 2(4) of the Charter entailing a presumption that it is illegal. A mere threat of attack thus does not warrant military action...' (*The Law of War*, Second Edition, (Cambridge, 2000), p86).

24. Cassese considers that, '[i]n the case of anticipatory self-defence, it is more judicious to consider such action as *legally prohibited* while admittedly knowing that there may be cases where breaches of the prohibition may be justified on moral and political grounds...' (*International Law*, (Oxford, 2001), p311).

25. To the extent that international law recognises that States *may* have the right to defend themselves by using force to pre-empt an imminent and serious attack, such use of force would have to be in accordance with the general rules and principles governing self-defence. These are well summarised by Oppenheim:

> 'The development of the law, particularly in the light of more recent state practice, in the 150 years since the <u>Caroline</u> incident suggests that action, even if it involves the use of

armed force and the violation of another state's territory, can be justified as self defence under international law where:

(a) an armed attack is launched, *or is immediately threatened*, against a state's territory or forces (and probably its nationals);

(b) there is an *urgent necessity* for defensive action against that attack;

(c) there is *no practicable alternative* to action in self-defence, and in particular another state or other authority which has the legal powers to stop or prevent the infringement does not, or cannot, use them to that effect;

(d) the action taken by way of self-defence is limited to what is necessary to stop or prevent the infringement, ie to the needs of defence...' (p412, emphasis added)

26. These principles would apply to the anticipatory use of force just as to any other use of force in self-defence.

Anticipatory self-defence is not justified in present circumstances

27. To the extent that international law recognises at all the right to use anticipatory force in self-defence, any such right, it only exists in situations of great emergency, as set out by Oppenheim.

28. The burden of proof is on the Government to demonstrate the existence of a pressing and direct threat. It would also need to show that there is no effective alternative to the use of force. Neither of those conditions is established by the dossier released on 24th September. The capacity to attack, combined with an unspecified intention to do so in the future, is not sufficiently pressing to justify the pre-emptive use of force. The threat must at least be imminent. The degree of proximity required must also be proportionate to the severity of the threat. A threat to use very serious weapons - nuclear weapons being the obvious example - *could* justify an earlier use of defensive force than might be justified in the case of a less serious threat. However, the existence of the threat, regardless of how serious that threat may be, must still be supported by credible evidence.

29. Iraq has engaged in negotiations with UN weapons inspectors, and has offered to lift restrictions upon the terms upon which such inspectors may return to Iraq. While the agreement may not be as extensive or complete as that sought by the United States and United Kingdom, its very existence tends to belie claims that there is no effective alternative to force.

Collective self-defence

30. As well as the individual use of force, Article 51 preserves the right of *collective* self-defence. This arises only in certain very narrow conditions. In the *Nicaragua* case, the ICJ stated that:

> 'it is the State which has been the subject of an armed attack which must form and declare the view that it has been attacked. There is no rule of customary international law permitting another State to exercise the right of collective self-defence on the basis of its own assessment of the situation. Where collective self-defence is invoked, it is to be expected that the State for whose benefit this right is used will have declared itself to be the victim of an armed attack.' (para 195)

31. In order to justify the use of force against Iraq on the basis of collective self-defence with the United States, there must first be credible evidence that Iraq has carried out, or intends to carry out, an armed attack on the United States or another of the United Kingdom's allies. The United Kingdom Government has supplied no evidence to show that Iraq carried out the terrorist attacks on 11 September 2001. It appears that those attacks were carried out by Al-Qa'ida, an international terrorist organisation with support and funds supplied from a number of countries and with particularly close links to the Taliban regime in Afghanistan, which was used as the basis for the military action taken by the United States, the United Kingdom and others in that country.

32. Further, even if it could be shown that Iraq has funded or otherwise assisted Al-Qa'ida, this does not necessarily justify the use of force in self-defence. According to the ICJ in the *Nicaragua* case:

> 'In the case of individual self-defence, the exercise of this right is subject to the State concerned having been the victim of an armed attack. Reliance on collective self-defence of course does not remove the need for this ... [T]he Court does not believe that the concept of 'armed attack' includes not only acts by armed bands where such acts occur on a significant scale but also assistance to rebels in the form of the provision of weapons or logistical or other support.' (para 195)

33. We are not aware of any proof that Iraq has provided 'weapons or logistical or other support' to Al-Qa'ida. Such support would not, in any event, amount to an armed attack. Unless Iraqi involvement in the September 11 terrorist attacks could meet the higher standard set out in the *Nicaragua* case, namely something *more* than the provision of weapons, logistical or other support, we do not consider that the attacks of September 11 in themselves justify the use of force against Iraq.

34. The issue of collective self-defence was highlighted by the statement of the North Atlantic Council of NATO, on 12 September 2001, that 'if it is determined that this attack was directed from abroad against the United States, it shall be regarded as an action covered by Article 5 of the Washington Treaty ... the United States' NATO allies stand ready to provide the assistance that may be required as a consequence of these acts of barbarism.' On 2 October 2001, NATO declared that it did, in fact, consider that the attacks came from abroad, and that they would therefore be regarded as falling within the scope of Article 5. Article 5 of the Treaty states that:

> 'The Parties agree that an armed attack against one or more of them in Europe or North America shall be considered an attack against them all and consequently they agree that, if such an armed attack occurs, each of them, in exercise of the right of individual or collective self-defence recognised by Article 51 of the Charter of the United Nations, will assist the Party or Parties so attacked by taking forthwith, individually and in concert with other Parties, such action as it deems necessary, including the use of armed force, to restore and maintain the security of the North Atlantic area.'

35. No force has in fact been used by NATO pursuant to the statement of 12 September. Although it has been determined that the acts of terrorism were 'directed from abroad at the United States', no proven link with Iraq has emerged.

36. Crucially, Article 5 is expressly subject to Article 51 of the Charter of the United Nations. All the restrictions on the use of collective self-defence in international law therefore apply. All that Article 5 does is to state in advance that, if the legal conditions for collective self-defence are met in a particular case, the members of NATO will act. Since one of the requirements for collective self-defence is a request from the attacked State, Article 5 provides a standing request from all NATO states for assistance in the event of an attack. The criteria applying to the use of force under Article 51 would still have to be met. It is our submission that as matters stand, they have not been met.

The Role of the Security Council

Article 42

37. The Security Council can authorise the use of force. In doing so it must comply with the constitutional principles of the United Nations, and with the objects and purposes of the Charter. It must be convinced that Iraq poses a 'threat to the peace', and that this threat cannot be averted in any way other than by the use of force (Article 39 of the Charter).

38. Iraq has recently engaged in the Vienna talks with the UN weapons inspectorate, and has made certain concessions which could facilitate a resumption of inspections after a four year lapse. It is at present, therefore, inappropriate to conclude that no alternatives to force are available. If it proves impossible to agree to a viable inspections regime, Iraq's continuing violations *may* lead the Security Council to conclude that peaceful means have failed to ensure compliance and peace, and that the use of force is necessary as a last resort. Having reached that conclusion, the Security Council could then pass a resolution under Article 42, clearly authorising the use of force against Iraq in order to ensure compliance.

39. One argument put forward by the United Kingdom in favour of taking action without consulting the Security Council is that the Security Council may decide *not* to authorise the use of force. The Prime Minister, speaking on 3 September 2002, stated that the UN had to be 'a way of dealing with it, not a way of avoiding dealing with it. It has to be done and we have to make sure there are not people who are simply going to turn a blind eye to this.'

40. This argument implies that the decision to use force is to be made by individual States, and that the Security Council need only endorse that decision. This ignores the constitutional position of the United Nations as a forum for collective decision-making, upon which we elaborate below. Two commentators writing in 1999 argue convincingly that:

> 'If the Security Council is dysfunctional or paralysed by the exercise of the veto, as arguably occurred during the Cold War, the case for implied authorisation might be stronger. However, Council practice since the Cold War simply does not support any greater need for a flexible reinterpretation of the Charter to support the actual behaviour of States. Five times in the past eight years the Security Council has authorised the use of force to address threats to world peace.'[4] (Jules Lobel and Michael Ratner, 'Bypassing the Security Council: Ambiguous Authorizations to use Force, Cease-fires and the Iraqi Inspection Regime' [1999] AJIL 124, at 127).

41. That the Security Council may decide that the use of force is not currently justified is not an argument for refusing to go through it. Only if the current resolutions themselves authorise the use of force could there be a legal basis for military action by the United Kingdom without a further Security Council resolution. In our submission, elaborated below, the existing resolutions give no such authorisation.

Existing Security Council resolutions do not authorise the use of force

42. The Security Council has not passed a resolution expressly authorising the use of force against Iraq since Resolution 678, passed at the start of the Gulf War. The United Kingdom appears prepared to argue that:

   (1)   The current Security Council resolutions implicitly authorise the use of force by Member States in the event of Iraq's persistent non-compliance;

   (2)   Further or alternatively, Iraq's failure to comply with the cease-fire requirements set out in Resolution 687, which brought to an end military action against Iraq during the Gulf War, and amplified subsequently, justify the renewed use of force under Resolution 678, without further authorisation from the Security Council.

43. Resolution 678, at paragraph 2, authorised Member States 'to use all necessary means to uphold and implement resolution 660 (1990) *and all subsequent relevant resolutions* and to restore international peace and security in the area.' (emphasis added) Resolution 660 had the sole aim of restoring the sovereignty of Kuwait. After that had been achieved, Resolution 687 imposed a formal cease-fire. That cease-fire was conditional on Iraq's acceptance of certain terms. It did accept those terms. The Security Council's current requirements of Iraq are contained in Resolution 687 and subsequent resolutions.

44. Those requirements include the destruction of all chemical and biological weapons and all ballistic missiles with a range greater than one hundred and fifty kilometres, the unconditional agreement not to acquire or develop nuclear weapons (Resolution 687, paras 8(a), 8(b), and 12), and full co-operation with the UN-appointed weapons inspectorate. Such inspections were initially the responsibility of the Special Commission and the International Atomic Energy Agency, and are now to be carried out by the United Nations Monitoring, Verification and Inspection Commission (UNMOVIC), established by Resolution 1284 (1999).

45. Shortly after the cease-fire, Resolution 688 dealt with the humanitarian issues arising from the situation in Iraq. It called upon Iraq to allow access to international humanitarian organisations. It is important to note that this resolution was *not* passed under Chapter VII of the Charter, and did not authorise the use of force to achieve its objectives. However, the United States, the United Kingdom and France used Resolution 688 as authority to establish 'safe havens' for Kurds and Shiites, and then to establish no-fly zones over Iraq. These developments are set out in detail in Christine Gray, *International Law and the Use of Force*, (Oxford, 2000) pp 191-192.

46. The United Kingdom and the United States have argued that Resolution 688 implicitly authorised Member States to respond to Iraq's actions, including by establishing no-fly zones, and thereafter to defend those zones by force. They argued that these zones were essential for humanitarian purposes and to monitor Iraq's compliance with the Security Council's requirements. These arguments are convincingly rejected by one legal commentator in the following terms:

> 'In fact there did not seem to be any adequate legal basis for the establishment of the safe havens by the coalition forces. Resolution 688, although referred to at the time by the States involved, clearly does not authorise forcible humanitarian intervention. It was not passed under Chapter VII and did not expressly or implicitly authorise the use of force. The USA, UK and France did not expressly rely on a separate customary law right of humanitarian intervention in any Security Council debates or in their communications to the Security Council at the time of the establishment of the safe havens. Such a right is notoriously controversial; since the Second World War it has always been more popular with writers than with States.' (Christine Gray, 'After the Ceasefire: Iraq, the Security Council and the Use of Force' [1994] BYIL 135, at 162.)

47. Iraq's obligations were further amplified in a series of Resolutions passed after Resolution 688. Among these, in Resolution 707, the Security Council noted Iraq's 'flagrant violation' and 'material breaches' of resolution 687. It considered that these constitute a 'material breach of the relevant provisions of that resolution which established a cease-fire and provided the conditions essential to the restoration of peace and security in the region' (para 1).

48. In Resolution 949, it stressed again that 'Iraq's acceptance of resolution 687 (1991) adopted pursuant to Chapter VII of the Charter of the United Nations forms the basis of the cease-fire' and that 'any hostile or provocative action directed against its neighbours by the Government of Iraq constitutes a threat to peace and security in the region', while 'underlining that it will consider Iraq fully responsible for the serious consequences of any failure to fulfil the demands in the present resolution.' These include, at paragraph 5, full co-operation with the Special Commission.

49. This demand was repeated in resolutions 1051, 1060, 1115, 1134, 1137 and 1154. The latter resolution states that the Security Council is 'determined to ensure immediate and full compliance by Iraq without conditions or restrictions with its obligations under resolution 687 (1991) and the other relevant resolutions'. Significantly, the Security

Council also

> '[s]tresses that compliance by the Government of Iraq with its obligations, repeated again in the memorandum of understanding, to accord immediate, unconditional and unrestricted access to the Special Commission and the IAEA in conformity with the relevant resolutions is necessary for the implementation of resolution 687 (1991), but that any violation would have severest consequences for Iraq.'

50. The Security Council also decides 'to remain actively seized of the matter, in order to ensure implementation of this resolution, and to secure peace and security in the area.'

51. On 5 August 1998, Iraq suspended co-operation with the Special Commission and the IAEA. In resolution 1194, the Security Council stated that this 'constitutes a totally unacceptable contravention of its obligations under [resolution] 687' This condemnation was repeated in resolution 1205, which also demands that Iraq co-operate fully with the Special Commission, and in which the Security Council again remains 'actively seized of the matter.'

52. The key question is whether Resolution 678 still allows Member States to use 'all necessary means' to ensure compliance with subsequent resolutions, or alternatively whether the 'severest consequences' envisaged by the Security Council in Resolution 1154 (now backed up by the demands in Resolution 1205) include the use of force by Member States. In our submission it does not.

53. The International Court of Justice, in the *Namibia Advisory Opinion* (1971) ICJ Reports 15, 53 stated that 'The language of a resolution of the Security Council should be carefully analysed ... having regard to the terms of the resolution to be interpreted, the discussions leading to it, the Charter provisions invoked and, in general, all circumstances that might assist in determining the legal consequences...' This has been described as 'one of the very few authoritative guides to the interpretation of Security Council resolutions' (Michael Byers, 'Terrorism, The Use of Force and International Law after 11 September' (2002) 51 ICLQ 401, at 402).

54. The current resolutions do not, it is submitted, implicitly authorise the use of force. The wording of the Gulf War resolutions shows that, when the Security Council intends to authorise the use of force, it does so in clear terms. Resolution 678 referred to the use of 'all necessary means', phrasing which does not appear in any subsequent Resolution relating to Iraq. The phrase 'all necessary means' has also been used when the Security Council authorised intervention in Rwanda, Bosnia, Somalia

and Haiti. Significantly, that phrase is used in the draft resolution now placed before the UN Security Council by the United States and the United Kingdom. The very concern of these two countries to secure the passing of a resolution in these terms underlines that the existing resolutions do not at present justify the use of all necessary means, and hence armed force, to enforce compliance by Iraq.

55. Resolution 686, para 4, which marked the provisional cessation of hostilities, expressly preserved the right to use force under Resolution 678. However, Resolution 687, which marked the permanent ceasefire, uses no such terms. This demonstrates a clear recognition that the right to use force requires express terms if it is to be continued. The absence of any clear terms in any resolution after 686 leads to the conclusion that no such use of force was authorised.

56. Further, Resolution 687 states that the Security Council '[d]ecides to remain actively seized of the matter and to take such further steps as may be required for the implementation of the present resolution and to secure peace and security in the region.' This clearly contemplates that the Security Council remains seized of the matter and will *itself* decide what further steps may be required for the implementation of that resolution.

57. The Secretary General of the United Nations has made it clear that Resolution 678 was directed at a unique and specific situation:

> 'The Iraqi invasion and occupation of Kuwait was the first instance since the founding of the Organisation in which one Member State sought to completely overpower and annex another. The unique demands presented by this situation have summoned forth innovative measures which have given practical expression to the Charter's concepts of how international peace and security might be maintained.' (The United Nations Blue Book Series Vol IX, The United Nations and the Iraq-Kuwait Conflict 1990-1996 (1996), at 3)

58. Those 'unique demands' relating to the invasion and occupation are no longer in existence. The Secretary General's remarks underline how exceptional the United Nations considers the use of force, and how dependent the decision to use force was on the fact that Iraq had actually *invaded* another Member State. No such action has been taken by Iraq since then.

59. Further, shortly after the end of the Gulf War, US officials gave evidence to the House Committee on Foreign Affairs that the military incursions into Iraq were authorised only because they were 'pursuant to the liberation of Kuwait, which was called for in the UN resolution',

and the United Kingdom declared that the sole purpose of the operation was to liberate Kuwait (Lobel and Ratner, *op cit*, p140).

60. Much reliance is placed, particularly by the United States but also by the United Kingdom, on Resolution 1154. The warning of 'severest consequences' in Resolution 1154 is a clear reference to the use of force. However, it is addressed to Iraq, not the Member States, and is not worded as an authorisation. At the meeting which led to the adoption of Resolution 1154, the 'automaticity' issue was debated: whether UN members would, without more, have the right to use force if Iraq failed to comply with the Resolution. Niels Blokker, in 'Is the Authorization Authorized? Powers and Practice of the UN Security Council to Authorize the Use of Force by 'Coalitions of the Able and Willing' (2000) 11 EJIL 541, summarises the debate as follows:

> 'No agreement was reached on this issue. The US and the UK did not receive support for the view that UN members would have such an automatic right. The other members of the Council, including the other permanent members, emphasized the powers and authority of the Security Council and in some cases explicitly rejected any automatic right for members to use force. Sweden emphasised that "the Security Council's responsibility for international peace and security, as laid down in the Charter of the United Nations, must not be circumvented." Brazil stated that it was "satisfied that nothing in its [the Resolution's] provisions delegates away the authority that belongs to the Security Council under the Charter and in accordance with its own resolutions." And Russia concluded that, "there has been full observance of the legal prerogatives of the Security Council, in accordance with the United Nations Charter. The resolution clearly states that it is precisely the Security Council which will directly ensure its implementation, including the adoption of appropriate decisions. Therefore, **any hint of automaticity with regard to the application of force has been excluded; that would not be acceptable for the majority of the Council's members.**"' (Emphasis added)

61. The intentions of the majority of States which passed Resolution 1154 could hardly be clearer: it gives Member States no authority whatsoever to use force in the event of non-compliance. The United States attempted to persuade the Security Council to include an express authorisation of force. It failed, as the above analysis shows. It cannot now be asserted by any State that, on its correct interpretation, Resolution 1154 does after all authorise the use of force.

62. The potentially serious consequences of ignoring the clear intent expressed by Permanent Members of the Security Council have been highlighted by Dame Rosalyn Higgins, the British Judge on the ICJ. Writing in a different but related context - whether UN resolutions gave NATO the implied authorisation to intervene in Kosovo[5] - she states that:

> 'One must necessarily ask whether [the implied authorisation argument] is not to stretch too far legal flexibility in the cause of good. In the Cold War legal inventiveness allowed peacekeeping instead of collective security enforcement. Then, at the end of the Cold War, we saw enforcement by coalition volunteers instead of UN military action under Article 42 of the Charter. In our unipolar world, does now the very adoption of a resolution under chapter VII of the Charter trigger a legal authorisation to act by NATO when it determines it necessary? If that is so, then we may expect that in the future Russia will again start exercising its veto in the Security Council, to make sure resolutions are not adopted, thus undercutting the possibility of useful political consensus being expressed in those instruments.' ('International Law in a Changing Legal System' [1999] CLJ 78 at 94, based on the text of the Rede Lecture, delivered in the University of Cambridge on 22 October 1998).

63. The issue of implied authorisation was further debated in the Security Council, following *Operation Desert Fox*, a British and American series of air strikes on Iraq in December 1998. The United Kingdom and the United States argued that Resolution 1205 implicitly revived the authorisation of the use of force contained in Resolution 678. The matter was debated at the 3930th meeting of the Security Council on 23 September 1998, when the majority of states speaking in the debate argued that the use of force by the United Kingdom and the United States under the purported authorisation of Resolutions 678, 1154 and 1205 was unlawful.

64. At that debate, Boris Yeltsin, President of the Russian Federation, stated that '[t]he UN Security Council resolutions on Iraq do not provide any grounds for such actions. By use of force, the US and Great Britain have flagrantly violated the UN Charter and universally accepted principles of international law, as well as norms and rules of responsible conduct of states in the international arena ... In fact, the entire system of international security with the UN and the Security Council as its centre-piece has been undermined.' China also expressed the view that the actions violated international law, and France ended its role in

policing the no-fly zones. The French Minister for Foreign Affairs stated that France had ended its participation since the operation changed from surveillance to the use of force: he considered that there was no basis in international law for this type of action. (See Christine Gray, 'From Unity to Polarisation: International Law and the Use of Force against Iraq' (2002) 13 EJIL 1, at 22, and Constantine Antonopoulos, 'The Unilateral Use of Force by States After the End of the Cold War', [1999] JACL 117, at 155).

65. This analysis of the Security Council debates shows that most Member States, including three Permanent Members, do not consider that the Resolutions can bear the meaning argued for by the United Kingdom and the United States, and consider that the proposed interpretation is incompatible with the framework laid down for collective decision-making. The arguments of the United Kingdom and United States have been said by one legal commentator to distort the language of the Security Council's resolutions:

> 'It is no longer simply a case of interpreting euphemisms such as "all necessary means" to allow the use of force when it is clear from the preceding debate that force is envisaged; the USA, the UK and others have gone far beyond this to distort the words of resolutions and to ignore the preceding debates in order to claim to be acting on behalf of the international community.' (Christine Gray, 'From Unity to Polarization: International Law and the Use of Force against Iraq' (2002) 13 EJIL 1, at 10).

66. The issue of implied authorisation was further debated after the United Kingdom and the United States attacked Iraqi radar installations and command and control centres in and outside the no-fly zones in February 2001. The UN Secretary-General stressed that only the Security Council could determine the legality of actions in the no-fly zones: only the Security Council was competent to determine whether its resolutions were of such a nature and effect as to provide a lawful basis for the no-fly zones and the action taken to enforce them. (Reported in Christine Gray, 'From Unity to Polarization: International Law and the Use of Force against Iraq', (2002) 13 EJIL 1, at 12, and recorded at www.un.org/News/dh/atest/ <http://www. un.org/News/dh/latest/>page2.html). Russia, China and France all rejected the legality of the air strikes, and Gray concludes that: 'The enforcement of the unilaterally proclaimed no-fly zones has thus come to be seen as illegitimate, despite UK protestations of humanitarian necessity.' (*Ibid*, at 12)

67. It should however be noted that, in relation to air attacks carried out in January 1993 by the USA, the UK and France, directed at destroying Iraqi missiles in the no-fly zones, the UN Secretary-General stated that:

> 'The raid yesterday and the forces that carried out the raid have received a mandate from the Security Council according to Resolution 678, and the cause of the raid was the violation by Iraq of Resolution 687 concerning the ceasefire. So, as Secretary General of the United Nations, I can say that this action was taken and conforms to the resolutions of the Security Council and conforms to the Charter of the United Nations.' (Ibid, at 167.)

68. This may appear to offer some support for the United Kingdom's position. However, the Secretary General has condemned the unilateral use of force before and since that statement. His statement to the press cannot be determinative of the legality of the action, and never again has the Secretary General given such support to unilateral military action against Iraq. In the light of the willingness of the Secretary General publicly to support such action in 1993, the fact that no support was given for the later attacks strongly suggests that the 1993 incident was an isolated one. The Secretary General's statement also runs contrary to the views of the UN Legal Department. In relation to the attacks in January 1993, it stated that 'the Security Council made no provision for enforcing the bans on Iraqi warplanes.' (Quoted in Lobel and Ratner, *op cit*, at p133).

69. Given the objects of the Charter, one of which is to preserve peace as far as possible, clear terms must be required to authorise the use of force. Bearing in mind that ambiguities in interpretation should be resolved in compliance with the Charter's objectives, it is submitted that the use of force is not justified until the Security Council says so in clear terms, and does so in terms directed at the current situation. The Charter's overriding commitment to the use of force only as a last resort entails that explicit authorisation be required, rather than seeking to make resolutions bear meanings clearly at odds with the intentions of large numbers of the States which drafted them, including Permanent Members of the Security Council.

70. The constitutional importance of the United Nations, and the constraints this places on interpretations of the relevant resolutions, is well expressed by Lobel and Ratner:

> 'To resolve these issues [whether the current Resolutions implicitly authorise the use of force], two interrelated principles underlying the Charter should be considered. The first is that force be used in the interest of the international community, not

individual states. That community interest is furthered by the centrality accorded to the Security Council's control over the offensive use of force. This centrality is compromised by sundering the authorisation process from the enforcement mechanism, by which enforcement is delegated to individual states or a coalition of states. Such separation results in a strong potential for powerful states to use UN authorisations to serve their own national interests rather than the interests of the international community as defined by the United Nations.' (Jules Lobel and Michael Ratner, 'Bypassing the Security Council: Ambiguous Authorizations to use Force, Cease-fires and the Iraqi Inspection Regime' [1999] AJIL 124, at 127.

71. Further, the Gulf War ended with a Security Council commitment to remain 'actively seized' of the situation. This strongly implies that they will apply their judgment *afresh* to any new proposals for the use of force. As Lobel and Ratner express it,

'It should not be presumed that the Security Council has authorised the greatest amount of violence that might be inferred from a broad authorisation. For example, Resolution 678 clearly authorised force to oust Iraq from Kuwait, but the broad provision on restoring international peace and security ought to be read in the context of that purpose. It should not be interpreted to authorise an escalation of the fighting that would remove the Government or enforce weapons inspections.' (129).

72. Thus far it has been argued that the terms of the relevant resolutions, their natural meaning and the intentions behind them offer no support to the argument that the wording of the Security Council resolutions implicitly authorises the use of force.

73. There is a further, more specific argument relied upon by the United Kingdom. This argument involves the interpretation to be placed on cease-fire agreements specifically, rather than Security Council Resolutions more generally. The United Kingdom appears to consider that breach of the terms accepted by Iraq in the ceasefire resolution (Resolution 687) entitles Member States without more to use force to end those violations.

74. Assuming that Iraq has in fact significantly breached the Security Council's requirements, this raises two questions of law: (1) whether material breach of requirements contained in a ceasefire agreement allows the use of force in response; (2) whether Member States are entitled unilaterally to determine the existence of such a breach and to use force without Security Council authorisation.

75.   Resolution 687 is an agreement between Iraq and the United Nations. It does two things. First, it brings the Gulf War to a permanent end. Secondly, it sets out a series of requirements for Iraq. The cease-fire was conditional on Iraq's *acceptance of* those terms. It did accept those terms. From the moment of ceasing hostilities, there exists a situation of peace, in which the obligation under Article 2(4) not to use force applies again in full. Lobel and Ratner give an example: 'no one would seriously claim that member states of the UN command would have the authority to bomb North Korea pursuant to the 1950 authorisation to use force if in 1999 North Korea flagrantly violated the 1953 armistice.' (*Op cit*, p145)

76.   It would be contrary to the Charter's objectives if, once the Security Council authorises the use of force, that authorisation constitutes a permanent mandate to Member States to use force as and how they determine it to be necessary. Statements made at the time of other cease-fires directly contradict the United Kingdom's argument. When the Security Council imposed a cease-fire on the parties to the conflict between Israel and various Arab governments in 1948, Count Bernadotte, the UN mediator, instructed that the UN cease-fire resolution was to mean that: '(1) No party may unilaterally put an end to the truce. (2) No party may take the law into its own hands and decree that it is relieved of its obligations under the resolution of the Security Council because in its opinion the other party has violated the truce.' The Security Council then reiterated that 'no party is permitted to violate the truce on the ground that it is undertaking reprisals or retaliations against the other party.' (Lobel and Ratner, *op cit*, p146).

77.   The objections to the United Kingdom's argument were powerfully stated by Professor Thomas Franck at proceedings of the American Society of International Law in 1998:

'[B]y any normal construction drawn from the administrative law of any legal system, what the Security Council has done is occupy the field, in the absence of a direct attack on a member state by Iraq. The Security Council has authorised a combined military operation; has terminated a combined military operation; has established the terms under which various UN agency actions will occur to supervise the cease-fire, to establish the standards with which Iraq must comply; has established the means by which it may be determined whether those standards have been met (and this has been done by a flock of reports by the inspection system); and has engaged in negotiations to secure compliance. After all these actions, to now state that the United Nations has not in fact occupied the field, that there remains under Article 51 or under Resolution 678, which authorised the use of force, which authorisation was terminated in Resolution 687, a collateral total freedom on the part of any UN member to use military force against Iraq at any point that any member considers there to have been a violation of the conditions set forth in Resolution 678, is to make a complete mockery of the entire system.' (ASIL Proceedings, 1998, 'Legal Authority for the Possible Use of Force Against Iraq', at 139).

78. It is far from clear that material breaches of a cease-fire agreement authorise the use of force in response. *If* such use of force can ever be justified, this is clearly a decision to be taken by the Security Council. The constitutional arguments considered above apply with equal force in this context. Given the purpose of the system of collective decision-making, the emphasis on peaceful resolution wherever possible, and the Security Council's active management of the Iraqi situation to date, neither breaches of the cease-fire agreement nor breaches of any other resolution authorise the unilateral use of force. Such use of force by the United Kingdom would therefore violate international law.

The proposed UN resolution

79. As matters stand, the United States and the United Kingdom are attempting to persuade the UN Security Council to adopt a strongly worded resolution giving the UNMOVIC and the International Atomic Energy Agency (IAEA) extensive powers of inspection of an unlimited range of sites in Iraq. The draft resolution would empower any permanent member of the Security Council to recommend to UNMOVIC and IAEA the sites to be inspected, persons to be interviewed, the conditions of such interviews and the data to be collected, and then to receive a report on the results. The proposed resolution also casts upon Iraq the obligation to make full disclosure 'an acceptable and currently accurate, full and complete declaration of all aspects of its programmes to develop chemical, biological and nuclear weapons, ballistic missiles, and unmanned aerial vehicles.'

80. The final clause of the proposed resolution states:

'...false statements or omissions in the declaration submitted by Iraq to the council and failure by Iraq at any time to comply and cooperate fully in accordance with the provisions laid out in this resolution, shall constitute a further material breach of Iraq's obligations, and that such breach authorises member states to use all necessary means to restore international peace and security in the area.' (clause 10 - emphasis added)

81. The very fact that the United States and the United Kingdom are making strenuous efforts to secure the adoption of the proposed resolution; and the wording of the resolution, in particular clause 10, illustrates that the proponents of the view that the existing resolutions authorise the use of force in present circumstances, or that the use of force is justified as a means of pre-emptive self-defence, themselves recognise that another resolution is needed which clearly authorises the use of force by the words "all necessary means." It would be an astonishing legal proposition if they failed to persuade the Security Council to pass a resolution in such terms and *still* contended later that they had authority to launch a unilateral attack on Iraq.

Necessity and Proportionality

82. It is clear that the laws of war also set limits to any force which may ultimately be used. If used in self-defence, force is limited to that which is strictly *necessary and proportionate* to repelling any attack. If used pursuant to a UN Security Council Resolution, the force could only be used in a manner, and for purposes, consistent with the United Nations Charter.

83. Force cannot be considered *necessary* to achieve compliance with the Security Council's requirements, and to secure peace, until (1) Iraq's current offer in relation to weapons inspections has been taken up and shown to be made in bad faith or otherwise ineffective; and (2) Iraq has been demonstrated to pose a pressing and immediate threat to another Member State or States.

A full invasion of Iraq with the aim of changing the government would not be proportionate to the aims of self-defence, or to the Charter's aim of maintaining peace and security. Iraq is a sovereign State: while the Security Council can demand that Iraq achieve certain results, it cannot dictate its choice of government. The Security Council Resolutions require Iraq to meet a long list of requirements. These *could* be met by Saddam Hussein's government. While the Security Council, or certain members of it, may not like that government, a change of regime cannot be considered absolutely necessary to achieving the Security Council's legitimate aims.[6]

Conclusion

84. It is submitted therefore that the Inquiry should conclude as follows:

'The Inquiry concludes that it would be unlawful for the United Kingdom to launch or take part in a military attack on Iraq under present circumstances without the express authorisation of a United Nations resolution.'

Rabinder Singh QC, Janet Kentridge
Matrix Chambers, Gray's Inn

London WC1R 5LN, 8th October 2002

INQUIRY INTO THE LEGALITY OF THE USE OF FORCE
BY THE UNITED KINGDOM AGAINST IRAQ

FOOTNOTES

1. This is the position recorded by UNSCOM in its 'Chronology of Main Events', which states '16 December 1998: The Special Commission withdraws its staff from Iraq.' (Available at:www.un.org/Depts/unscom/Chronology/chronologyframe.htm). This followed the report submitted by Richard Butler, Executive Chairman of UNSCOM, to the Security Council on 15 December 1998, in which he reported that on that inspection, 'Iraq did not provide the full co-operation it promised on 14 November 1998.' (UN reference: S/1998/1172, 15 December 1998).

2. See also the 1987 *Declaration on the Non-Use of Force* GA Res 42/22 (1988) and Christine Gray *International Law and the Use of Force* (2000, Oxford) pp 4-6.

3. It should be noted that Sir Robert Jennings was the British Judge on the ICJ and was its President.

4. Those occasions were: SC Res 678, authorising the use of 'all necessary means' to liberate Kuwait; SC Res 794, authorising 'all necessary means to establish as soon as possible a secure environment for humanitarian relief operations in Somalia', SC Res 940, authorising 'all necessary means to facilitate the departure from Haiti of the military leadership', SC Res 929, authorising France to use 'all necessary means' to protect civilians in Rwanda, SC Res 770, authorising states to take 'all measures necessary' to facilitate humanitarian assistance and enforce the no-fly zone in Bosnia.

5. It should be noted that, in the case of Kosovo, it is arguable that the use of force was justified in international law on another ground – the doctrine of humanitarian intervention – but, for present purposes, it is only the suggestion that the use of force against Serbia was justified by the doctrine of implied authorisation by Security Council Resolutions which we need consider.

6. The *Financial Times* on Monday 7th October 2002 reported that the Government had received legal advice from the Attorney General and the Solicitor General to the effect that the use of force against Iraq in order to achieve a change of regime would be contrary to international law. A similar report appeared in *The Guardian* of Tuesday 8th October 2002, p 12.

Editors' Note: this Chapter augments and updates the *Opinion on the Use of Force Against Iraq* provided by Rabinder Singh QC and Alison MacDonald on September 10 2002 for the Legal Inquiry Steering Group.

2. THE CASE FOR WAR: JULIAN KNOWLES

9 October 2002

****

In the Matter of an Inquiry into the Legality of the Use of Force by the United Kingdom against Iraq

Skeleton Argument on behalf of Legal Inquiries Support Group (LISG)

A.   INTRODUCTION

1.   The terms of reference for this Inquiry are as follows:

"To examine whether in the light of present circumstances any decision by the UK Government to use force in the war against terror, and specifically Iraq, would be consistent with the rules of *jus ad bellum*"

2.   However, the real issue as crystallised in the Skeleton Argument filed by 'Peacerights' is whether an armed attack on Iraq would be compatible with international law, rather than the legality of the use of force in the 'war against terror'. There can be no doubt that the military operations in Afghanistan following 9/11 are lawful under international law. Accordingly, this Skeleton Argument will address the issue of an attack on Iraq.

3.   This Inquiry, in order to be meaningful, has to assume that an attack is to take place without the benefit of a UN Security Council Resolution, which (it is common ground) would render lawful military action in accordance with its terms.

4.   The LISG will invite the inquiry to conclude:

a.   That an attack on Iraq would not be unlawful under international law if the evidence in the possession of the relevant governments, when scrutinised by an appropriate international body or tribunal, were to demonstrate the necessity of destroying Iraq's capability to develop or deploy weapons of mass destruction (WMD) in order to preserve international peace and security.

b.   The proper interpretation of post-Gulf War Resolutions allows force to be used a further specific Resolution.

B.   SUMMARY OF SUBMISSIONS

5.   In summary, LISG will contend:

a.   It is not possible for this Tribunal to determine the hard-edged question of whether or not an attack on Iraq would or would not be unlawful under the doctrine of anticipatory self-defence.

That is because this question is essentially one of fact. This Tribunal is not, does not purport to be, and cannot be, a fact-finding tribunal. Nevertheless, the following matters support the view that the requirements of this doctrine are satisfied here.

b. Article 51 of the UN Charter preserves the inherent right of state self-defence;

c. This right includes the right to take pre-emptive action where the evidence suggests that an armed attack is anticipated;

d. It is sufficient if the attack is on a UN member state.

e. The concept of 'imminence' must be judged by reference to the form of armed attack that is contemplated. In the case of ballistic missiles equipped with nuclear, chemical or biological warheads capable of being fired at short notice, imminence must be given a flexible interpretation. This view is supported by examples of state practice in the form of attacks on Iraqi nuclear facilities by US forces which have not been condemned by the UN Security Council as being unlawful despite there being no overt evidence of any imminent attack.

f. The document 'Iraq's Weapons of Mass Destruction: The Assessment of the British Government' ('the Dossier') demonstrates inter alia that Saddam Hussein is a homicidal and genocidal dictator of the utmost ruthlessness who has not hesitated (i) to begin aggressive wars, and (ii) to use WMD against real and perceived enemies without provocation in the past.

g. The view of the attacking government as to whether sufficient evidence exists must be given significant weight in determining whether sufficient evidence does exist.

h. The Secretary-General of the UN has stated that Resolution 687 permits military force without further Resolutions.

C. THE DOSSIER

6. The evidence contained in the Dossier demonstrates the following:

a. The threat from Iraq does not depend solely on its weapons capabilities, described below. It arises also because of the violent, unpredictable, and aggressive nature of Saddam Hussein's regime. The UK Government's informed judgment is that   Saddam's record of internal repression and external aggression gives rise to unique concerns about the threat he poses.

b.   Part 3 of the Dossier charts Saddam's rise to power; the nature of his regime and his history of regional aggression; his human rights abuses; his record of torture, mass arrests and summary executions. These include:

    i.   4000 prisoners executed at Abu Ghraib Prison in 1984.

    ii.   3000 prisoners executed at the Mahjar Prison between 1993 and 1998.

    iii.   About 2500 prisoners executed between 1997 and 1999 in   a "prison cleansing " campaign.

    iv.   122 male prisoners executed at Abu Ghraib prison in February/March 2000. A further 23 political prisoners were executed there in October 2001.

    v.   In October 2000 dozens of women accused of prostitution were beheaded without any judicial process. Some were accused for political reasons. Women prisoners at Mahja are routinely raped by their guards.

c.   Saddam Hussein utilises the most perverted forms of cruelty to enforce his will. His regime has demonstrated genuine creativity in devising methods of inflicting pain and death on real and perceived opponents. These include: using electric drills to mutilate prisoners' limbs; prolonged suspension by the arms and legs; beatings on the soles of the feet; electric shocks to the genitals; pulling out of fingernails; mutilation with knives; sexual attacks; and official rape.   Prisoners at the Qurtiyya Prison in Baghdad and elsewhere are kept in metal boxes the size of tea chests. If they do not confess they are left to die.

d.   Under Saddam Hussein, Iraq developed chemical and biological weapons, acquired missiles allowing it to attack neighbouring countries with these weapons and persistently tried to develop a nuclear bomb. Saddam has used chemical weapons, both against Iran and against his own people. Following the Gulf War, Iraq admitted all of this.

e.   In the ceasefire of 1991 Saddam agreed unconditionally to give up his weapons of mass destruction.

f.   Evidence in the public domain points to Iraq 's continuing possession, after 1991, of chemical and biological agents and weapons produced before the Gulf War. Iraq has refurbished sites formerly associated with the production of chemical and biological agents. Iraq remains able to manufacture these agents, and to use bombs, shells, artillery rockets and ballistic missiles to deliver them.

g. An independent review of this public evidence was provided by the International Institute for Strategic Studies (IISS) on 9th September. The IISS report also suggested that Iraq could assemble nuclear weapons within months of obtaining fissile material from foreign sources.

h. Significant additional information is available to the Government from secret intelligence sources. This intelligence provides a fuller picture of Iraqi plans and capabilities. It shows that Saddam Hussein attaches great importance to possessing weapons of mass destruction which he regards as the basis for Iraq 's regional power. It also shows that he does <u>not</u> regard them only as weapons of last resort. He is ready to use them, including against his own population, and is determined to retain them, in breach of Security Council Resolutions.

i. Intelligence also shows that Iraq is preparing plans to conceal evidence of these weapons, including incriminating documents, from renewed inspections. And it confirms that despite sanctions and the policy of containment, Saddam has continued to make progress with his illicit weapons programmes.

j. Iraq 's weapons of mass destruction are in breach of international law. Under a series of Security Council Resolutions Iraq is obliged to destroy its holdings of these weapons under the supervision of UN inspectors. Part 2 of the Dossier sets out the key UN Security Council Resolutions. It also summarises the history of the UN inspection regime and Iraq 's history of deception, intimidation and concealment in its dealings with the UN inspectors.

D. DISCUSSION

7. It is common ground between the parties that article 51 of the Charter preserves states' rights to self-defence. By referring to 'inherent rights', it plainly recognises the continued existence of the right in customary international law for states to defend themselves. It states:

> Nothing in the present Charter shall impair the inherent right of individual or collective self-defence if an armed attack occurs against a member of the United Nations, until the Security Council has taken measures necessary to maintain international peace and security. Measures taken by Members in the exercise

of this right of self-defence shall be immediately reported to the Security Council and shall not in any way affect the authority and responsibility of the Security Council under the present Charter to take at any time such action as it deems necessary in order to maintain or restore international peace and security.'

8.	Therefore states may take military action:

a.	In individual or collective self-defence (which is a right under customary international law preserved by article 51).

b.	Pursuant to a UN Security Council resolution, in accordance with article 2(4).

*(i)	Anticipatory self-defence*

9.	The right to self - defence includes the right of a state to take action in anticipation of an attack either on itself or a third party UN member. This is known as 'anticipatory self-defence' and has been recognised as a principle of customary international law:

> ... while anticipatory action in self-defence is normally unlawful, it is not necessarily unlawful in all circumstances, the matter depending on the facts of the situation including in particular the seriousness of the threat and the degree to which pre-emptive action is really necessary and is the only way of avoiding that serious threat; the requirements of necessity and proportionality are probably even more pressing in relation to anticipatory self-defence than they are in other circumstances.' (R Jennings QC and A Watts QC (eds), Oppenheim's International Law: Ninth Edition 1991)

10.	The extracts from *Detter* and *Cassese*, relied on by Peacerights at para. 23 *et seq*, which appear to deny the existence of this doctrine, represent an extreme view not borne out by examples of state practice where anticipatory self-defence has been utilised without condemnation by the international community: see Fleck, The Handbook of Humanitarian Law in Armed Conflicts, p3. Importantly, *Oppenheim* goes on to state, in a passage not included in Peacerights' Skeleton Argument:

> In conditions of modern hostilities it is unreasonable for a state always to have to wait until an armed attack has begun before taking defensive action. States have in practice invoked the plea of self-defence to justify action begun to forestall what they regard as an imminent threatened attack.

11.	These extracts from *Oppenheim* make good:

a.	The proposition that anticipatory self-defence exists as a recognised exception to the prohibition on the use of force;

b.	The proposition set out above at para. 5(a), namely, that this Inquiry is not equipped to make the necessary factual findings in order to answer in terms the question posed by its terms of reference. No disrespect is meant by this observation; it is merely intended to point out the difficulty involved in assessing the degree of risk in the absence of an opportunity to make factual findings.

(ii) Justification

12.	It is entirely accepted that the burden of proof will be on the Government to justify by reference to evidence that the situation is such that an anticipatory attack is justified. However, support for the view that the necessary conditions are in place is to be found in the Dossier and the other publicly available material. These are: (i) that Iraq has the capacity to attack with WMD; (ii) it has attacked with WMD before, killing tens of thousands; (iii) it is ruled by a tyrant whose behaviour is unconstrained by any recognisable notions of morality and whose political strategy has included waging two aggressive wars in the last 22 years.

13.	Whilst the classical formulation of the doctrine of anticipatory self-defence refers to an 'imminent attack', the degree of proximity required must obviously be proportionate to the severity of the threat and the speed with which an attack could be launched. Threats to use WMD are capable of justifying the earlier use of defensive force than might be justified in the case of a less serious threat. The doctrine as enunciated in the *Caroline* was laid down in the age of the musket and the horse, whereas the present danger arises in the age of the thermonuclear ballistic missile. Moreover, Saddam Hussein is unlikely to publish his intentions in advance.

14.	As an example, in 1981 Israel attacked Iraqi nuclear facilities, fearing that they were to be used to make nuclear weapons. It was condemned by *inter alia* the British Government and the Security Council for doing so. A telegram to the Security Council from the International Atomic Energy Agency recited: *"Mindful of the fact that Iraq fully subscribes to the Agency's safeguards system and is a party to the Treaty on the Non-proliferation of nuclear weapons... Noting the statement of the Director-General to the effect that Iraq has fulfilled its obligations under Agency safeguards, pursuant to the non-proliferation Treaty"*. Sir Anthony Parsons, the British Ambassador, emphasised in his speech how Iraq had cooperated with weapons inspections.

15.	In 1981, of course, Saddam Hussein was fighting the Iran-Iraq war and was the friend of the West. He had not yet invaded Kuwait, and had not yet committed genocide against the Kurdish people. He had not yet used chemical and biological weapons to kill thousands of Iranian soldiers. The full extent of his tyranny had not yet been established.

16. The situation now is very different to 1981. This has been reflected in the different reaction to US attacks on Iraq's nuclear facilities during the 1990s, which did not meet with international condemnation: see O'Connell, *Evidence of Terror*, Journal of Conflict and Security Law, p26; *The Legality of the 1993 US Missile Strike on Iraq and the Right of Self-Defence in International Law* (1996) 45 I.C.L.Q. 162.

17. Given this acceptance by the international community of the US's 1993 attack as a legitimate act of self-defence, that self - defence being an *ex post facto* attack following the Iraqi sponsorship of an assassination attempt on former President Bush, the present factual scenario lends strong support for the view that a proportionate attack to remove WMDs and prevent their rebuilding would fall within accepted parameters. As a result of its intelligence gathering, the Government's Joint Intelligence Committee's judgment is that Saddam has:

   a.   continued to produce chemical and biological agents;

   b.   military plans for the use of chemical and biological weapons, including against its own Shia population. Some of these weapons are deployable within 45 minutes of an order to use them. There are command and control arrangements in place to use chemical and biological weapons. Authority to use these weapons resides with Saddam Hussein personally, save where he has delegated his power to family members.

   c.   developed mobile laboratories for military use, corroborating earlier reports about the mobile production of biological warfare agents;

   d.   pursued illegal programmes to procure controlled materials of potential use in the production of chemical and biological weapons programmes;

   e.   tried covertly to acquire technology and materials which could be used in the production of nuclear weapons;

   f.   sought significant quantities of uranium from Africa, despite having no active civil nuclear power programme that could require it;

   g.   recalled specialists to work on its nuclear programme;

   h.   illegally retained up to 20 al-Hussein missiles, with a range of 650km, capable of carrying chemical or biological warheads;

   i.   started deploying its al-Samoud liquid propellant missile, and has used the absence of weapons inspectors to work on extending its range to at least 200km, which is beyond the limit of 150km imposed by the United Nations in Resolution 687;

j. started producing the solid-propellant Ababil-100, and is making efforts to extend its range to at least 200km,which is beyond the limit of 150km imposed by the United Nations;

k. constructed a new engine test stand for the development of missiles capable of reaching the UK Sovereign Base Areas in Cyprus and NATO members (Greece and Turkey),as well as all Iraq 's Gulf neighbours and Israel;

l. pursued illegal programmes to procure materials for use in its illegal development of long range missiles;

m. learnt lessons from previous UN weapons inspections and has already begun to conceal sensitive equipment and documentation in advance of the return of inspectors.

18. The argument that because Iraq has engaged in negotiations with UN weapons inspectors, and has offered to lift restrictions upon terms whereby the inspectors may return to Iraq, there is an effective alternative to force, is naive in the extreme and refuted by the evidence in the Dossier.

19. In summary, there is clear support for the view that conditions for an anticipatory attack on Iraq to remove WMD, and to remove the capability of making them again (which may extend to removing the people responsible for their creation and deployment) are met in this case.

(iii) Existing Security Council resolutions

20. Resolution 678, passed at the start of the Gulf War, authorised the use of force against Iraq. There have been many others, discussed below. The position taken by the UK Government is that:

a. Existing Resolutions implicitly authorise the use of force by Member States in the event of Iraq's continued and persistent non-compliance;

b. Further or alternatively, Iraq's failure to comply with the cease-fire requirements set out in Resolution 687, which brought to an end military action against Iraq during the Gulf War, and amplified subsequently, justify the renewed use of force under Resolution 678, without further authorisation from the Security Council.

21. The existing Resolutions can be summarised as follows:

a. Paragraph 2 of Resolution 678 authorises Member States 'to use all necessary means to uphold and implement resolution

660 (1990) and all subsequent relevant resolutions and to restore international peace and security in the area.' (emphasis added).

b.   Resolution 660 aimed to restore the sovereignty of Kuwait. After that had been achieved, Resolution 687 imposed a formal cease-fire. The cease-fire was conditional on Iraq's acceptance of terms which it did not accept.

c.   The Security Council's current requirements of Iraq are contained in Resolution 687 (dubbed 'the Mother of All Resolutions') as well as subsequent Resolutions. These require the destruction of all chemical and biological weapons and all ballistic missiles with a range greater than 150km, the unconditional agreement not to acquire or develop nuclear weapons (Resolution 687, paras 8(a), 8(b), and 12), and full co-operation with the UN-appointed weapons inspectorate. Such inspections were initially the responsibility of the Special Commission and the International Atomic Energy Agency, and are now to be carried out by the United Nations Monitoring, Verification and Inspection Commission (UNMOVIC), established by Resolution 1284 (1999).

22.   Iraq's obligations were spelt out in a series of Resolutions after Resolution 688. In Resolution 707, the Security Council noted Iraq's 'flagrant violation' and 'material breaches' of resolution 687. It considered that these constitute a 'material breach of the relevant provisions of that resolution which established a cease-fire and provided the conditions essential to the restoration of peace and security in the region' (para 1).

23.   In Resolution 1154 the Security Council said it was 'determined to ensure immediate and full compliance by Iraq without conditions or restrictions with its obligations under resolution 687 (1991) and the other relevant resolutions'. The Security Council also said that any violation by Iraq with its obligations to accord immediate, unconditional and unrestricted access to the Special Commission and the IAEA in conformity with the relevant resolutions is necessary for the implementation of resolution 687 (1991), but that any violation would have severest consequences for Iraq.' The Security Council also decided 'to remain actively seized of the matter, in order to ensure implementation of this resolution, and to secure peace and security in the area.'

24.   On 5th August 1998, Iraq suspended co-operation with the Special Commission and the IAEA. In resolution 1194, the Security Council stated that this 'constitutes a totally unacceptable contravention of its

obligations under [Resolution] 687...' In resolution 1205 the Security Council demanded that Iraq co-operate fully with the Special Commission, and said that it again remained 'actively seized of the matter.'

25. It is submitted that these series of Resolutions implicitly justify the use of force in order to implement the terms of Resolution 687 because that allows Member States to use 'all necessary means' to ensure compliance with it and with subsequent resolutions. Furthermore, the 'severest consequences' envisaged by the Security Council in Resolution 1154 (now backed up by the demands in Resolution 1205) obviously includes the use of force by Member States.

26. Before offering justification for this position, it should be noted that the point taken by Peacerights, namely, that the current proposed Resolution demonstrates in clear terms the lack of any current authority, is manifestly bad. It ignores the fact that the UN Security Council is a political and not a judicial body and that proposals for Resolutions may be motivated by a number of considerations quite apart from jurisprudential ones.

27. Clear and unambiguous support for the proposition that military action prompted (as it would be) by Iraqi violations of Resolution 687 would be authorised by Resolution 678 comes from no lesser figure than the then Secretary-General of the UN himself. He said, in relation to the air attacks carried out in January 1993 by the USA, the UK and France, directed at destroying Iraqi missiles in the no-fly zones:

> 'The raid yesterday and the forces that carried out the raid have received a mandate from the Security Council according to Resolution 678, and the cause of the raid was the violation by Iraq of Resolution 687 concerning the ceasefire. So, as Secretary General of the United Nations, I can say that this action was taken and conforms to the resolutions of the Security Council and conforms to the Charter of the United Nations', quoted in Christine Gray, From Unity to Polarization: International Law and the Use of Force against Iraq, ' (2002) 13 EJIL [1]

28. In relation to this statement, the LISG submits as follows:

   a. The best guide to the proper meaning and interpretation of UN Security Council Resolutions is the Secretary-General of the UN;

   b. However, equally obviously, this statement cannot be taken as a mandate for any and all forms of attack against Iraq. The factual context here, as in anticipatory self-defence, is everything.

   c. Therefore, the fact that other forms of unilateral action may have been condemned by the Secretary-General in no way diminishes the highly authoritative status of this interpretation of the Resolutions.

d. However, it should be borne in mind that the putative military action in this case is aimed <u>directly</u> at enforcing the terms of the ceasefire. Action to make Iraq give up its WMD and allow inspections was one of the primary goals of Resolution 687. The statement of the Secretary-General (presumably considered, presumably issued with the benefit of legal advice) must therefore be regarded as reflecting the UN's own view that the Resolutions have continuing effect and the proposed military action falls within the continuing mandate given to Member States

29. This statement by the Secretary-General also meets the argument that the statement in Resolution 687 that the Security Council '[d]ecides to remain actively seized of the matter and to take such further steps as may be required for the implementation of the present resolution and to secure peace and security in the region' requires the Security Council itself to decide when to further authorise the use of force is unsound.

30. The Secretary-General's interpretation of Resolution 687 is reinforced by the reference in Resolution 1154 to 'severest consequences'. This is an obvious reference to the use of force. Whilst Resolution 1154 is addressed to Iraq, once it is accepted that force continues to be authorised by Resolution 687, 'severest consequences' can be read perfectly properly as a warning to Iraq of the possible consequences of continued [non-compliance]. The fact that in subsequent debates, the Security-Council has not agreed on the proper interpretation does not undermine this interpretation.

31. Such an interpretation is in no way inconsistent with the object of the UN Charter, namely, the preservation of peace. By framing the ceasefire conditions in the form which it did, the Security-Council must be taken to have decided that the preservation of peace required a continuing threat of military force in order to secure compliance by Iraq of terms deemed necessary for a greater and more lasting peace in the region, and the world.

D.   CONCLUSION

32. For these reasons, the Inquiry is respectfully invited to reach the conclusions set out above at para. 4.

JULIAN B. KNOWLES
Matrix Chambers
Gray's Inn
9th October 2002

IN THE MATTER OF AN INQUIRY INTO THE LEGALITY OF THE USE OF FORCE BY THE UNITED KINGDOM AGAINST IRAQ

SKELETON ARGUMENT ON BEHALF OF LEGAL INQUIRIES SUPPORT GROUP (LISG)

Silks Solicitors
368 High Street
Smethwick
West Midlands
B66 3PG

3. ADJUDICATION OF PROFESSOR COLIN WARBRICK, 30 OCTOBER 2002

****

Legal Inquiry into a Prospective Use of Force by the United Kingdom against Iraq

1. Introduction

The Legal Inquiry into the legality of the use of force by the United Kingdom against Iraq was held on 11 October 2002. It could only take into account the situation as it was on that date. The British Government had indicated that it was contemplating the use of force against Iraq and had said that any force that was used would be compatible with international law. Even though the government conceded a recall of Parliament, it has been notably unwilling to elaborate in detail on the case in support of the international legality of any proposed action against Iraq.

Because of the constitutional arrangements in the United Kingdom governing the disposition of the armed forces, it is difficult to imagine that a UK court would be prepared to examine the international legality of any action contemplated by the Government. The result is that the Government's claim for the legality of its plans, clearly made for the purpose of persuading people of the legitimacy of any action amounts to no more than an assertion of a proposition which is contested. As an international lawyer, one is glad to see that not only does the Government regard compliance with international law as a component of its policy-making but that it considers international law also to be a consideration of persuasive force with public opinion.

The purpose of this Inquiry is to examine the constraints which international law places on any military action by the government against Iraq. The method which was adopted for the Inquiry was the presentation of the arguments by counsel before me. I was asked to make a report after hearing them. To give a focus to the Inquiry, I was asked by counsel on behalf of "Peacerights" to reach the following conclusion:

that it would be unlawful for the United Kingdom to launch or take part in a military attack on Iraq under present circumstances without the express authorisation of a United Nations resolution.

It was made clear that "United Nations resolution" meant a resolution of the Security Council clearly authorising the use of force.

The adoption of an adversarial process and the appearance of a judgment at the end of it is apt to mislead. It is important to emphasise that none of us engaged in the Inquiry regard it as the last word on the matter of the legality of the use of force against Iraq: this was not a trial of the British government. The Inquiry had the advantage of the presentation of argument by experienced counsel for and against the conclusion cited above. It did not have (and could not have had, of course) the benefit of the consideration of these submissions by a judge of like experience. I am not, and I was not pretending to be, a judge. I was not assuming the position of an English judge, with his potential remedial powers but with complex limitations on his jurisdictional authority, especially with regard to the sources of international law. Nor do I presume to the authority of an international judge. While it is true that the International Court of Justice has decided a case involving the use of force in the absence of one of the parties, I know of no instance when an international judge has been expected to reach his decision in the absence of both of them. It is necessary to underline that the proposition which I am asked to consider, though it has the appearance of an asymmetrical request, does in fact implicate the position of two States-the United Kingdom and Iraq.[1] Mr Singh, for Peacerights, did not purport to represent the position of the government of Iraq and Mr Knowles, responding, was not speaking for the British government. Mr Singh put his case against the legality of any action on behalf of Peacerights, a non-governmental organisation. Mr Knowles relied on information in the public domain to argue the contrary but was not instructed by nor privy to any information from the British government not otherwise available.

I express my appreciation of the measured tone of the written arguments of counsel and the clarity of their oral submissions, an appreciation which I am sure is shared by those who heard them. We all recognise that if this had been a real international law case, the resources available to counsel for the elaboration of their cases and the time for their presentation would have been much greater than was possible on this occasion. Furthermore, it is manifestly the case that all the evidence which would be relevant to determining the issues at stake is not available and, if one needed another cause for caution, we are dealing with a prospective use of force: assumptions have to made in considering the question now which might be confounded by events. Even taking these contingencies into account, I am persuaded that the exercise was one that was worth undertaking. To repeat an earlier point, the British government has said that it will act only in conformity with international law. It has put some evidence into the public debate concerning the case that it would have to make if force were used. But it has been reticent to elaborate its case in international law (though nobody should imagine that the matter will not have been extensively canvassed within government). In these circumstances, it seems to me a reasonable thing to do, to see how what we know about the government's position comports with international law. Nonetheless, I reiterate what was said above - the proceedings were not a trial and this is not a judgment.

2. **The factual and legal background**

   It is not, I think, necessary to elaborate at length the facts on which this Inquiry is founded. In August 1990, Iraq invaded the territory of Kuwait, a State and a member of the United Nations. The attack was condemned by the Security Council which took a number of decisions in response, in the initial phase culminating in Resolution 678, which, so far as relevant here:

   Authorises Member States co-operating with the Government of Kuwait, unless Iraq on or before 15 January 1991 [leaves Kuwait and complies with other Resolutions] to use all necessary means [emphasis added] to uphold and implement [Iraq's obligations] and to restore international peace and security in the area.

   A number of States had already come to Kuwait's assistance (the "Coalition") and had been asked by Kuwait to use force in collective self-defence with Kuwait to repel the invasion and restore the authority of the government of Kuwait. It was understood that the emphasised words in Resolution 678 - "all necessary means" included the use of force. The purposes of the Council and the wishes of Kuwait were realised by military action which commenced with air-raids on 16 January 1991, followed by a ground invasion on 24 February 1991 and terminated on 28 February with a cease-fire agreed by Iraq. [Although nothing turns on it, there remains an uncertainty about whether the action of the Coalition was an exercise of collective self-defence or was done under the authorisation of the Council.] The Council first laid down the terms of a temporary cease-fire in Resolution 686 (which specifically continued the authority to use force in Resolution 678) and then set out the terms of a permanent cease-fire in Resolution 687. All the Iraq resolutions were under Chapter VII of the Charter and all were binding on Iraq, whether or not it accepted them. In fact, Iraq did accept the terms of Resolution 687. Certain of the measures in the earlier resolutions, notably the regime of economic sanctions against Iraq, were expressly kept in place by Resolution 687 but the authorisation to the Coalition to use force was not among them. The Resolution covers many matters, some Kuwait-specific, such as the delimitation of the Iraq-Kuwait border; some related to the invasion directly, like the arrangements for securing compensation for those States, individual and companies injured by Iraq's illegal actions; and some of a more general character, affecting Iraq's capacity to engage in various kinds of military activity in the future, against whichever State it were directed. These last, disarmament provisions, were accompanied by a regime of implementation - UN inspectors were to identify weapons, components and facilities covered by the Resolution and destroy or disable them. Iraq was expected to co-operate with UNSCOM, the UN organ charged with these tasks. Its co-operation was less than whole-hearted and eventually deteriorated into obstruction. The UNSCOM inspectors were withdrawn in 1998, in the face of Iraqi allegations that they were abusing their powers. After a period (in which unilateral military action - aerial bombardment (see below) - was taken against Iraq by the US and the UK), an agreement was reached for the readmission of inspectors to Iraq, a new UN body, UNMOVIC, being set up to carry out the work, under Resolution 1284. Continued disagreements about the terms on which the inspectors would operate and persisting Iraqi dissatisfaction about the prolongation of the sanctions regime have meant that the inspectors have not returned to Iraq. Instead, a somewhat diffuse policy of containment has been pursued, some of it (the sanctions regime) under the authority of the UN, some of it (the no-fly zones) on the basis of claims of unilateral right. The no-fly zones, the legality of which is not an issue relevant to the Inquiry, are areas of Iraq airspace designated by the US and the UK (and initially also by France) as forbidden to Iraqi planes. They are patrolled by allied aircraft, which claim a right of self-defence against attacks from the ground. The only matter of importance is that the "allies" taking this action are not the "Coalition" which went to the aid of Kuwait.

The stasis continued. It was shattered in the wake of the events of 11th September 2001. President Bush included Iraq in an "axis of evil" States, which, he said, maintained or sought weapons of mass destruction and their means of delivery and which supported terrorist movements directed against the US and its allies. Of these States, only Iraq was under an international regime of supervision of its weapons programmes. Its failure to submit fully to the demands of Resolution 687 and Resolution 1284, were held against it, both as breaches of its obligations and as evidence that it was seeking or had obtained weapons of mass destruction, weapons which directly or indirectly by transmission to terrorists would be turned against the US. The US expressed its determination to do something about this situation, using military force if necessary, to secure "regime change" in Iraq if need be. The contemplated use of force which is our present concern is any that the British government would take in support of US action.

The charges against Iraq provided three kinds of claim for justification for employing military force:

1. Self-defence, including collective self-defence, as a further element in the war against terrorism, Iraq being implicated in future incidents in the campaign of terrorism against the US of which "11th September" events were the most prominent example;

2. Self-defence, including collective self-defence, to meet a threat from Iraq to use weapons of mass destruction against the US or its allies sometime in the future;

3. Enforcement of Iraq's obligations under various Security Council resolutions, the claim being made that existing resolutions contained sufficient authority for the use of force by States on their own initiative.[2]

3. The Legal Background

Starting in earnest with the Covenant of the League of Nations, international law has sought to impose limitations on the use of force by States. The Kellogg-Briand Pact of 1928 aimed at eliminating force as a means of achieving political goals. The lessons of the Great War which prompted these steps were reinforced by the experiences of World War II. The United Nations Charter is much more than a treaty, a political compact for world order in which the preservation of peace was seen as the priority. Besides setting up the UN and its organs, the Charter also lays down some fundamental rules for States. High among them are the obligations to settle disputes peacefully and not to resort to force, Articles 2(3) and 2(4) of the Charter. The proscription against the use of force is extensive. It is subject only to two exceptions - the right to use force in Article 51 and the right to use force under the authority of the Security Council (see below). The Charter puts the prohibition of force above considerations of justice and of law - while States have surrendered their own power to use force to secure compliance with international law, there is no power in the Charter of forcible implementation of international law (General Assembly Resolution 2625). What there is and what is the other part of the compact, is the vesting of authority in the Security Council to maintain international peace and security by a system of collective security. The Council has the power to take binding decisions, subject to a nine-from-fifteen majority and the absence of opposition from any of the five permanent members of the Council, if the Council determines that a situation threatens international peace (Article 39). These decisions not only bind the members of the UN but take precedence over other treaty obligations of those States (Article 103). The Council, at anyone time only fifteen members of the UN, possesses, therefore, an exceptional authority. It may require States to take non-forcible action under Article 41, such as economic sanctions. The Charter envisaged that the Council could deploy UN forces under Article 42, a power which was dependent upon agreements between States and the UN to provide these forces. This power in the Charter has never been available for want of any agreements. Instead, there has developed a practice of the Council authorising willing

States to use their national forces or the forces of inter-national organisations to secure the implementation of mandates conferred by the Council (N Blokker, "Is the Authorisation Authorised?... (2000) 11 EJIL 541). The authorisation given to the "states co-operating with Kuwait" under Resolution 678 was the first occasion the Council did this after the end of the Cold War.[3] The authorisation is notable for its breadth of purpose (including, as mentioned, action to restore international peace and security in the area), for its time-unlimited character and for the lack of accountability obligations of the States to the UN. As the practice has developed during the 1990s, it has been the case that the mandates have been more tightly defined and subject to temporal limits and that the overall authority of the UN has been affirmed. These elements of control, it is argued, are not merely desirable politically but necessary legally to constitute a valid delegation of authority from the Council to the participating States. This is not quite the Charter scheme as it was envisaged but one which has been crafted in practice and accepted by States as the most feasible and functionally effective option available.

The right of States to use force in self-defence is specifically recognised by the Charter (Article 51). Even if the collective security arrangements under Chapter VII had worked impeccably from the very beginning, a right of self-defence would still have been necessary in those instances in which one State attacked another but before the collective security forces could be put in the field. The language of the Charter is not entirely clear and its ambiguities were much relied upon because of the imperfections of the collective security response following the divisions in the Council as a consequence of the Cold War. Much is often made of the use of the word "inherent" - "Nothing in the Charter shall impair the **inherent** right to... self-defence...". Although it is not without controversy, I accept that this refers to a right of self-defence in customary international law, as it was in 1945 and as it may have developed since (Nicaragua (Merits) case, (1986) ICJ Rep 14). For the moment, though, I want to draw a further implication from the word. "Inherent" suggests that the right is an incident of Statehood, a right which a State or States might choose to limit but as to which limitations should not readily be presumed. The legal basis for each limitation will, in each case, have to be demonstrated. This is not to say that the right of self-defence is a non-justiciable prerogative of a State which can never be subject to external scrutiny. In particular, a State claiming to act in self-defence is obliged to report the matter to the Security Council. The ICJ has said that a failure to do so may be taken into account in assessing the legality of a State's claim of self-defence. If a situation is reported to the Council, it is hardly conceivable that the defending State would not explain its case. Quite apart from any legal complexity, which may be beyond resolving in the Council, the need to bring plausible evidence in support of a State's case will expose a significant part of its argument to scrutiny. Because self-defence is not equivalent to state necessity, it has both inherent and specific limitations upon it.

In contrast to self-defence, authorisation by the Council to a State to use force requires a two-fold justification: the authorisation must be within the substantive power of the Council, taken according to the procedural mechanisms identified in the Charter; and the authorisation to the State must be clear - if it is not express, the necessity of any implication must be strong, otherwise States could usurp the power of the Council and, with the support of a permanent member veto, could then thwart any attempt by the Council to retrieve its authority [4]

4. The Legal Argument

The Inquiry took the form of a challenge to any prospective UK military action. Accordingly, Mr Singh had to anticipate arguments which the Government might make and to consider whether they could be sustained by any evidence publicly available and then whether they were legally defensible. Mr Knowles took Mr Singh's arguments at each level and sought to refute them. He did not put any claim not proposed by Mr Singh.

I begin by noting that Mr Singh did not suggest that the British government would put forward an argument falling within category 1 above, viz that an attack against Iraq could be justified as an exercise of collective self-defence within the continuing campaign of the war on terrorism, a claim which would necessitate the demonstration that Iraq has or immediately will facilitate terrorist attacks by Al Qaeda against the UK or its allies. I consider this no further.

Mr Singh made arguments within the broad categories 2 and 3 above. He said that the Government would contend that it could use force against Iraq, because it had a right of self-defence against an attack by Iraq on its (Iraq's) own behalf against the UK (or against a State which would seek UK assistance as collective self-defence) - the "self-defence" argument. Alternatively, the Government would say that it was authorised by existing Security Council Resolutions to use force because of Iraq's failure to comply with its disarmament obligations under Resolution 687 - the "Security Council" argument. It is important to disentangle two aspects of the situation with respect to Iraq's undoubted delinquency under Resolution 687. On the one hand, it is put forward as a source of a right to use force against Iraq - this is the "Security Council" argument. On the other, it is regarded as a source of evidence as to Iraq's capacity (and even intention) to use its weaponry held in contravention of Resolution 687 against the UK or one of its allies - the "self-defence" argument. Its evidential value is not enhanced simply by reason that Iraq is in breach of its obligations to the UN.

The Self-defence Argument

I take the argument from self-defence first and I start with the question of evidence. Mr Knowles suggested that the inquiry had no option but to defer to the Government's contention that it had adequate evidence of a threatened attack by Iraq of such magnitude and immediacy as to justify a military response. I have some sympathy with this position. However, the Government's enlistment of international law on its side and its engagement in the debate about the facts of the situation in Iraq invite consideration of its position, of course on the understanding that an authoritative conclusion about the legality of its plans cannot be arrived at. That is the basis on which this Inquiry is undertaken. I am asked to consider the question "in the present circumstances" and I have indicated that I take that to include the evidential circumstances - that which is in the public domain on the 11th October 2002. I do not rule it out, indeed I think it most likely, that the government has evidence that it has not revealed by reason of the sensitivity of its sources but which would reinforce the case the Government seeks to make. Equally, more evidence might become available or events might show that that which is presently tentative or speculative does in fact have some forensic value. What I do here is rely on the evidence used by counsel, derived from public sources, and apply it to the arguments based on self-defence as I understand them. Any conclusions I reach are, of course, vulnerable to the production of other evidence in the future.

So, I turn now to the law of self-defence. On one point, at least, there was agreement between counsel: there is no present "armed attack" against the UK or any other relevant State by Iraq or any other state or group with which Iraq is associated. In other words, a claim of self-defence could be made out now only if the law allowed some action in anticipation of an actual "attack". However, even then there were immediate difficulties. Counsel had some problem in determining when "attacks" started: neither of them were able to say quite when, at the earliest, Kuwait (or its allies) would have been permitted to respond to Iraq's undoubted armed attack in 1990. Yet, it seems clear that an "attack" cannot be confined to the actual passage of the first hostile tank, aircraft or missile across the international boundary. Equally, once an "attack", even if it were so narrowly circumscribed, has started, the defending State is entitled to respond, within the parameters of immediacy and necessity, if the attack is part of a continuing campaign against it. None of this would avail the UK at present.

The British government needs to rely on a wider notion of anticipation. Any such right must find its source in the "inherent" right because other the language of the Charter - "if an armed attack occurs" - inclines against it. Equally, it seems to me, if some notion of anticipatory defensive action is permissible, it must be related to something more than a situation of concern or, especially, mere capacity on the part of the alleged putative attacker. Although it was not a juridical determination and although Mr Knowles tried to limit the analysis to the precise facts of the situation, the Council did condemn the raid by Israel on the Osirak reactor in 1981 (Resolution 487), with some members of the Council regarding it precisely in terms of an excessive (that is to say, wholly precautionary) notion of anticipation. It is the nearest example we have to what is claimed in the present case. The writers are divided about what was the state of customary international law in 1945 (such as might be embraced by the "inherent" right in Article 51) but I accept the view of Dr Gray that any uncertainty about what the position was has been increasingly narrowed by practice since then, a practice marked by a reluctance of even those States which assert a right in the abstract to rely on it in particular situations (Gray, above, pp.111-115). To extend self-defence so far in anticipation excludes from it the essential element of immediacy. Mr Knowles argued that the idea had to be considered in its context, taking into account both the seriousness of any threat (here the use of weapons of mass destruction) and the practical possibility of responding. He maintained that the prospect of widespread damage from the clandestine delivery of a weapon of mass destruction created an immediate need to destroy any possibility of an eventual attack. On this basis, of course, there would be no need even to show that the other State presently had the capacity to attack (that is, that it actually had any weapons), only that it was seeking to get them and, if it did, it had the intention to use them against the defending State. Mr Knowles's analysis would put all the weight on intention (though he did not concede that there was no evidence of a present capability of Iraq to deliver a biological or chemical weapons attack). There are principled and pragmatic reasons why the practice has developed against this proposition - in principle and subject to any international obligations that it has accepted or any decision of the Council to the contrary, a State is entitled to develop, obtain and deploy any weapons as an exercise of its sovereignty. Even if a State develops weapons in breach of a treaty, say the Nuclear Non-proliferation Treaty, there is no right in international law for a State to use forcible counter-measures against the wrong-doing State by reason of the illegality alone. The pragmatic reason runs directly contrary to Mr Knowles's case: the very danger on which he places so much weight is increased if an attack by one State, assertedly in self-defence to pre-empt the other's use of weapons of mass destruction, precipitates an exchange of these weapons. On such is the whole theory of deterrence based.

Mr Singh was able to concede that Iraq might have weapons of mass destruction, might even have the means to use them for an attack beyond its immediate neighbours but, in the absence of any evidence that Iraq intended to use its capacity in this way, it was not possible to claim that there was any right of self-defence. That being the case, considerations of the necessity and proportionality of any response were beside the point, indeed impossible to calculate, for neither the threat (which remained putative) nor the response (which was at present in the future) could be identified. To the extent that he thought these were questions within the competence of the Inquiry, Mr Knowles relied mainly on the Government's "Dossier" - "Iraq's Weapons of Mass Destruction". However, much of the evidence which seeks to go beyond establishing Iraq's capacity to use weapons of mass destruction against targets which would give rise to a right of self-defence in the UK, does little more than point to Saddam Hussein's propensity to use force, including chemical weapons, against domestic opponents and an external enemy without the capacity to respond in kind (Iran during the first Gulf War). That Hussein is a very bad man with aggressive tendencies is beyond doubt: that there is evidence here that he has taken steps towards instituting an armed attack against the UK such as to give rise to a right of self-defence is unconvincing. Indeed, the thrust of this opinion is that such threat as Hussein's capacities and propensities pose is a threat to which "the international community" has to "stand up" and against which it should act. Self-defence, even collective self-defence being a unilateral act, does not appear to be the appropriate answer to the concerns of the "international community".

The Security Council Argument

Now, reference to the "International Community", at least in a legal context, often gives one cause for pause. However, where the use of force is involved, the "International Community" has a legal manifestation - it is the Security Council which acts for the international community in these matters. The Council has acted with respect to Iraq: a catalogue of 16 Resolutions was brought to my attention (there are 29 in all). There is no question that the Council has dealt and is dealing with the situation in Iraq. It is exercising the powers of the "International Community". The Security Council may authorise the use of force by member States willing to discharge the mandate proposed by the Council and, since the Council may respond to "situations" which threaten international peace and security, its powers clearly go beyond circumstances which would justify a state from resorting to self-defence. It is usually the case these days that the Secretary-General assembles his "coalition of the able and the willing" before the Security Council formally approves the mandate and other details for which the forces may act. We have seen that the Council did authorise the use of force ("all necessary measures") by the "States co-operating with Kuwait") in Resolution 678. This mandate included the power to act "for the restoration of peace and security in the area". We should recognise that if the Coalition had been willing to proceed to Baghdad in 1991 and overthrow Hussein's regime, the language of Resolution 678 is apposite to have permitted it to have done so. It is also the case that, in the Preamble to Resolution 687, the Council recalls all previous Resolutions relating to Iraq's invasion of Kuwait and, since Resolution 687 refers to "the objective of restoring international peace and security in the area" and refers to Chapter VII, the argument goes that States may use the authorisation in Resolution 678 to achieve the objective in Resolution 687. The contention could be strengthened by noting that the Council has found Iraq to be in breach of its obligations under 687 and has warned Iraq of "the severest consequences" if it failed to remedy them (Resolution 1154).

However, a close scrutiny of Council practice since Resolution 687 shows an alternative line of argument. First is the distinction between Resolutions 686 and 687 on the reference back to the power to use force under 678, present in the former but not in the latter. Indeed, in Resolution 687, para 6, the Council noted that the deployment of the UN force on the Kuwait-Iraq border would allow the Coalition to withdraw from Iraq, according to the terms of Resolutions 678 and 686. Furthermore, Resolution 687 declares that a formal cease-fire will arise between Iraq on the one hand and Kuwait and the Coalition on the other on "official notification by Iraq..." of its acceptance of the provisions of the Resolution and decides that the Council will remained seized of the matter and it will "take such further steps as may be required for the implementation of the present resolution and to secure peace and security in the region" (para 34). This pattern of language has continued through the subsequent resolutions on the situation in Iraq. Even Resolution 1154, which threatens Iraq with the "severest consequences" in the event of violations,

Decides, in accordance with its responsibilities under the Charter, to remain actively seized of the matter, in order to ensure its implementation of this resolution , and to secure peace and security in the area.

This is language which clearly refers to the power of the Council and not of member states. Any unilateral right to use force must be based on something other than these resolutions. The argument that the power in Resolution 678 both survives and is adequate to justify unilateral State action will not stand up to examination. This authorisation is to "the States co-operating with the government of Kuwait" to take action effectively to restore the authority of the government of Kuwait (no longer an issue) and to restore international peace and security in the area (potentially a wider authority) - but the Coalition is no longer in existence and the power being sought is related to the implementation of resolutions subsequent to Resolution 678, not obviously intended when Resolutions 686 and 687 are compared and when the language of those subsequent resolutions is considered. (See Lobel (below), Gray (above)). In particular, Resolution 1154 is an assertion of plenary authority by the Council over the situation in Iraq insofar as it is covered by Council Resolutions. The argument that Resolution 678 is a residuary right to use force fails to take into account the original reassertion of authority over the situation by the Council in Resolution 687. There are no longer "States co-operating with the Government of Kuwait" to restore its authority. It might even be argued that Resolution 678 is no longer a "relevant" resolution in the terms of Resolution 1154.

The British government's explanation for the legality of Operation Desert Fox, the US/UK bombing operation after the withdrawal of UNSCOM in 1998 was characterised by its opacity. Take for instance the statement of Foreign Office Minister Baroness Symmonds:

It is important to remember that we are considering a highly complex network of United Nations Security Council Resolutions. Perhaps I may remind your Lordships that there is Resolution 678 demanding that Iraq left Kuwait. There is Resolution 687, which set out the ceasefire arrangements, the position of UNSCOM and the necessity for Iraq to comply with it on an unconditional basis. There is also Resolution 1154, which concerns the memorandum of understanding with the United Nations Secretary General and which speaks of the severest consequences if that memorandum was broken. There is Resolution 1205, which speaks of the flagrant violation which the Security Council believes has been committed by Iraq.

I believe I have been very clear that Her Majesty's Government were not in any doubt that there was a clear legal basis for the planned military action at the weekend ((1998) British Yearbook of International Law 590).

Perhaps the most important feature of her statement are the words, "... there is Resolution 678 demanding that Iraq left Kuwait...". Iraq has, of course done that (or been made to do it). None of the other resolutions cited by the Minister authorise the unilateral use of force, indeed to the contrary, they assert the authority of the Council. Her belief that "I have been very clear... that there was a clear legal basis for the planned military action" is unfounded. Nor is much further assistance to be gained from the statement of the British representative to the Security Council when he referred to three Council resolutions - 1154, 1205, and 687 - and said "by that resolution" the Council implicitly revived the authorisation to use force" in 678 (id, 591). It is not clear which resolution "that" one is or how breach of any of them could have, even implicitly, the effect maintained. Certainly, it was an interpretation rejected by other members of the Council [C Gray, "From Unity to Polarisation... (2002) 13 EJIL 1]. Indeed, one feels that the very lack of a clear statement of its case counts against the Government. One need not expect that it could be made succinctly but it must be made persuasively.

The strongest single item of evidence in favour of Mr Knowles's proposition is the Secretary General's statement of January 1993 saying that air raids carried out by the US, the UK and France directed against Iraqi missiles in the no-fly zones was justified under Resolution 678 in answer to Iraq's breach of the cease-fire Resolution 687. To that Mr Singh said that it was an isolated remark, given in a press statement, which had not been repeated and which had been contradicted since by the UN Legal Department (referring to J Lobel and M Ratner, "Bypassing the Security Council... (1999) 93 AJIL 124, 133). I should add that the Secretary General's comment does not reflect the British justification for use of force to protect planes in the no-fly ones and that what is contemplated at present seems to be for a wholly different purpose and of a wholly different order.

This isolated statement apart, there is a dispute between members of the Council about what the resolutions mean. An authoritative interpretation from a tribunal is scarcely conceivable; an interpretation by the Council is unlikely because of the capacity of either side to veto an unfavourable conclusion. The present Legal Adviser to the Foreign & Commonwealth Office has indicated how troublesome the interpretation of Security Council resolutions can be (M Wood, "The Interpretation of Security Council Resolutions", 2 Max Planck Yearbook of United Nations Law 73). Taking too formal an approach may miss the point but, unless the language is held to disguise the absence of agreement, the words of the resolutions in their Charter context must be taken to represent the political compromise reached by the Members of the Council. The mere fact that a State takes (or, indeed, has taken) a different view ought not to avail it against the resolution. Any conclusion of mine is, of course, far from authoritative but, based on the structure of the Charter as well as on the language of the resolutions, the Charter requiring a State claiming authorisation to use force to make its case, the resolutions demonstrating an intention of the Council to take control of affairs after Resolution 687, and the absence of "States co-operating with Kuwait" (the ones authorised to use force by Resolution 678, as an identifiable category), my position is that the use of unilateral force to secure the implementation of Resolution 687 and subsequent resolutions requires a new mandate from the Council, a mandate which could take account of the post-Kuwait practice of the Council in establishing clear mandates and setting time-limits for any authorisation actually given.

I do not attach much weight to the fact that the US and UK are actively seeking a new Security Council resolution which would expressly authorise the use of force against Iraq. Those States are entitled to argue that the resolution is legally superfluous, though it might be politically significant in engendering support from those States who doubt or even reject the argument that the US and UK may act in any event against Iraq.

There is no right of States to use force to secure the implementation of international law. Iraq's obligations under Resolution 687 are obligations under international law. Something more, then, is required to allow the use force than the mere fact of Iraq's non-compliance (even if it is described as a "material breach"). In my view the burden of showing this "something more", viz Security Council authorisation, rests on the States claiming to use force, a claim that the UK has not made out. I am particularly sceptical of claims that the failure of diplomacy justifies resort to force "as a last resort". The whole process of the development of international law from the Kellogg-Briand Pact through the Charter and General Assembly Resolution 2625 demonstrates a trend to the contrary, a trend confirmed by the ICJ in the Nicaragua case. Nor do I find convincing in legal terms the claim that if a new resolution authorising the use of force fails to be passed by the Security Council (whether or not because of the veto), some residual right of individual States to secure Iraq's compliance with its obligations then emerges.

5. Conclusion:

On the above view of the law of self-defence, even if weight is given to the "inherent" quality of the right of self-defence, such that a State is entitled to respect for its decision to act (at least until such time as the Security Council has considered the matter) and, perhaps, even if some notion of anticipatory self-defence is accepted, the British government has not produced evidence necessary to establish a plausible case that there is a threat of armed attack by Iraq against the UK commensurate with a right of self-defence. This is not to say that there might not be such evidence which the Government would be able to reveal later if it actually needed to use force rather than simply contemplate using it or that circumstances could soon change so as to make the claim a plausible one.

There is no explicit authority of the Council to the UK to use force for the implementation of Council resolutions, notably 687 or 1154. Resolution 678, which does contain an explicit authorisation, refers to the "States co-operating with Kuwait". The case cannot be sensibly made that any forcible action against Iraq now of the kind contemplated by the US and the UK has anything to do with Iraq's attack on Kuwait or that the two States see themselves as acting in assistance to Kuwait. In the absence of explicit authorisation, one should be wary of claims that there is implicit authority to use force, given that the powers of the Council are limited and that its practice has been developing to condition any authorisations it does make in order to secure at least a degree of accountability of the authorised States to the Council. An implicit power, in the nature of things, cannot be circumscribed in this way. Furthermore, the language of 687 and all subsequent resolutions asserts the power of the Council to secure implementation of whatever obligations of Iraq are under consideration. Although the US and the UK claimed that there was a unilateral right to use the force applied against Iraq in 1998, these claims were weakly explained as to their legal justification and the legality of the bombings was strongly contested by a number of members of the Council. The interpretation of Council resolutions is not to be definitively determined by a majority of its members (any more than it is by a minority), so one must do the best one can. The conclusion against authorisation seems to me to fit best the structure of authority in the UN and the pattern of language of the resolutions.

Colin Warbrick, 30.10.02

FOOTNOTES

1. Realistically, if it does use force, the position of the UK is likely to be associated with the use of force by the US. We did not assume that the UK would necessarily support the US and so would necessarily take any argument for legality put forward by the US.

2. I have not addressed the objective of "regime change," since the case for this as a legitimate objective was not put to me. It is enough, perhaps to note that Security Council Resolution 687 affirms "the commitment of all Member States to the sovereignty, territorial integrity and political independence ofIraq."

3. For recent accounts of the law and practice, see C Gray, "International Law and the Use of Force" (2000), chs. 4 and 5; Y Dinstein, "War, Aggression and Self-Defence" (3rd ed, 2001), chs. 7-9).

4. The Croatia Subpoena case before the International Criminal Court for Yugoslavia shows that Tribunal taking a wide view of the powers of the Council (following the Tadic case on the setting up of the Tribunal) but a narrow view of the powers of organs so established, here no coercive powers against States for the Tribunal in the absence of an express conferring of the power by the Council. The analogy with the position of States claiming implied powers to use force against other states seems wrong.

PART II
CND LEGAL CHALLENGE TO THE GOVERNMENT

4. AN OPINION GIVEN TO THE CAMPAIGN FOR NUCLEAR DISARMAMENT (CND) : RABINDER SINGH QC AND CHARLOTTE KILROY, 15 NOVEMBER 2002

****

In the Matter of the Potential Use of Armed Force by the UK against Iraq and in the Matter of Reliance for that Use of Force on United Nations Security Council Resolution 1441

OPINION

---

1. We are asked to advise the Campaign for Nuclear Disarmament on whether the United Kingdom (**UK**) can rely on United Nations Security Council Resolution 1441 (**SCR 1441**), which was adopted on 8 November 2002, to use force against Iraq.

Summary of advice

2. In summary our opinion is that:

    (1) Security Council Resolution 1441 does not authorise the use of force by member states of the UN.

    (2) The UK would be in breach of international law if it were to use force against Iraq in reliance on Resolution 1441 without a further Security Council Resolution.

The text of the resolution

3. SCR 1441 was sponsored jointly by the UK and the United States (**US**). The resolution states at paragraph 1 that the Security Council acting under Chapter VII of the United Nations Charter

    "Decides that Iraq has been and remains in material breach of its obligations under relevant resolutions, including resolution 687 (1991), in particular through Iraq's failure to cooperate with United Nations inspectors and the IAEA, and to complete the actions required under paragraphs 8 to 13 of resolution 687 (1991;".

4. Consequently SCR 1441 offers Iraq a *'final opportunity to comply with its disarmament obligations'* and sets up what is described at paragraph 2 as

    'an enhanced inspection regime with the aim of bringing to full and verified completion the disarmament process established by resolution 687 (1991) and subsequent resolutions of the Council'.

5. Paragraphs 4, 11 and 12 of SCR 1441 deal with the event of non-compliance by Iraq with the terms of the resolution. By these paragraphs the Security Council.

    "4. Decides that false statements or omissions in the declarations submitted by Iraq pursuant to this resolution and failure by Iraq at any time to comply with, and cooperate fully in the implementation of, this resolution shall constitute a further material breach of Iraq's obligations and will be reported to the Council for assessment in accordance with paragraphs 11 and 12 below;

    11. Directs the Executive Chairman of UNMOVIC and the Director-General of the IAEA to report immediately to the Council any interference by Iraq with inspection activities, as well as any failure by Iraq to comply with its disarmament obligations, including its obligations regarding inspections under this resolution;

    12. Decides to convene immediately upon receipt of a report in accordance with paragraphs 4 or 11 above, in order to consider the situation and the need for full compliance with all of the relevant Council resolutions in order to secure international peace and security".

6. By paragraph 13 of SCR 1441 the Security Council

    "Recalls, in that context, that the Council has repeatedly warned Iraq that it will face serious consequences as a result of its continued violations of its obligations".

Background to the resolution

The draft resolutions

7. A draft of the resolution was first circulated at the United Nations at the beginning of October. That first draft contained the following paragraph:

    "The Security Council...

    Determined to secure full compliance with its decision

    Acting under Chapter VII of the Charter of the United Nations...

    Decides that false statements or omissions in the declaration submitted *by Iraq to the Council and the failure by Iraq at any time to comply and cooperate fully in accordance with the provisions laid out in this resolution, shall constitute a further material breach of Iraq's obligations, **and that such breach authorises member states to use all necessary means to restore international peace and security in the area**.*" (Emphasis added)

8.   This paragraph was highly controversial, receiving the notable opposition of Russia and France, two of the five permanent members of the Security Council. As a result, on 23 October 2002, the UK and US presented a draft to the Security Council which had been modified to remove any reference to authorisation to '*member states to use all necessary means*'. The paragraph (which was now paragraph 4) read instead:

"*4. Decides that false statements or omissions in the declarations submitted by Iraq pursuant to this resolution and failure by Iraq at any time to comply with, and cooperate fully in the implementation of, this resolution shall constitute a further material breach of Iraq's obligations.*"

9.   In addition paragraph 12 was inserted into the resolution.

10.   Further negotiations and discussions amongst the Security Council members led to a new draft being submitted to the Security Council on 6 November 2002. That draft was identical to the form of the resolution which was finally adopted save for two changes. Paragraph 4 stated that a breach of Iraq's obligations would *"be reported to the Council for assessment in accordance with paragraphs 11 **or** 12 below"*; and paragraph 12 concluded with the words *"in order to **restore** international peace and security."*

Statements of the Ambassadors to the UN

11.   Following the adoption of SCR 1441 on 8 November 2002 the ambassadors to the United Nations from the 15 members of the Security Council made public statements including the following.

12.   Ambassador Greenstock from the UK stated:

"*....We heard loud and clear during the negotiations the concerns about "automaticity" and "hidden triggers" - the concern that on a decision so crucial we should not rush into military action; that on a decision so crucial any Iraqi violations should be discussed by the Council. Let me be equally clear in response, as a co-sponsor with the United States of the text we have adopted. There is no "automaticity" in this Resolution. If there is a further Iraqi breach of its disarmament obligations, the matter will return to the Council for discussion as required in Operational Paragraph 12. We would expect the Security Council then to meet its responsibilities ....*

if Iraq chooses defiance and concealment, rejecting the final opportunity it has been given by the Council in Operational Paragraph 2, the UK – together, we trust, with other Members of the Security Council – will ensure that the task of disarmament required by the Resolutions is completed.

13. Ambassador Negroponte from the US stated:

"As we have said on numerous occasions to Council members, this Resolution contains no "hidden triggers" and no "automaticity" with respect to the use of force. If there is a further Iraqi breach, reported to the Council by UNMOVIC, the IAEA, or a member state, the matter will return to the Council for discussions as required in paragraph 12. The Resolution makes clear that any Iraqi failure to comply is unacceptable and that Iraq must be disarmed. And one way or another, Mr. President, Iraq will be disarmed. If the Security Council fails to act decisively in the event of a further Iraqi violation, this resolution does not constrain any member state from acting to defend itself against the threat posed by Iraq, or to enforce relevant UN resolutions and protect world peace and security."[1]

14. The statements from the ambassadors of France, Russia and China, in common with those of many other of 15 Security Council members, welcomed the inclusion in the resolution of the 'two-stage approach' whereby the Security Council in the words of the French ambassador '*maintains control of the process at each stage*', and the absence of all *traces of 'automaticity'. In a later* joint statement issued on 8 November 2002 France, Russia and China stated

"Resolution 1441 (2002) adopted today by the Security Council excludes any automaticity in the use of force. In this regard, we register with satisfaction the declarations of the representatives of the United States and the United Kingdom confirming this understanding in their explanations of vote, and assuring that the goal of the resolution is the full implementation of the existing Security Council resolutions on Iraq's weapons of mass destruction disarmament. All Security Council members share this goal.

In case of failure by Iraq to comply with its obligations, the provisions of paragraphs 4, 11 and 12 will apply. Such failure will be reported to the Security Council by the Executive Chairman of UNMOVIC or the Director General of the IAEA. It will be then for the Council to take position on the basis of that report.

Therefore, this resolution fully respects the competences of the Security Council in the maintenance of international peace and security, in conformity with the Charter of the United Nations."

64

Press statements of UK Ministers

15. Despite these clear statements on the meaning of SCR 1441, several Ministers of the UK Government and US officials have indicated that, in the event of non-compliance with SCR 1441 by Iraq, the UK and the US would be entitled to take military action against Iraq even without a further Security Council resolution.

16. Colin Powell is reported[2] as saying: *"The United States believes because of past material breaches, current material breaches and new material breaches there is more than enough authority for it to act.....I can assure you if he doesn't comply this time we are going to ask the UN to give authorisation for all necessary means, and if the UN isn't willing to do that, the United States with like-minded nations will go and disarm him forcefully."*

17. Jack Straw, meanwhile, stated on 10 November 2002 that: *'military action is bound to follow if Saddam Hussein does not fully cooperate with the terms of this resolution'.*[3]

18. Furthermore, in response to MPs' questions[4] on the resolution in the House of Commons on 7 November 2002 Mr Straw stated,

     "I do not want to anticipate what will happen if there is a breach, except to say that although we would much prefer decisions to be taken within the Security Council, we have always made it clear that within international law we have to reserve our right to take military action, if that is required, within the existing charter and the existing body of UN Security Council resolutions, if, for example, a subsequent resolution were to be vetoed."[5]

Issues

19. The question therefore arises from the statements set out above to what extent the UK is entitled to rely on either:

     1) SCR 1441,

     2) The existing body of UN Security Council resolutions,

     3) The UN Charter, and/or

     4) Customary International law as the basis for the use of force against Iraq, *without* a further Security Council resolution.

20. Peacerights has already received an opinion on the extent to which the UK can rely on the existing body of UN Security Council resolutions, the UN Charter and/or customary international law as authorising the use of force without a Security Council Resolution. That opinion concluded:

(1)   The use of force against Iraq would not be justified under international law unless:

(a)   Iraq mounted a direct attack on the United Kingdom or one of its allies and that ally requested the United Kingdom's assistance; or

(b)   an attack by Iraq on the United Kingdom or one of its allies was imminent and could be averted in no way other than by the use of force; or

(c)   the United Nations Security Council authorised the use of force in clear terms.

(2)   Iraq has not attacked the United Kingdom or one of its allies, and no evidence is currently available to the public that any attack is imminent.

(3)   Existing Security Council resolutions do not authorise the use of force against Iraq. Such force would require further clear authorisation from the Security Council.

(4)   At present the United Kingdom is therefore not entitled, in international law, to use force against Iraq.

21.   We adopt that opinion which is attached (**OP1**). We also note the views of Professor Colin Warbrick after an inquiry into these issues on 11 October 2002, which in substance accord with ours (that document is also attached).

22.   In this advice therefore we will address only the question of whether the UK can rely on SCR 1441 as authorising the use of force..

Legal Background

23.   As pointed out in OP1 at paragraphs 6-14 the United Nations Charter provides the framework for the use of force in international law.

24.   Article 1 states:

"The Purposes of the United Nations are:

(1)   To maintain international peace and security, and to that end: to take effective collective measures for the prevention and removal of threats to the peace, and for the suppression of acts of aggression or other breaches of the peace, and to bring about by peaceful means, and in conformity with the principles of justice and international law, adjustment or settlement of international disputes or situations which might lead to a breach of the peace."

25.   Articles 2(3) and 2(4) then set out the fundamental principles governing

the settlement of international disputes and the use of force. Article 2(4) states:

"All Members shall refrain in their international relations from the threat or use of force against the territorial integrity or political independence of any state, or in any other manner inconsistent with the Purposes of the United Nations."

26.   In classifying the prohibition on the use of force contained in Article 2 (4) as a principle of customary international law, the International Court of Justice (*Nicaragua v United States*, [1986] ICJ Reports 14, at para 190) referred to the widely held view that this principle was *ius cogens*, in other words a peremptory norm of international law from which states cannot derogate.

27.   Chapter V of the Charter governs the constitution and powers of the Security Council. Article 24 of the Charter states:

1.   In order to ensure prompt and effective action by the United Nations, its Members confer on the Security Council primary responsibility for the maintenance of international peace and security, and agree that in carrying out its duties under this responsibility the Security Council acts on their behalf.

2.   In discharging these duties the Security Council shall act in accordance with the Purposes and Principles of the United Nations. The specific powers granted to the Security Council for the discharge of these duties are laid down in Chapters VI, VII, VIII and XII....

28.   Chapter VII confers on the Security Council the duty of determining the existence of any threat to the peace, breach of the peace, or act of aggression, and the duty of deciding what action should be taken to maintain or restore international peace and security (Article 39).

29.   Article 41 gives the Security Council the power to take peaceful measures to give effect to its decisions, and by Article 42, where the Security Council considers that those measures would be, or have proved to be, inadequate it may take such action by air, sea, or land forces as may be necessary to maintain or restore international peace and security.

30.   Chapter VII[6] originally envisaged that the Security Council would carry out such enforcement action itself using the armed forces of Member States. As a consequence there is no express authority for the Security Council to delegate to Member States[7] the competence to carry out enforcement action under their own command and control (see Danesh Sarooshi, The United Nations and the Development of Collective Security, (Oxford, 1999), at p143).

31. The only express reference in Chapter VII to the use of force by Member States acting alone is at Article 51 which states: "*Nothing in the present Charter shall impair the inherent right of individual or collective self-defence if an armed attack occurs against a Member of the United Nations, until the Security Council has taken measures necessary to maintain international peace and security.*"

32. Nonetheless a practice has arisen of authorising Member States to carry out enforcement action on the Security Council's behalf. It is important to emphasise, however, that there is no express authority in the UN Charter for Member States to carry out actions under Article 42 under their own command and control either with or without a Security Council Resolution.

Does SCR 1441 authorise the use of force?

Express authorisation

33. It is clear that SCR 1441 does not expressly authorise Member States to use force in the event of non-compliance. A study of resolutions adopted by the Security Council, including Resolution 678, shows that that the language used to authorise force is bold and consistent. Member states are '*authorised*' to '*use all necessary means*' or '*take all necessary measures*' in pursuit of a specified goal.[8] (See OP1 at paragraph 52).

34. As can be seen from the excerpts of the draft resolutions set out above, the UK and the US sought express authorisation in such terms in the first draft of their resolution. Such express authorisation is manifestly lacking in the final draft. This was for reasons which the other Security Council permanent members Russia, China and France made clear: they did not want the resolution to authorise force.

35. Instead SCR 1441 provides at paragraphs 4, 11 and 12 that in the event of non-compliance the matter will be referred to the Security Council, which will convene to consider the need for full compliance with all of the relevant Security Council resolutions. This clearly contemplates that it is the Security Council which will decide on any further action to be taken against Iraq.

36. Paragraph 13 states that the Security Council "*Recalls, in that context, that the Council has repeatedly warned Iraq that it will face serious consequences as a result of its continued violations of its obligations.*" We consider that the words '*in that context*', which appeared first in the 6 November draft, clearly indicate that any serious consequences which Iraq will face are to be decided upon in the context of the discussion by the Security Council envisaged by paragraph 12. In any event, we are of the view that the phrase "serious consequences" does not itself authorise

the use of force but is a reference to previous warnings which this part of the Resolution "recalls".

Implicit authorisation

37. OP1 at paragraphs 40- 76 addresses the arguments put forward by the UK and the US in the past that the Security Council resolutions previously adopted in respect of Iraq provide authorisation either expressly or impliedly for the resumption of the use of force against Iraq.

38. In particular OP1 describes at paragraph 58 the debate over whether Resolution 1154 gave Member States the automatic right to use force in the event of non-compliance. On that occasion no agreement was reached on the issue with the UK and the US maintaining that they did have such a right and other members such as Russia explicitly rejecting the argument that 'automaticity' was included in the resolution.

39. It appears to be because of the subsequent attempt of the UK and the US to invoke Resolution 1154 together with Resolutions 678 and 1205 as authority for its use of force (see OP1 paragraph 61) that Russia, France and China insisted on detailed changes to the final draft of SCR 1441 to ensure the same arguments could not be used again. On this occasion, as can be seen above, agreement was reached on the issue of "automaticity" and "hidden triggers" with Russia, China, France, and even the UK and the US ambassadors agreeing that both were absent from SCR 1441.

40. It would be extraordinary if, having failed to obtain an express authorisation for the use of force, having incorporated minute changes to the final draft whose sole purpose was to exclude the possibility of 'automaticity' and 'hidden triggers' and to preserve the role of the Security Council, and having publicly agreed in their explanation of the vote for adoption of SCR 1441 that there was no such implied authorisation for force, the UK and the US were to be able to use SCR 1441 as authority for the use of force without a further Security Council Resolution.

41. For the reasons set out below and in OP1 our view is that any use of force by the UK in reliance on SCR 1441 without a further Security Council Resolution would be a violation of the Purposes of the UN Charter set out in Article 1, and of Article 2(4).

The Charter

42. OP1 at paragraphs 60-70 sets out the reasons why use of implied authorisation of force is in conflict with the fundamental objectives of the Charter set out in Articles 1 and 2 to preserve peace and to prohibit force save in specified circumstances. First, the fundamental nature of

the prohibition against the use of force in Article 2(4) means that any ambiguities in interpretation should be resolved in favour of that prohibition. Secondly, the power given to the Security Council alone under Chapter VII to decide to use force to restore peace is intended to ensure that any decisions on the use of force are reached collectively. The implied authorisation arguments of the UK and the US permits states to make unilateral decisions on the use of force, which is precisely what Chapter VII and the Charter as a whole are designed to avoid.

43. Furthermore, as pointed out above, it is only the Security Council which has the power under Article 39 to determine whether there has been a breach of the peace or threat to the peace and to decide whether to take action under Articles 41 and 42.

44. Danesh Sarooshi argues that, since the Security Council is exercising powers delegated to it by Member States under Article 24 of the UN Charter, powers which it must exercise in compliance with the Purposes and Principles of the United Nations, it cannot delegate certain of its functions under Chapter VII to a Member State, and must retain effective authority and a tight control over those functions which it does delegate (Danesh Sarooshi, The United Nations and the Development of Collective Security, (Oxford, 1999), at pp154-5; see also Niels Blokker, *Is the Authorisation Authorised? Powers and Practice of the UN Security Council to Authorise the Use of Force by 'Coalitions of the Able and Willing'* EJIL 2000 Vol 11 No 3 at 552). Sarooshi also argues that the limitations on delegation mean that the terms of a resolution which delegates Chapter VII powers are to be interpreted narrowly (The United Nations and the Development of Collective Security, above, at p 44). We agree.

45. It is clear that a practice has grown up of delegating the carrying out of enforcement action to Member States, but it is equally clear that in so doing the Security Council has increasingly sought to retain overall control of the operation with clear mandates, time-limited authorisations and reporting requirements (See Blokker, ibid, at 561-5).

46. In our view the implied authorisation arguments put forward by the UK and the US would undermine the control exercised by the Security Council which is an essential feature of lawful delegation under the Chapter VII. These arguments would effectively allow Member States to take unilateral decisions on the interpretation of resolutions, reading into them authorisation to take action which does not appear clearly on the face of the resolution. This leaves the Security Council with little or no control of the functions it has delegated and, in our view, unacceptably waters down the protections built into Chapters V and VII which enshrine the principle of collective decision-making.

47. The fact that states have sought to rely on implied authorisation in circumstances where Members of the Security Council have made it quite clear in adopting the resolution that they do not intend that authorisation to be present only emphasises the flawed nature of the argument.

48. We conclude therefore that both the fundamental objectives and the constitutional framework of the Charter mean that the use of force by a Member State is not justified unless the Security Council authorises it in the clearest of terms. Use of force without such clear authorisation would therefore violate international law.

Interpretation of resolutions under Chapter VII

49. For the reasons set out above and in OP1 at paragraphs 60-70, we consider that an implied authorisation to use force is not compatible with the framework and the objectives of the Charter. Even if such implied authorisation were in principle compatible with the Charter it is in our view clear both from the terms of SCR 1441 and from the discussions of the Security Council members prior to the adoption of SCR 1441 that authorisation to use force cannot be derived from the terms of this particular resolution.

50. As stated above paragraphs 4, 11 and 12 of SCR 1441 provide a clear mechanism in the event of Iraq's non-compliance with its obligations under SCR 1441. Given that there is such a clear mechanism on the face of the resolution it is difficult to see on what basis it could be argued that an alternative mechanism should be implied into the resolution.

51. Furthermore, while the Ambassadors' statements set out above are not a definitive guide to their meaning, they provide the strongest possible evidence of the intentions of the Security Council members in adopting SCR 1441. In the *Namibia Advisory Opinion*, (1971) ICJ Reports 15, at p 53 the International Court of Justice stated that the language of a resolution should be carefully analysed before a conclusion could be made as to its binding effect under Article 25 of the Charter. The question of whether the powers under Article 25 had been exercised was to be determined *"having regard to the terms of the resolution to be interpreted, the discussions leading to it, the Charter provisions invoked and, in general all circumstances that might assist in determining the legal consequences of the resolution...."*

52. We consider that the same exercise should be employed where the terms of a resolution are ambiguous or unclear. The suggestion that ambiguity or uncertainty should permit Member States to reach a unilateral view on the meaning of a resolution is in our view untenable. If the discussions and revisions leading up to the adoption of SCR 1441 are

taken into account, it is clear that they rule out any arguments to the effect that paragraphs such as paragraph 13, which warns of serious consequences, and paragraph 2, which talks of affording Iraq a final opportunity, implicitly authorise the use of force.

53. On the basis of the arguments set out above we consider that any attempt by the UK to rely on SCR 1441 as the basis for taking military action against Iraq without a further Security Council resolution would be in violation of the terms both of the Charter.

54. We consider briefly below some of the other arguments which the UK and the US have hinted they might use if a further Security Council resolution were not forthcoming in the event of Iraq's non-compliance with SCR 1441.

The 'Material breach' argument

55. SCR 1441 at paragraph 1 declares Iraq to be in material breach of its obligations under relevant resolutions and at paragraph 4 states that Iraq's failure to comply with this resolution shall be a further material breach.

56. Colin Powell has stated that '*past material breaches, current material breaches and new material breaches*' provide more than enough authority for the US to act even without a fresh Security Council resolution. The UK approach is more muted but Jack Straw in his response to MPs' questions set out above indicates that he believes that the UK has the right to act within the Charter and the existing body of UN resolutions.

57. OP1 at paragraphs 71-76 addresses the material breaches argument and concludes at paragraph 76 that neither breaches of the cease-fire agreement nor breaches of any other resolution authorise the unilateral use of force.

58. It is important to emphasise in this regard that there is no authority anywhere in the Charter for a Member State to decide to use force in order to enforce against breaches of Security Council resolutions. On the contrary that power is reserved to the Security Council at Article 42. It is only with an express delegation of that power that a Member State may use force against another Member State to force it to comply with a Security Council resolution.

59. Without that authorisation any use of force would be in clear contravention of the basic principle prohibiting the use of force in Article 2(4) of the Charter.

Authorisation in the event of the Security Council's failure to reach a resolution

60. Both UK and US ambassadors to the UN and government ministers have made statements saying they expect the Security Council to '*meet its responsibilities*' (Ambassador Greenstock). Jack Straw in his answer to MPs' questions set out above alluded to the right to use force in the event of a veto of a further resolution from the Security Council.

61. It is plain that this is not the correct approach to the interpretation of the Charter. It is the Security Council which is the final arbiter of whether to take measures and what measures to take under Articles 39, 41 and 42. As explained above and in OP1 this collective decision-making process is at the heart of the powers conferred on the Security Council by the Charter. It would be in contradiction to the fundamental objectives and the framework of the Charter for a Member State to review the decisions of the Security Council and take action in its stead if it does not agree with them.

62. Professor Colin Warbrick, at page 14 of his opinion, states,

"I am particularly sceptical of claims that the failure of diplomacy justifies resort to force "as a last resort". The whole process of the development of international law from the Kellogg-Briand Pact through the Charter and General Assembly Resolution 2625 demonstrates a trend to the contrary, a trend confirmed by the ICJ in the <u>Nicaragua</u> case. Nor do I find convincing in legal terms the claim that if a new resolution authorising the use of force fails to be passed by the Security Council (whether or not because of the veto), some residual right of individual States to secure Iraq's compliance with its obligations then emerges."

Why does SCR 1441 not expressly require the US and the UK to obtain a new resolution?

63. Some reports have suggested that government officials are asserting that the fact that there is no language in SCR 1441 explicitly ruling out the use by the UK or the US of force without a further Security Council resolution means that they are not "handcuffed" by the SCR 1441 into obtaining such a resolution.[9] In our view, this argument is flawed. Jules Lobel and Michael Ratner address a similar argument adopted by the US in relation to Resolution 1154: "*the failure to adopt a resolution opposing US action cannot be deemed dispositive when any such resolution would have been fruitless in the face of the US and UK veto power. Still the Council did the next best thing: it adopted a resolution that did not provide the United States with the authority it sought and the members stated their understanding that the resolution was intended*

to preclude any such authority." (*Bypassing the Security Council: Ambiguous Authorisations to use Force, Cease-fires and the Iraqi Inspection Regime.*' [1999] AJIL 124).

64. In any event, in our view, for the reasons set out above, it is unnecessary to insert wording in a resolution expressly requiring Member States to obtain an authorisation to use force, when the Charter makes it quite clear that with the exception of the inherent right of self-defence in Article 51, only the Security Council can make a decision to use force and only in the circumstances set out in Chapter VII.

65. The US Ambassador may be right when he says that SCR 1441 itself '*does not constrain any member state from acting to defend itself against the threat posed by Iraq, or to enforce relevant UN resolutions and protect world peace and security*' (*see above*). Member states are, however, constrained as explained above and in OP1 by customary international law and by the UN Charter.

The preamble

66. We have also been asked to consider whether the wording of the preamble in particular paragraphs 4, 5, 10 and 11 allows the UK to use force without a further resolution. The preamble to a resolution may be used as a tool of interpretation of the operative part of the resolution (see *Namibia Advisory Opinion* at p 53) but carries no operative force itself. This means that it cannot be relied upon to authorise action of any kind. Nor in our view may it be used to reinterpret resolutions previously adopted. Their meanings must be assessed according to their terms and the discussions which led up to their adoption.

67. For the reasons set out above, we consider that it is clear that SCR 1441 does not authorise military action by a member state against Iraq. In our view there is nothing in the preamble which alters this view. Indeed it is notable that a late insertion into the Preamble was the commitment of all Member States to the sovereignty and territorial integrity of Iraq, Kuwait and the neighbouring States.

Rabinder Singh QC
Charlotte Kilroy
15 November 2002

FOOTNOTES

1. It will be noted that the last words used by the Ambassador refer to the possibility of the use of force outside the scope of authority by a UN Security Council resolution on two bases: first, self-defence and, secondly, to enforce UN resolutions. While the right of self-defence is in principle recognised in international law, reliance on it will depend on the particular circumstances in which a state finds itself. We do not consider that there is any right in an individual member of the UN or the Security

Council to use force to enforce UN resolutions without clear authorisation from the Security Council itself.

2. Daily Telegraph 11 November 2002

3. In an interview with Radio 4

4. Hansard 7 November 2002,Col 435; Jack Straw's statement appears to have been made on the basis of the penultimate draft of the resolution not the version which was eventually adopted.

5. Note the important caveat "within international law".

6.   A recently formed non-governmental organisation concerned with issues of international law and international human rights law particularly in the context of weapons of mass destruction and the peaceful resolution of conflict

7. See Articles 43-49

8. See Jules Lobel and Michael Ratner 'Bypassing the Security Council: Ambiguous Authorisations to use Force, Cease-fires and the Iraqi Inspection Regime.' [1999] AJIL 124 at 126; Danesh Sarooshi, The United Nations and the Development of Collective Security, 1999, at pp142-3

9. See inter alia S/Res/940 (Haiti), S/ Res/1264 (East Timor), S/Res/1080 (The Great Lakes)

10. See Anton La Guardia, 11 November 2002 in the Daily Telegraph

11. As in OP1, we have not considered in detail the possibility of reliance upon another doctrine of international law (the doctrine of humanitarian intervention), whose precise status and contours are themselves controversial. This is because, as we understand it, no state has suggested that it can be relied upon in present circumstances to justify an attack on Iraq.

5. CLAIM FORM AND GROUNDS FOR THE JUDICIAL REVIEW OF MICHAEL FORDHAM, RABINDER SINGH QC AND CHARLOTTE KILROY

8 November 2002

****

IN THE HIGH COURT OF JUSTICE

QUEEN'S BENCH DIVISION

ADMINISTRATIVE COURT

IN THE MATTER OF AN APPLICATION FOR JUDICIAL REVIEW

BETWEEN:

THE QUEEN

on the application of the Campaign for Nuclear Disarmament

Claimant

and

THE PRIME MINISTER

First Defendant

SECRETARY OF STATE FOR FOREIGN AND COMMONWEALTH AFFAIRS

Second Defendant

Third Defendant

DETAILED STATEMENT OF GROUNDS

PART I. SUMMARY OF CLAIMANT'S CASE

Introduction

1. By this claim for judicial review the claimant asks the Court to rule on the question, by means of an advisory declaration, whether the United Kingdom Government would be acting within international law were it to take military action against Iraq on the basis of Iraq's non-compliance with United Nations Security Council Resolution 1441 **(SCR 1441)** without a further UN Security Council resolution. The claim is self-evidently both novel and important.

2. On 8 November 2002 the United Nations Security Council adopted SCR1441 **(Bundle B405-408)**. The Resolution imposed a framework of obligations on Iraq, including (paragraph 3) imposing a timetable for compliance, the first significant deadline for which is 8 December 2002.

As to the consequences of non-compliance, the Resolution said this (at paragraph 4)[1]:

> failure by Iraq at any time to comply with, and cooperate fully in the implementation of, this resolution shall constitute a further material breach of Iraq's obligations and will be reported to the Council for assessment in accordance with paragraphs 11 and 12 below.

The Resolution did not authorise military action.

3. The United Kingdom Government has publicly stated that any military action against Iraq would be taken only having regard to and acting compatibly with international law. On 24 September 2002, asked about the legal position and legal advice as to whether a further UN Resolution would be necessary, the Prime Minister had said this **(B110)**:

of course, we will always act in accordance with international law.

On 7 November 2002, and in the context of Resolution 1441, the Foreign Secretary said **(B246)**:

> we have always made it clear that within international law we have to reserve our right to take military action, if that is required, within the existing charter and the existing body of UN Security Council resolutions, if, for example, a subsequent resolution were to be vetoed.

4. There are essentially two questions:

(1) The preliminary issue: does the subject-matter of the case render it "inappropriate as a matter of principle" for the Court to rule on the legal merits of the issue of substance?

(2) The substantive issue: does international law prohibit military action without a further Security Council resolution?

5. The claimant's case on these issues is outlined in this section, and further supplemented in Parts II and III (respectively) of these grounds. The factual position is further described in the Witness Statement of Carol Naughton and in the statement of facts, to which attention is invited.

The preliminary issue

6. In deciding whether the subject-matter renders it inappropriate as a matter of principle for the Court to rule on the legal merits of the substantive issue, three considerations arise to be addressed: (1) justiciability; (2) standing; and (3) prematurity.

7. As to justiciability, the context is that there is a relevant question of law which is in the circumstances cognisable in public law terms and which

properly engages the Court's supervisory jurisdiction:

(1)   The claimant accepts that decisions whether to take military action have conventionally been identified as among those functions of prerogative power where judicial restraint is warranted on constitutional grounds.[3] But it does not follow, especially under the now more developed state of the constitutional and administrative law, that there is any absolute or blanket immunity for such exercises of prerogative power. This has been recognised in other related areas, such as the prerogative of mercy (see most recently *Lewis v Attorney-General of Jamaica* [2001] 2 AC 50) or foreign affairs (most recently *R (on the application of Abbasi) v Secretary of State for Foreign and Commonwealth Affairs* [2002] EWCA Civ 1598). As Lord Phillips MR (for the Court of Appeal) said in *Abbasi* at [85]:

the issue of justiciability depends, not on general principle, but on subject matter and suitability in the particular case.

(2)   The proper focus is therefore a contextual one. The law asks whether the case engages any justiciable <u>issue</u>, such as a relevant issue of <u>law</u>, engaged in the particular case. Certainly, questions of factual merits will not engage the review function of the Court. But questions of law can. As Laws LJ recently explained in *R (on the application of International Transport Roth GmbH) v Secretary of State for the Home Department* [2002] EWCA Civ 158 [2002] 3 WLR 344 at [85]:

*It is well settled that executive decisions dealing directly with matters of defence, while **not immune from judicial review (that would be repugnant to the rule of law)** cannot sensibly be scrutinised by the courts **on grounds relating to their factual merits.***

Similarly, in *Secretary of State for the Home Department v Rehman* [2001] UKHL 47 [2001] 3 WLR 877 Lord Hoffmann recognised at [54] (in discussing *Chandler v DPP* and SIAC national security appeals) that there could be relevant:

issues which at no point lie within the exclusive province of the executive.

(3)   Thus, even a decision as to military action can be justiciable if it engages a relevant question of <u>law</u>. That would include,for example, human rights questions (*Rehman* at [54]), as by reference to the Human Rights Act (see *R (on the application of Marchiori) v Environment Agency* [2002] EWCA Civ 03

[2002] EuLR 225 at [38], [40]). It would also include questions of legality, whether or not relating to human rights, arising by reference to any relevant statutory source[4]. But justiciability is not limited to a prohibition arising by domestic statute. As the Court of Appeal said in *Abbasi* at [57]:

> this court ***does not need the statutory context*** in order to be free to express a view in relation to what it conceives to be ***a clear breach of international law***...

As this observation indicates, it is by no means fatal to the claim that, in the present case, the critical issue is one arising out of international law.

(4)   The question whether action would be compatible with international law is a question of law, not foreign policy (cf. *Rehman* at [53]). Whether that is cognisable will depend in particular on one or both of two key things: (a) the approach taken by the Government itself and (b) the nature and status of the international law standard said to be breached.

(5)   As regards the approach taken by the Government, here it was specifically stated that regard would be had to international law, and indeed that action must be compatible with international law: see paragraph 3 above.

    (a)   The effect of that approach is that a source of law, even if it might otherwise be cognisable only on the international law plane, becomes a source which the Court can properly address on judicial review. That is because, having chosen to act according to a legal standard, the Court can consider whether the Government has directed itself correctly as to what that legal standard requires.

    (b)   This was the approach where, prior to the Human Rights Act, the Secretary of State chose to take into account the European Convention on Human Rights, prior to its incorporation into domestic law. The Court on judicial review had a proper role in asking whether the Secretary of State had misdirected himself as to the requirements of that (international law) instrument: see *R v Secretary of State for the Home Department, ex p Launder* [1997] 1 WLR 839 per Lord Hope at 867C-F; endorsed by Lord Steyn in *R v Director of Public Prosecutions, ex p Kebilene* [2000] 2 AC 326 at 367E-H.

(6)   Further, as to the nature and status of the international law standard, the issue of international law incompatibility in this case engages a fundamental rule of customary international law, namely the prohibition on the use of force contained in Article 2(4) of the United Nations Charter (paragraph 14(1) below).

    (a)   That principle is recognised as a principle of customary international law having the status of *ius cogens*: see paragraph 14(2) below.

    (b)   A legal principle of this fundamental status thereby readily informs and engages municipal law (cf. *Abbasi* at [28], [68]-[69]); Oppenheim's International Law, Ninth Edition, at 56-57.).

8.   The suggestion as set out in the Defendants' response to the Claimant's letter before action (B359Q-R) that the Government should be entitled to keep silent the entire country in the dark as to its view of the true meaning and effect of international instruments because any view taken might have a bearing upon its conduct and its relations with other countries is unsustainable and in any event is nothing to the point. Neither *Abbasi*, nor *Everett* nor *CCSU* provide support for this proposition, and nor do they support an argument that the court should be prevented from considering questions of international law. In *Abbasi*, the court recognized the appropriateness of reaching and stating its conclusion on the international law issue.

9.   The Government has said it will always act in accordance with international law. That assurance is meaningless if it is unwilling to state what its understanding of international law is, and this in any event serves to emphasise the appropriateness of the Court ensuring that the correct understanding is judicially expressed.

10.   If the matter is justiciable (paragraph 7 above), it should not fail on grounds of sufficient interest or timing. The claimant's standing to raise the issue should be recognised by the Court, in particular for these reasons:

    (1)   The claimant has a sincere and well-founded interest in the subject-matter to which the claim relates, reflected in its coordinating role as to the public debate (including a march in September 2002) and in the exchange of correspondence with the Government. Cf. *R v Secretary of State for Foreign & Commonwealth Affairs, ex p Rees-Mogg* [1994] QB 552;

    (2)   If the matter is non-justiciable the claim will fail for that reason. But if it is justiciable, it would be unjust and contrary

to the public interest for the claim to fail for want of standing. That would indeed be a grave lacuna, in circumstances where justiciability reflects the need to uphold "the rule of law" (paragraph 7(2) above).[5]

11. As to prematurity:

    (1)   The claimant accepts that the Government has not yet decided (or at least publicly announced) to take military action, and has not unambiguously said that it considers that action to enforce against a breach of SCR 1441 without a further UN Resolution would be permissible under international law. However, the matter is plainly imminent and is under direct consideration, as the Foreign Secretary Jack Straw MP's statement and responses to questions in the debate in the House of Commons on 25 November 2002 demonstrate (B260-278). The matter has also been raised in pre-action correspondence (B359A-359L).

    (2)   There is nevertheless no doubt that nothing in relation to the timing of this matter robs the Court of the <u>jurisdiction</u> to entertain the claim for judicial review. The Administrative Court is equipped with jurisdiction[6] to give an "advisory" declaration in an appropriate case.

    (3)   The claimant submits that the hallmark of an appropriate case for the exercise of this jurisdiction will be a case where (a) the issues are important and the case serves a useful purpose in the public interest (London Borough of Islington v Camp 20th July 1999 unrep.) or (b) there is a pressing reason why it would not be satisfactory to await and consider the issues after the event and why from a practical point of view clarification at the start is to be preferred.[7]

    (4)   Here, <u>both</u> factors are present. The issues are undoubtedly important. Moreover, if the Court is to rule on the matter, it is plain that for that ruling to inform the Government's approach it would necessarily need to precede the taking of military action. If the matter is justiciable, there is and should be no bar relating to timing.

12. The analysis on the points relating to the preliminary issue is further developed in Part II of these Grounds, below.

The substantive issue

13. The position in international law is as follows: military action taken by the United Kingdom to enforce the terms of Security Council Resolution 1441 would indeed require a further Resolution.

14. That is so for the following main reasons.

    (1)   Article 2(4) of the United Nations Charter contains the following general prohibition **(Legislative Provisions Bundle p 2)**:

All Member States shall refrain in their international relations from the threat or use of force against the territorial integrity or political independence of any state...

    (2)   The prohibition on the use of force contained in Article 2(4) is a principle of customary international law, having the status of ius cogens (a peremptory international law norm from which no derogation is permissible): see *Nicaragua v United States* [1986] ICJ Reports 14 at [190].

    (3)   There are two exceptions, reflected in the Charter itself, to the prohibition on the use of force. The first is the recognition of the function of the Security Council in taking such action. Article 24(1) and (by Art 24(2)) Chapter VII of the Charter confer and govern the responsibility of the Security Council to decide on action in order to maintain or restore international peace. Article 24(1) provides:

In order to ensure prompt and effective action by the United Nations, its Members confer on the Security Council primary responsibility for the maintenance of international peace and security, and agree that in carrying out its duties under this responsibility the Security Council acts on their behalf.

    (4)   The second exception is the direct right of self-defence. The Charter does permit use of force by a Member State acting without reference to the Security Council, but only by recognising a right arising in deliberately narrowly-formulated circumstances. Article 51 provides:

Nothing in the present Charter shall impair the inherent right of individual or collective self-defence if an armed attack occurs against a Member State of the United Nations, until the Security Council has taken measures necessary to maintain international peace and security.

The terms of this provision are incompatible with the existence of any general entitlement to take military action, beyond circumstances of self-defence or absence of Security Council measures.

    (5)   Accordingly, military action to enforce against breach of Security Council resolutions could only fall outside the

prohibition contained in Article 2(4) if and to the extent that the action has been sanctioned by the Security Council (Article 24 and Chapter VII). Unless it be said that SCR 1441 already sanctions military action for non-compliance with its terms, no Security Council authority exists for such action and such authority would need to be sought.

(6)   That Resolution 1441 does not authorise military action for breach of its terms is clear. The Resolution does not on its face provide for military action, in the case of non-compliance. It could and would easily have done so, were this its intention. Moreover, the Resolution does deal with consequences, but does so by providing expressly for that matter to be referred to the Security Council: paragraph 2 above.

(7)   Indeed, the 'travaux preparatoires' of the Resolution included draft Resolutions which would have authorised military action in circumstances of non-compliance. Such a provision was conspicuously and deliberately absent from the final text of the Resolution. That, moreover, was because Security Council permanent members (Russia, China and France) were opposed to such inclusion.

(8)   In these circumstances, there is no authorisation (whether express or "implied"). Absent authority conferred by the Security Council military action to enforce the terms of SCR 1441 would not be compatible with international law and the Court should so rule.

15.   It is important to emphasise that an examination of whether the UK government can rely on SCR 1441 as authorizing the use of military action in the event of its breach is a pure question of interpretation of that resolution. This does not in any way address or pre-empt the question of whether the Government would be justified under the self-defence exception contained in Article 51 of the Charter in taking military action based on circumstances which may arise in the future. That is a separate question. This case is about action based on non-compliance with SCR 1441 which is not the subject of this application (c.f. Mr Jack Straw's statement in the House of Commons debate of 25 November 2002 at Col 60 (B274-276).

16.   The analysis on the substantive issue is further developed in Part III of these Grounds, below.

Conclusion

17.   The Court is asked to grant permission for judicial review, or direct a rolled-up hearing so that the issues in this case can be properly

ventilated and the Court assisted with argument on both sides, and subsequently the declaratory relief sought.

18. The claimant does not seek an order to injunct military action. However, if the United Kingdom Government were to decide to proceed with such action when that would be in contravention of international law, it should face up squarely to that fact[8]. The Court has a legitimate and important role in ruling on whether action would constitute such a contravention. This is a proper case for the Court to be being asked to consider making an advisory declaration.

PART II: THE PRELIMINARY ISSUE

FURTHER DISCUSSION

JUSTICIABILITY

The Law

The prerogative

19 In *R (Abbasi) v Secretary of State for Foreign and Commonwealth Affairs & Secretary of State for the Home Department* [2002] EWCA Civ 1598 , the Court of Appeal considered the question of whether the response of the Secretary of State for Foreign and Commonwealth Affairs to a request for diplomatic assistance was justiciable. It was argued before the court that decisions taken by the executive in its dealings with foreign states regarding the protection of British nationals abroad are non-justiciable.

20. The court reviewed the authorities on the question of whether the mere fact that a power derived from the Royal Prerogative excludes it from the scope of judicial review. After citing extracts from *Council of Civil Service Unions v Minister for Civil Service* [1985] AC 374 the court stated (at paragraph 18) that the issue of justiciability depends, not on general principle but on subject matter and suitability in the particular case.

21. The court summarised the propositions established by the authorities as follows:

(i) *"It is not an answer to a claim for judicial review to say that the source of the power of the Foreign Office is the prerogative."*..

(iii) *...there is no reason why its decision or inaction should not be reviewable if it can be shown that the same were irrational or contrary to legitimate expectation; but the court cannot enter the forbidden areas, including decisions affecting foreign policy.*

22. In *R v Secretary of State for the Home Department ex parte Bentley* [1994] QB 349 (see also the Privy Council in *Lewis v Attorney-General of Jamaica* [2001] 2 AC 50) the court considered the prerogative of mercy which had, along with other prerogative powers prior to the *CCSU* case [1985] AC 374, been considered immune to judicial review. It accepted the applicant's argument that it 'would be surprising and regrettable if the decision of the Home Secretary were immune from legal challenge irrespective of the gravity of the legal errors which infected such a decision'. The court stated (at 363A)

"*The CCSU case [1985] AC 374 made it clear that the powers of the court cannot be ousted merely by invoking the word "prerogative". The question is simply whether the nature and subject matter of the decision is amenable to the judicial process. Are the courts qualified to deal with the matter or does the decision involve such questions of policy that they should not intrude because they are ill-equipped to do so.*"

23. The court concluded that some aspects of the exercise of the Royal Prerogative were amenable to the judicial process. The court also stated that it was not precluded from reaching this conclusion by the fact that Lord Roskill in *CCSU* had listed the prerogative of mercy as among the prerogative powers which he did not think could properly be subject to review; this passing reference was obiter.

24. Lord Roskill's list included (at 418) making treaties, and the defence of the realm. He stated "*the courts are not the place wherein to determine whether a treaty should be concluded or the armed forces disposed in a particular manner...*".

25. Lord Roskill's list was considered in a number of subsequent decisions, including *R v Secretary of State for Foreign and Commonwealth Affairs ex parte Everett* [1989] QB 811 at 820 where Taylor LJ stated "*At the top of the scale of executive functions under the prerogative are matters of high policy...making treaties, making war...mobilising the armed forces. Clearly those matters and no doubt a number of others are not justiciable....*" This extract from the decision was cited in *Abbasi*.

26. Nonetheless the court has recently accepted that "*No matter how grave the policy issues involved, the courts will be alert to see that no use of power exceeds its proper constitutional bounds.*" (Laws LJ in *R (on the application of Marchiori) v Environment Agency* [2002] EWCA Civ 03 at [40]. That is why a statute such as the Human Rights Act 1998 could for example require the court to review even high policy decisions (*Marchiori* at [40]).

Submissions

27. The Claimant is requesting the court to consider whether at international

law a breach of SCR 1441 by Iraq would entitle the UK to take military action without a further UN Security Council resolution. This is a question of pure law which the court is eminently able to decide. It is not in any sense a request that the court decide on the issue of whether troops should be deployed or not, and it does not involve the court going into any of the forbidden areas of high policy. If the issue came before an international court, there would be no doubt that it would be capable of judicial determination.

28. The question arises before the domestic courts because the UK government has clearly stated to a domestic audience that whatever action it takes will be in accordance with international law. It has directed itself that it will act in accordance with international law and in particular as to the legal effect of Resolution 1441. It is therefore appropriate for a domestic court to review any misdirection in law on which the government relies in making its decision to go to war.

29. In *R. v Secretary of State for the Home Department Ex p. Launder* (No.2). [1997] 1 W.L.R. 839 the House of Lords held that although the European Convention on Human Rights (**ECHR**) had not been incorporated into UK law, since the Secretary of State stated that he had taken into account the respondent's representations that his extradition would be in breach of the ECHR, it was right to examine whether he had done so correctly. In *R. v DPP Ex p. Kebilene* [2000] 2 AC 326 at 341Lord Bingham CJ confirmed that where a decision-maker had made it clear that he had relied on advice regarding the ECHR, it was appropriate to review the correctness of that advice. He stated:

> "*It is, therefore, as it seems to me, appropriate for this court to review the soundness of the legal advice on which the Director has made clear, publicly, that he relied; for if the legal advice he relied on was unsound he should, in the public interest, have the opportunity to reconsider the confirmation of his consent on a sound legal basis.*"

30. Furthermore in *Abbasi* the court accepted (paragraphs 68-69) the applicant's proposition that customary international law was part of the common law. Customary international law includes the prohibition on the use of force against another state save in recognised circumstances such as self-defence.

31. The Defendants' reliance on *R v Lyons* [2002] UKHL 44 in their response to the Claimant's letter before action (B359Q-359R.) is therefore misplaced. In that case the House of Lords simply repeated the finding in *JH Rayner (Mincing Lane) Ltd v Department of Trade and Industry* [1990] 2 AC 418 that a domestic court could not enforce the United Kingdom's obligations under international treaties (per Lord Hutton at [69]). The case concerned rights under the ECHR before it

was incorporated which had been precluded by statute.[9] There had been no statement from the Government that it intended to act in accordance with the ECHR, and furthermore the terms of the domestic statute were clear.

32. The case of *Bentley* makes it clear that the crucial question in deciding the justiciability of the exercise of the prerogative is whether the courts are qualified to deal with the matter. There is no automatic bar on the review of any prerogative; this was established by *CCSU*. The lists which appear in that case and in *Everett* of types of prerogative which are considered to be non-justiciable, simply reflect a view on the suitability of reviewing the subject matter which would normally be at issue in the exercise of that particular prerogative, namely matters of high policy. The content of the lists in *CCSU*, *Everett* and *Abbasi* are obiter, as *Bentley* demonstrates, and the court is not precluded from addressing the question of whether on the subject matter of the particular case review is appropriate.

33. As the court in *Abbasi* makes clear as long as the court's review does not impinge on any forbidden area, the decision is reviewable. Decisions dealing with matters of defence and high policy cannot be scrutinised on grounds relating to their factual merits; this does not mean that they are immune from judicial scrutiny (see *R (on the application of International Transport Roth GmbH) v Secretary of State for the Home Department* [2002] EWCA Civ 158 [2002] 3 WLR 344 at [85], above). It is important *'neither to blur nor to exaggerate the area of responsibility entrusted to the executive'* (see Lord Hoffman in *Rehman* at [54]).

34. As stated above the question of whether the government is misdirecting itself on international law is not a question which in any way impinges on the matters of high policy which the government undoubtedly has to address in deciding whether to go to war. The review simply ensures that the government does not make that high policy decision against the background of a misconceived and erroneous view of the law.

35. In the final paragraph of their response to the Claimant's letter before action (B359Q-359R) the Defendants state that a decision to issue a <u>reasoned statement</u> concerning the true meaning and effect of international instruments which apply not just to the United Kingdom but also to other states is a matter bearing upon the substantive conduct of this country's international affairs and affecting its relations with other countries. The Defendants suggest therefore that this decision is non-justiciable on the authority of *Everett*, *Abbasi* and *CCSU*. Insofar as the Defendants are suggesting that the interpretation of international law is a matter of high policy, this argument is unsustainable.

36. The question of whether an action is lawful or not is clearly one over which the courts have jurisdiction (see *Marchiori* at [40]). This applies as much to international law as to domestic law (see the *Expenses* case ICJ Reports (1962), 151; *Abbasi* at [57] and at [64]; *R v Home Secretary ex parte Adan* [2001] 2 WLR 143). In *Adan* the House of Lords rejected a similar argument put forward in relation to the Refugee Convention 1951: the risk that a UK ruling on the interpretation of the Convention might contain an implicit criticism of the interpretation put on it by other state parties could not prevent the court from applying its own concluded view of the Convention (see Lord Steyn at 155-6).

37. The Government has given an assurance to the British public that it will act in accordance with international law. That assurance is meaningless if the Government is unwilling to state its view on what its international law obligations require it to do, and only emphasises the appropriateness of the Court ensuring that the correct understanding is judicially expressed.

STANDING

38. CND has sufficient interest to bring this application both in the public interest and as an organisation which has been engaged in correspondence with the Government about the legal issues involved.

39. It is self-evident that the legality of the government's decision to go to war with Iraq is a matter of the highest public interest. Not only does the decision involve the commitment of UK troops and resources but such a war could by its nature have serious and unforeseen consequences for the peace and security of the UK. Public disquiet about the potential war with Iraq has been intense, with the Stop the War March in London on 28 September 2002 illustrating the extent of the unease.

40. Given that the UK has obligations under international treaties and under customary international law which determine the legality of its decision to go to war and given that the UK government has expressly declared to the British public its intention to comply with those obligations, it is clearly in the public interest for a court to assess whether the course of action the government is considering is indeed compatible with the UK's obligations under international law. Further, the UK Government assured CND by a letter of 24 May 2002 that "in the context of Iraq.. any action will continue to be justified under international law". (B374)

41. Carol Naughton, the Chair of the Campaign for Nuclear Disarmament (**CND**), sets out in her witness statement (**CNWS**) (B360-364) the history of CND. She explains that the focus of CND's campaigns have evolved so that they are now concerned with the global abolition of nuclear weapons and the overall defence policies of nuclear weapon states.

42. CND's concerns about a potential war with Iraq began in December 2001 and were intensified when Secretary of State for Defence, Mr Geoff Hoon, stated to the House of Commons Defence Committee on 20 March 2002 that in the right conditions nuclear weapons would be used against Iraq. CND's subsequent activities in campaigning against a war with Iraq are set out in CNWS at paragraphs 4-9 and included a detailed letter to Mr Geoff Hoon (B366-373) dated 25 March 2002 questioning the legality of any attack on Iraq and the co-organisation of the Stop the War March in London on 28 September 2002.

43. There can be no doubt therefore about the sincerity of CND's concern about the issue of the legality of a war against Iraq (see *R v Secretary of State for Foreign and Commonwealth Affairs ex parte Rees-Mogg* [1994] 2 WLR 115 at 119) and the sufficiency of their expertise and interest in this area (*R v Secretary of State for Foreign and Commonwealth Affairs ex parte World Development Movement Ltd* [1995] 1 WLR 386 at 395H-396A, followed in *R v Somerset County Council ex p. Dixon* [1998] Env LR 111 at 118-121).

TIMING

44. The government has not yet taken a decision to go to war; and it has stated that it has not yet made a decision to commit troops (see the article on *Guardian* website, 20 November, referring to a statement by Mr Geoff Hoon)[10]. Nor has the government said unequivocally that it considers that the UK would be entitled to attack Iraq without a further UN Security Council Resolution upon Iraq's breach of its obligations under SCR 1441, although it has made statements which could be interpreted in that way (see Statement of Facts).

45. It is quite clear, however, from the statements of Ministers set out in the Statement of Facts firstly that the government considers that a decision on war against Iraq is imminent, and would in one way or another follow upon breach of SCR 1441, and secondly that the legality of such an attack, if for example a further UN Security Council Resolution were to be vetoed, is a matter of constant debate and some confusion (see the Prime Minister's monthly press conference on 25 November 2002 at B70A-D, and the debate of 25 November 2002 in the House of Commons at B244-341).

46. The Claimant in its letter before action explicitly asked the Defendants to state whether they agreed that action against Iraq for non-compliance with SCR 1441 without a further UN Security Council Resolution would be in breach of international law. The Defendants in their response to (B359Q-R) refuse to give a reply, stating that there is no obligation on them to engage in a debate about legal analysis or to provide an explanation with reasons. The Defendants do not explain

why it is that they cannot even state what their position is, let alone engage in a debate or provide reasons for that position.

47. A material breach of SCR 1441 within the meaning of paragraph 4 of the resolution might be deemed to take place, if Iraq were to obstruct the weapons inspections provided for by paragraph 5, thereby triggering a report to the Security Council under paragraph 11. The principal date for compliance, however, as the timetable set out above demonstrates, is 8 December 2002 (paragraph 3 of SCR 1441), and it appears to be in expectation of a breach on this date that the US is making its preparations for war and encouraging its allies to do the same.

48. It is clear then that the timetable set in motion by SCR 1441 is extremely tight, and that if the UK does decide to go to war without a further UN Security Council Resolution a decision could be made in a matter of weeks. It is equally clear that once a decision on war is made, there will be little point asking the court for a declaratory judgment to the effect that the government misdirected itself as to the legality at international law of its actions.

49. The Claimant is not suggesting that the court may arrest the process of war either before or after a decision is taken. The Claimant is simply asking the court to inform the government's decision-making process with a declaration on the legality of the course of action the government is considering, the government having made it clear that it considers legality at international law to be a necessary and relevant element of any decision it makes.

50. There are four reasons why the court should consider itself to have the jurisdiction in judicial review to make such a declaration in advance of the decision being taken:

(1)   practicality: a declaratory judgment at this stage serves a purpose as it informs the government and the general public on the legality of an action that is proposed. If it is accepted that the issue is justiciable then it makes no sense to wait until an irreversible decision has been taken on the basis of an erroneous view of the law. As Sedley J (as he then was) stated in R v Secretary of State for Transport, ex parte London Borough of Richmond Upon Thames and Others [1995] Env LR 409 at 413

"...the want of an identifiable decision is not fatal to an application for judicial review: see R v Secretary of State for Employment, ex p. Equal Opportunities Commission [1995] 1 AC 1, 26 (per Lord Keith) and 34-36 (per Lord Browne-Wilkinson). If it is arguable that the new consultation is

> *proceeding on a false basis which is justiciable in law, there will be every reason to lean in favour of deciding the issue sooner rather than later."*

(2)   This is no mere hypothetical issue. Nor is it an abstract or theoretical debate. It is clear that this very question is being considered by the government with a view to taking a decision on it. It may even be that the government has a reached a clear view on this question but is reluctant to publicise it (see the Defendants' response to the Claimant's letter before action at B359Q-359R). *In Rusbridger v Attorney General and DPP*, Divisional Court, judgment of 22 June 2001, an application for declaratory relief on the compatibility of section 3 of the Treason Felony Act with the Human Rights Act 1998 was refused permission on the basis that there was no decision which was susceptible to challenge[11], and that the claimants were not victims of any unlawful act of the Defendant. In that case, however, there was no suggestion that a decision or action was even being considered.

Here, although the government statements on the legality of attacking Iraq without a further UN Security Council Resolution are equivocal, they give a strong indication that the government is minded to attack without a further resolution. It is clear therefore that there is a live dispute between the Claimant and the Defendants based on the very real possibility of an attack on Iraq (see Zamir & Woolf, The Declaratory Judgment, Third Edition, 2002 at 140-162; see also *Ruislip-Northwood Urban District Council v Lee* (1935) 145 LT 208).

In *R v British Advertising Clearance Centre ex parte Swiftcall Ltd* 16 November 1995, unreported, Carnwath J stated:

> *"as to whether there is a reviewable decision, BACC says with some force that it has done no more at this stage than respond to BT's complaint by seeking Swiftcall's views and suggesting possible amendments, but that no conclusive view has been reached. However, this is an area in which decisions are made very quickly. Looking at the letters and affidavits realistically, they give a clear indication of how BACC is minded to act [and] as Swiftcall argue [that] the course they are suggesting is fundamentally unlawful, the sooner that is decided the better."*

(3)   There is no advantage to be gained, and every disadvantage to be had, in awaiting a decision. The court is in as good a position now to examine the legality of any proposed action as

it would be once the decision to take military action is made. This is not a case where the subject-matter of the review is a discretion whose exercise depends on factual circumstances which can only be determined at the time of the decision itself (see *R (Pretty) v Director of Public Prosecutions* [2002] 1 AC 800).

(4)   Even if the dispute between the Claimant and the Defendants cannot be characterised as a live dispute, the public importance and urgency of the issue is such that the court should exercise its discretion to grant declaratory relief. Clive Lewis, Judicial Remedies in Public Law, Second Edition, 2000 at 7-043 - 7-045

".. restrictions flow from the general principle that declarations will only be granted where a genuine justiciable issue arises for determination, and relief will not be granted if the matter is hypothetical or academic. These restrictions are increasingly seen as discretionary barriers rather than absolute jurisdictional bars".

He continues:

"There is a strong argument that the courts ought to have jurisdiction in limited circumstances at least to grant advisory declarations in appropriate circumstances.

At Chapter 9 of Zamir & Woolf, The Declaratory Judgment, there is a discussion of the advantages of extending the scope of advisory declarations. It concludes:

*"Both the Law Commission in its report on Administrative Law: Judicial Review and Statutory Appeals, and the Bowman Committee in its Review of the Crown Office List recommended that it should be possible to obtain advisory declarations in matters of public importance, provided the parties affected have been given an opportunity to be represented. It is disappointing that this reform has yet to be implemented. **However, statutory intervention is not needed. What is required is a willingness for the courts to be prepared to make a much broader use of the remedies they have now been given.** An essential change of approach is required. The courts should use the opportunity of the introduction of the Civil Procedure Rules to develop the ability to assist parties constructively by not only resolving legal disputes but also facilitating solutions to complex problems."* (Emphasis added)

The court has in any event accepted that in certain

circumstances advisory opinions are appropriate (see for example, *Sedley LJ in London Borough of Islington v Camp*, 20 July 1999 unreported.)

PART III: THE SUBSTANTIVE ISSUE

FURTHER DISCUSSION

DOES UN SCR 1441 ENTITLE THE UK TO USE FORCE AGAINST IRAQ IN THE EVENT OF ITS BREACH WITHOUT A FURTHER UN SECURITY COUNCIL RESOLUTION?

Legal Background

51. The United Nations Charter provides the framework for the use of force in international law.

Article 1 states:

"The Purposes of the United Nations are:

(1)   *To maintain international peace and security, and to that end: to take effective collective measures for the prevention and removal of threats to the peace, and for the suppression of acts of aggression or other breaches of the peace, and to bring about by peaceful means, and in conformity with the principles of justice and international law, adjustment or settlement of international disputes or situations which might lead to a breach of the peace.*"

52. Articles 2(3) and 2(4) then set out the fundamental principles governing the settlement of international disputes and the use of force. Article 2(4) states:

"*All Members shall refrain in their international relations from the threat or use of force against the territorial integrity or political independence of any state, or in any other manner inconsistent with the Purposes of the United Nations.*"

53. In classifying the prohibition on the use of force contained in Article 2 (4) as a principle of customary international law, the International Court of Justice (*Nicaragua v United States*, [1986] ICJ Reports 14, at para 190) referred to the widely held view that this principle was *ius cogens*, in other words a peremptory norm of international law from which states cannot derogate.

54. Chapter V of the Charter governs the constitution and powers of the Security Council. Article 24 of the Charter states:

1.   In order to ensure prompt and effective action by the United Nations, its Members confer on the Security Council primary responsibility for the maintenance of international peace and

> *security, and agree that in carrying out its duties under this responsibility the Security Council acts on their behalf.*
>
> 2.   *In discharging these duties the Security Council shall act in accordance with the Purposes and Principles of the United Nations. The specific powers granted to the Security Council for the discharge of these duties are laid down in Chapters VI, VII, VIII and XII....*

55.

56.   Chapter VII confers on the Security Council the duty of determining the existence of any threat to the peace, breach of the peace, or act of aggression, and the duty of deciding what action should be taken to maintain or restore international peace and security (Article 39).

57.   Article 41 gives the Security Council the power to take peaceful measures to give effect to its decisions, and by Article 42, where the Security Council considers that those measures would be, or have proved to be, inadequate it may take such action by air, sea, or land forces as may be necessary to maintain or restore international peace and security.

58.   Chapter VII[13] originally envisaged that the Security Council would carry out such enforcement action itself using the armed forces of Member States[14]. As a consequence there is no express authority for the Security Council to delegate to Member States the competence to carry out enforcement action under their own command and control (see Danesh Sarooshi, <u>The United Nations and the Development of Collective Security,</u> (Oxford, 1999), at p143).

59.   The only express reference in Chapter VII to the use of force by Member States acting alone is at Article 51 which states: "*Nothing in the present Charter shall impair the inherent right of individual or collective self-defence if an armed attack occurs against a Member of the United Nations, until the Security Council has taken measures necessary to maintain international peace and security.*"

60.   Nonetheless a practice has arisen of authorising Member States to carry out enforcement action on the Security Council's behalf. It is important to emphasise, however, that there is no express authority in the UN Charter for Member States to carry out actions under Article 42 under their own command and control either with or without a Security Council Resolution.

Does SCR 1441 authorise the use of force?

<u>Express authorisation</u>

61.   It is clear that SCR 1441 does not expressly authorise Member States to

use force in the event of non-compliance. A study of resolutions adopted by the Security Council, including Resolution 678, shows that that the language used to authorise force is bold and consistent. Member states are '*authorised*' to '*use all necessary means*' or '*take all necessary measures*' in pursuit of a specified goal.[15]

62.   As can be seen from the excerpts of the draft resolutions set out in the Statement of Facts, the UK and the US sought express authorisation in such terms in the first draft of their resolution. Such express authorisation is manifestly lacking in the final draft. This was for reasons which the other Security Council permanent members Russia, China and France made clear: they did not want the resolution to authorise force.

63.   Instead SCR 1441 provides at paragraphs 4, 11 and 12 that in the event of non-compliance the matter will be referred to the Security Council, which will convene to consider the need for full compliance with all of the relevant Security Council resolutions. This clearly contemplates that it is the Security Council which will decide on any further action to be taken against Iraq.

64.   Paragraph 13 states that the Security Council "*Recalls, in that context, that the Council has repeatedly warned Iraq that it will face serious consequences as a result of its continued violations of its obligations.*" The words '*in that context*', which appeared first in the 6 November draft, clearly indicate that any serious consequences which Iraq will face are to be decided upon in the context of the discussion by the Security Council envisaged by paragraph 12. In any event, it is clear that the phrase "serious consequences" does not itself authorise the use of force but is a reference to previous warnings which this part of the Resolution "recalls".

Implicit authorisation

65.   As can be seen in the Statement of Facts, the question of whether SCR 1441 gave Member States an automatic right to use force in the event of its breach was extensively discussed, and agreement was reached on the issue of "automaticity" and "hidden triggers" with Russia, China, France, and even the UK and the US ambassadors agreeing that both were absent from SCR 1441 (**B63-7A**).

66.   Having failed to obtain an express authorisation for the use of force, having incorporated minute changes to the final draft whose sole purpose was to exclude the possibility of 'automaticity' and 'hidden triggers' and to preserve the role of the Security Council, and having publicly agreed in their explanation of the vote for adoption of SCR 1441 that there was no such implied authorisation for force, there is and

can be no basis for the claim that SCR 1441 can be interpreted as authority for the use of force without a further Security Council Resolution.

67. Furthermore any use of force by the UK in reliance on SCR 1441 without a further Security Council Resolution would be a violation of the Purposes of the UN Charter set out in Article 1, and of Article 2(4) for the reasons set out below.

The Charter

68. The use of implied authorisation of force is in conflict with the fundamental objectives of the Charter set out in Articles 1 and 2 to preserve peace and to prohibit force save in specified circumstances. First, the fundamental nature of the prohibition against the use of force in Article 2(4) means that any ambiguities in interpretation should be resolved in favour of that prohibition. The Charter's overriding commitment to the use of force only as a last resort entails that explicit authorisation be required.

69. Secondly, the power given to the Security Council alone under Chapter VII to decide to use force to restore peace is intended to ensure that any decisions on the use of force are reached collectively. The implied authorisation arguments of the UK and the US permits states to make unilateral decisions on the use of force, which is precisely what Chapter VII and the Charter as a whole are designed to avoid.

70. Furthermore, as pointed out above, it is only the Security Council which has the power under Article 39 to determine whether there has been a breach of the peace or threat to the peace and to decide whether to take action under Articles 41 and 42. Since the Security Council is exercising powers delegated to it by Member States under Article 24 of the UN Charter, powers which it must exercise in compliance with the Purposes and Principles of the United Nations, it cannot delegate certain of its functions under Chapter VII to a Member State, and must retain effective authority and control over those functions which it does delegate. (see Danesh Sarooshi, The United Nations and the Development of Collective Security, (Oxford, 1999), at pp154-5; see also Niels Blokker, *Is the Authorisation Authorised? Powers and Practice of the UN Security Council to Authorise the Use of Force by 'Coalitions of the Able and Willing'* EJIL 2000 Vol 11 No 3 at 552),

71. It is clear that a practice has grown up of delegating the carrying out of enforcement action to Member States, but it is equally clear that in so doing the Security Council has increasingly sought to retain overall control of the operation with clear mandates, time-limited authorisations and reporting requirements (See Blokker, ibid, at 561-5).

72. The implied authorisation arguments put forward by the UK and the US would undermine the control exercised by the Security Council which is an essential feature of lawful delegation under the Chapter VII. These arguments would effectively allow Member States to take unilateral decisions on the interpretation of resolutions, reading into them authorisation to take action which does not appear clearly on the face of the resolution. This leaves the Security Council with little or no control of the functions it has delegated and unacceptably waters down the protections built into Chapters V and VII which enshrine the principle of collective decision-making.

73. Finally the limitations on delegation mean that the terms of a resolution which delegates Chapter VII powers are to be interpreted narrowly (See Sarooshi, The United Nations and the Development of Collective Security, above, at p 44).

74. In conclusion, the fundamental objectives and the constitutional framework of the Charter mean that the use of force by a Member State is not justified unless the Security Council authorises it in the clearest of terms. Use of force without such clear authorisation would therefore violate international law.

Interpretation of resolutions under Chapter VII

75. Even if implied authorisation were in principle compatible with the Charter it is clear both from the terms of SCR 1441 and from the discussions of the Security Council members prior to the adoption of SCR 1441 that authorisation to use force cannot be derived from the terms of this particular resolution.

76. As stated above paragraphs 4, 11 and 12 of SCR 1441 provide a clear mechanism in the event of Iraq's non-compliance with its obligations under SCR 1441. Given that there is such a clear mechanism on the face of the resolution there is no basis for arguing that an alternative mechanism should be implied into the resolution.

77. Furthermore, while the Ambassadors' statements to the Security Council after the adoption of SCR 1441 **(B63-67)** are not a definitive guide to their meaning, they provide the strongest possible evidence of the intentions of the Security Council members in adopting SCR 1441. In the *Namibia Advisory Opinion*, (1971) ICJ Reports 15, at p 53 the International Court of Justice stated that the language of a resolution should be carefully analysed before a conclusion could be made as to its binding effect under Article 25 of the Charter. The question of whether the powers under Article 25 had been exercised was to be determined *"having regard to the terms of the resolution to be interpreted, the discussions leading to it, the Charter provisions invoked and, in general*

all circumstances that might assist in determining the legal consequences of the resolution...."

78. The same exercise should be employed where the terms of a resolution are ambiguous or unclear. The suggestion that ambiguity or uncertainty should permit Member States to reach a unilateral view on the meaning of a resolution is untenable. If the discussions and revisions leading up to the adoption of SCR 1441 are taken into account, it is clear that they rule out any arguments to the effect that paragraphs such as paragraph 13, which warns of serious consequences, and paragraph 2, which talks of affording Iraq a final opportunity, implicitly authorise the use of force.

79. In conclusion, any attempt by the UK to rely on SCR 1441 as the basis for taking military action against Iraq without a further Security Council resolution would be in violation of the terms both of the Charter and of customary international law.

The 'material breach' argument

80. SCR 1441 at paragraph 1 declares Iraq to be in material breach of its obligations under relevant resolutions and at paragraph 4 states that Iraq's failure to comply with the terms of SCR 1441 shall be a further material breach.

81. There is no authority anywhere in the Charter for a Member State to decide to use force in order to enforce breaches of Security Council resolutions. On the contrary that power is reserved to the Security Council at Article 42. It is only with an express delegation of that power that a Member State may use force against another Member State to ensure that it complies with a Security Council resolution.

82. Without that authorisation any use of force would be in clear contravention of the basic principle prohibiting the use of force in Article 2(4) of the Charter.

Authorisation in the event of the Security Council's failure to reach a resolution

83. Both the UK and US ambassadors to the UN and government ministers have made statements saying they expect the Security Council to '*meet its responsibilities*' (Ambassador Greenstock). Mr Jack Straw in his response to MPs' questions on 7 November 2002 set out in the Statement of Facts and at B267 alluded to the right to use force in the event of a veto of a further resolution from the Security Council.

84. It is plain that this is not the correct approach to the interpretation of the Charter. It is the Security Council which is the final arbiter of whether to take measures and what measures to take under Articles 39, 41 and 42. As explained above this collective decision-making process is at the heart of the powers conferred on the Security Council by the Charter. It

would be in contradiction to the fundamental objectives and the framework of the Charter for a Member State to review the decisions of the Security Council and take action in its stead if it does not agree with them.

No express requirement for the US and the UK to obtain a new resolution

85. In the debate in the House of Commons on 25 November 2002, Mr Jack Straw referred to the fact that SCR 1441 did not stipulate that a further Security Council resolution would be required, as a justification for his 'reserving his position' on whether military action could be taken to enforce SCR 1441. This argument is flawed. First of all any such proposed amendment would have been vetoed by the UK and the US so the non-inclusion of this requirement is no indication that Member States did not consider a further Security Council Resolution necessary. Secondly the other Member States made it quite clear that they did consider that a further Security Council resolution was necessary and required by the terms of the resolution (B67A). (See Jules Lobel and Michael Ratner *Bypassing the Security Council: Ambiguous Authorisations to use Force, Cease-fires and the Iraqi Inspection Regime.'* [1999] AJIL 124).

86. Thirdly, for the reasons set out above, it is unnecessary to insert wording in a resolution expressly requiring Member States to obtain an authorisation to use force, when the Charter makes it quite clear that with the exception of the inherent right of self-defence in Article 51[16], only the Security Council can make a decision to use force and only in the circumstances set out in Chapter VII.

CONCLUSION

87. It is clear from the above analysis that UN SCR 1441 does not authorise the use of force in the event of its breach. Any military action to enforce the terms of SCR 1441 would therefore need to be clearly authorised by a new Security Council Resolution in order to be compatible with international law.

88. The Claimant therefore invites the Court to give a ruling, which the Claimant respectfully suggests should be accompanied by a declaration, unless it be considered by the Court that the judgment itself suffices, that military action to enforce the terms of SCR 1441 without a further UN Security Council Resolution would be in breach of international law, and that the UK would be misdirecting itself in law if it were to take military action in these circumstances on the basis that it was acting compatibly with international law.

28.11.02

RABINDER SINGH QC
MICHAEL FORDHAM
CHARLOTTE KILROY

FOOTNOTES

1. Bold type in quotations connotes emphasis added.

2. Bold type in quotations connotes emphasis added.

3. *See Chandler v DPP* [1964] AC 763; *Council of Civil Service Unions v Minister for the Civil Service* [1985] AC 374, 418B-C.

4. Cf. *R (on the application of Bancoult) v Secretary of State for the Foreign and Commonwealth Office* [2001] QB 1067 (whether Ordinance compulsorily removing indigenous people from a former territory to make way for a US military base incompatible with Order under which made); *R v Secretary of State for Foreign and Commonwealth Affairs, ex p British Council of Turkish Cypriot Associations* [1998] COD 336 treating "the powers of the Crown, even in its diplomatic function", as justiciable "if it engages a question of domestic United Kingdom law", as where action was said to be "constrained by statute".)

5. *R v Inland Revenue Commissioners, ex p National Federation of Self-Employed and Small Businesses Ltd* [1982] AC 617, 644E-G; *R v Secretary of State for Foreign and Commonwealth Affairs, ex p World Development Movement Ltd* [1995]1 WLR 386, 395G-H.

6. *R v Secretary of State for the Home Department, ex p Mehari* [1994] QB 474, 491G-H.

7. Cf *R (On the application of Alconbury Developments Ltd) v Secretary of State for the Environment Transport and the Regions* [2001] UKHL 23 [2001] 2 WLR 1389 at [171].

8. Cf *R v Secretary of State for the Home Department, ex p Simms* [2000] 2 AC 115, 131E-F.

9. Lord Hoffman also stated (at [69]) that where the appellants claim to enforce a right which is not only given to them by the ECHR (prior to its incorporation into domestic law) but is also recognised by domestic law, the principle in *Rayner's* case did not require that the domestic court should not regard a judgment of the European court as providing clear guidance and that it should not follow that judgment unless required by statute to reach a difference conclusion.

10. Although in the recent debate in the House of Commons on 25 November 2002, Mr Geoff Hoon has made it clear that preparations are being made, Hansard, 25 November 2002, at cols. 127-8

11. The matter went to the Court of Appeal on a different point: *Rusbridger v Attorney General* [2002] EWCA Civ.

13. See Articles 43-49

14. See Jules Lobel and Michael Ratner *'Bypassing the Security Council: Ambiguous Authorisations to use Force, Cease-fires and the Iraqi Inspection Regime.'* [1999] AJIL 124 at 126; Danesh Sarooshi, The United Nations and the Development of Collective Security (Oxford, 1999), at pp 142-3

15. See inter alia S/Res/940 (Haiti), S/Res/1264 (East Timor), S/Res/1080 (The Great Lakes) (B53-62)

6. THE ARGUMENT AGAINST
A JUDICIAL REVIEW
****

Skeleton Argument of Philip Sales & Jemima Stratford
for the Treasury Solicitor, 5 December 2002

IN THE HIGH COURT OF JUSTICE

QUEEN'S BENCH DIVISION, ADMINISTRATIVE COURT

IN THE MATTER OF AN APPLICATION FOR PERMISSION

TO APPLY FOR JUDICIAL REVIEW

Ref. No. CO/542912002

BETWEEN THE QUEEN

On the Application of the Campaign for Nuclear Disarmament

Proposed Claimant

and -

THE PRIME MINISTER

Proposed First Defendant

THE SECRETARY OF STATE FOR FOREIGN AND COMMONWEALTH
AFFAIRS

Proposed Second Defendant

THE SECRETARY OF STATE FOR DEFENCE

Proposed Third Defendant

SKELETON ARGUMENT OF THE PROPOSED DEFENDANTS

Time Estimate: 1 - 1 1/2days

Pre-Reading: skeleton arguments; witness statement of Peter Ricketts;
Detailed Statement of Grounds

Pre-Reading Time Estimate: 3 hours

INTRODUCTION

1. This is an application by the Proposed Claimant, the Campaign for Nuclear
   Disarmament ("CND") for permission under CPR Part 54 to bring a claim for
   judicial review. The application relates to UN Security Council Resolution
   1441 on Iraq, adopted on 8 November 2002 ("SCR 1441").

2. Following a directions hearing before Mr Justice Maurice Kay on 29
   November 2002, the, Court has ordered that the hearing on permission

on 9 December 2002 may (if permission is granted) proceed directly to a substantive hearing, but limited to the preliminary issues raised by the proposed claim. Accordingly, the substantive issue which this application seeks to raise before the Court (addressed at paras 13-16 and 51-88 of the Detailed Statement of Grounds) is not addressed in this skeleton argument. As was made clear to the Court, the Government submits that it has no obligation in law to engage in a debate with CND about the substantive issues of international law referred to in the claim, and considers that it would be detrimental to the national interest for it to engage in a substantive debate on those issues at the present time.

3.   CND seeks:

"A declaration that UN Security Council Resolution 1441 does not authorise the use of force in the event of its breach and that a further UN Security Council Resolution would be needed to authorise such force." (Section 6 of the Claim Form).

Section 3 of the Claim Form does not identify any particular decision to be re-viewed. Instead it alleges that the challenge is to "a misdirection of law as to the effect of [SCR 1441]". In fact, as CND is forced to acknowledge in its Detailed Statement of Grounds (e.g. paras 44 and 50 (2)), the United Kingdom Government has deliberately, and after careful consideration, refrained from making a definitive statement of its legal position under international law in relation to these highly sensitive issues concerning the international relations of the United Kingdom [Ricketts 1, in particular paras 3 and 8]. Accordingly, the suggestion of "a misdirection of law" is purely speculative. The true target and purpose of this application is to require the Government to make such a definitive statement.

4.   For the reasons which are developed below, the Proposed Defendants[1] respectfully submit that this claim is misconceived, and that in view of insuperable legal obstacles facing CND no permission should be granted.

In the alternative, if permission is granted, the claim should be dismissed for the reasons set out below.

NON-JUSTICIABLE

5.   CND present the preliminary issue as being whether it is "inappropriate as a matter of principle" for the Court to rule on the legal merits of the substantive issue (Detailed Statement of Grounds, para 4(1)). In fact, as the Court of Appeal has recently emphasised in *R (Abbasi) v Sec. of State for Foreign and Commonwealth Affairs and anor.* [2002] EWCA Civ. 1598 (6.11.02), the issue of justiciability depends, not on general principle, but on subject matter and suitability in the particular

case" (para 85). Accordingly, it is necessary to consider the particular context of this case, its subject matter and the suitability of the Court being asked to make the declaration which is sought.

6. The claim is founded on an assertion that the United Kingdom Government has misdirected itself as to international law. There is no such misdirection, and CND are unable to point to one. The furthest that the United Kingdom has gone is to reserve its position [Ricketts 1, para 7]. This potential challenge is therefore in fact to the decision of the Government to date not to make a definitive statement of its legal position under international law. Any decision by the Government to issue a definitive statement of its views on a matter of international law involves sensitive judgments as to the effect of such a statement on this country's international relations [Ricketts 1, paras. 3-4 and 6-8]. That is particularly true in the position adopted by this country in relation to a difficult international to situation such as that addressed by SCR 1441. Thus the proposed claim is in substance an attempt by CND to dictate the conduct of foreign policy.

7. As a matter of domestic law, decisions as to the conduct of the United Kingdom's foreign policy and international relations with other states are entrusted to the executive, who are subject to democratic accountability in Parliament. The executive Government is best placed to assess all the multifarious ramifications for this country of decisions in the conduct of foreign relations. As Lord Hoffmann recently identified in the parallel (and, in this case, closely related) field of national security, the principle of the separation of the powers requires the courts to respect the executive's responsibility in this area: *Secretary of State for the Home Department v. Rehman* [2001] 3 WLR 877 at paras. 50-54, 57 and 62. See also *International Transport Roth GmbH v Secretary of State for the Home Department* [2002] 3 WLR 344, paras. 80-87 (Laws LJ: in the minority in the result, but here stating general propositions with which the majority expressed no disagreement. In the COMBAR lecture 2001, "Separation of Powers" [2002] *Judicial Review* 137, Lord Hoffmann says that the conduct of foreign relations and the security of the State are matters which "are wholly within the competence of the executive" and thus "obviously not justiciable" (para. 11).

8. It is well recognised by the English courts that decisions on the conduct of the UK's international relations with foreign states are not justiciable by the courts: see e.g. *Council of Civil Service Unions v Minister for the Civil Service* [1985] 1 AC 374, 411C-F (Lord Diplock), 418A-D (Lord Roskill); *R v Secretary of State for Foreign & Commonwealth Affairs, ex p. Everett* [1989] 1 QB 811 esp. at 816F-817B per O'Connor LJ and 820B-G per Taylor LJ; *R v Secretary of State for Foreign and*

Commonwealth Affairs ex parte Ferhud Butt [1999] 116 International Law Rep. 608 (esp. 615 per Lightman J; and p. 622 in the Court of Appeal per Henry LJ); *R v Secretary of State for Foreign & Commonwealth Affairs, ex p. Pirbhai* (1985) 107 International Law Rep. 462 (CA), esp. at p. 479 per Sir John Donaldson MR ("... in the context of a situation with serious implications for the conduct. of international relations, the courts should act with a high degree of circumspection in the interests of all concerned. It can rarely, if ever, be for judge to intervene where diplomats fear to tread."); *In the Matter of Foday Saybana Sankoh,* CA, unrep., 27 Sept. 2000, para. 9 per Laws LJ ("... that involves the proposition that the court should dictate to the executive government steps that it should take in the course of executing Government foreign policy: a hopeless proposition").

9.   Those cases were referred to as "powerful" authority by the Court of Appeal in *Abbasi* (paras. 37-38 and 80). The limited circumstances in which the Court was there prepared to envisage that there might be scope for judicial review of a refusal to render diplomatic assistance to a British subject who is suffering violation of a fundamental human right as the result of the conduct of the authorities of a foreign state have no application or relevance to the present claim. Thus the Court of Appeal confirmed in *Abbasi* that the Government "must be free to give full weight to foreign policy considerations, which are not justiciable" (para 99).

10. CND seek to argue that it is appropriate for the Court to review "any misdirection in law" (there is none identified, see above) on which the Government "in making its decision to go to war" (Detailed Statement of Grounds, para 28). No such decision has in fact been made. However, quite apart from this flaw in the claim, this submission of CND does reveal the extent to which this claim is intimately connected with questions of military and defence policy. These are matters of high policy relating to a decision as to whether and when the United Kingdom would engage in military action against another state. Such matters are pre-eminently non-justiciable, as stated, eg, in *De Smith, Woolf & Jowell, Judicial Review of Administrative Action* (5th ed.) at para 6-045:

"There will be some questions of 'high policy' such as the making of treaties, the defence of the realm, the dissolution of Parliament and the appointment of Ministers where the courts as a matter of discretion do not intervene, because the matters are simply not justiciable." (footnote omitted)

11. Having cited this passage in *Marchiori v Environment Agency and ors.* [2002] EWCA Civ 03 (25.2.02), Laws LJ went on to summarise the effect of the case law as follows:

> "38.   Taking all these materials together, it seems to me, first, to be plain that the law of England will not contemplate what may be called a merits review of any honest decision of government upon matters of national defence policy... The court is unequipped to judge such merits or demerits... The graver a matter of State and the more widespread its possible effects, the more respect will be given, within the framework of the constitution, to the democracy to decide its outcome. The defence of the realm, which is the Crown's first duty, is the paradigm of so grave a matter. Potentially such a thing touches the security of everyone; and everyone will look to the government they have elected for wise and effective decisions......"

Lord Justice Laws' caveat to this statement of principle, on which CND seek to rely (Detailed Statement of Grounds, para 26 and 36) was in relevant part:

> "40   .... Judicial review remains available to cure the theoretical possibility of actual bad faith on the part of ministers making decisions of high policy."

CND have not sought to suggest, nor could they, that the present case discloses any actual bad faith on the part of ministers in making decisions of high policy.

12.   It is firmly established that international instruments such as SCR 1441 do not form part of English law, and that the courts do not have jurisdiction to rule upon the true meaning and effect of such obligations which apply only at the level of international law: see, most recently, *R v Lyons* [2002] 3 WLR 1562, in particular per Lord Hoffmann at para 27, citing *J H Rayner (Mincing Lane) Ltd v Dept of Trade and Industry* [1990] 2 AC 418.

13.   Moreover, it is well established that the English courts do not have jurisdiction to rule upon the obligations of foreign states under international instruments: see, e.g., *British Airways v. Laker Airways* [1985] AC 58 at 85-86 (per Lord Diplock). SCR 1441 directly affects the rights and obligations in international law of a range of other states, apart from the United Kingdom. To do so would also involve a breach of comity, which the courts are astute to avoid: see *Buck v. AG* [1965] 1 Ch 745 at 770-771 (per Lord Diplock) and *R. v. Secretary of State, ex parte British Council of Turkish Cypriot Associations* 112 ILR 735 at 740 (per Sedley J).

14.   None of these clear principles is affected, contrary to the contentions of CND (e.g. Detailed Statement of Grounds, para 31), by wholly unexceptional statements made to the effect that the Government will

always act in accordance with international law [e.g. p.110 of the Bundle]. The substantive issue on which CND seeks a ruling plainly concerns the interpretation of an international instrument, SCR 1441. Accordingly, the Court should for this additional reason hold that this application is not properly justiciable.

15. Indeed, even at the level of international law, the question whether military action will be justified against Iraq must depend upon the particular circumstances applicable at the time when any decision to take such action may be made. Therefore CND is wrong to state that if the issue came before an international court, there would be no doubt that it would be capable of judicial determination (Detailed Statement of Grounds, para 27). Any judgment, both by the United Kingdom Government and by any international court, would have to be made against the actual circumstances that arose: see Ricketts 1 para 10, citing a statement by the Foreign Secretary in the House of Commons on 25 November.

16. A decision by the United Kingdom Government, or by its courts, to issue a definitive and reasoned statement or judgment concerning the true meaning and effect of SCR 1441 would affect not only the United Kingdom, but also other states. This would itself be a matter bearing upon the substantive conduct of the international affairs of the United Kingdom and would affect its relations with other countries. It would be the fact of a decision being made to issue such a statement which would be a matter of high policy (c.f. Detailed Statement of Grounds, para 35). The Court of Appeal in *Abbasi* was mindful of such considerations in refusing any relief. Two of the four reasons noted at para 107 for refusing relief were:

"i)... if the Foreign and Commonwealth Office were to make any statement as to its view of the legality of the detention of the British prisoners, or any statement as to the nature of discussions held with United States officials, this might well undermine those discussions.

ii) On no view would it be appropriate to order the Secretary of State to make any specific representations to the United States, even in the face of what appears to be a clear breach of a fundamental human right, as it is obvious that this would have an impact on the conduct of foreign policy, and an impact on such policy at a particularly delicate time." (emphasis added)

17. The witness statement of Peter Ricketts, Director General for Political Affairs at the Foreign and Commonwealth Office, explains both the similar and the additional concerns held in relation to SCR 1441. In summary, he highlights the following principal points:

(a)   The assertion of arguments of international law by one state is in practice regarded by other states as a political act, which may arouse upset or, depending on the state, even enmity (para 3).

(b)   This is especially true in a situation which is sensitive and where tension is high on all sides, where the issue of international law affects many states, and where the successful conduct of international affairs may dictate that matters should be left open for diplomatic negotiation (para 4);

(c)   To disclose the Government's understanding of the legal position under international law relevant to an international negotiation could be prejudicial to the success of the Government in that negotiation, and could be of immense value to any potential adversary (para 5);

(d)   Accordingly, the greatest care should be exercised and sensitive diplomatic judgment be brought to bear before the Government commits itself to supporting arguments in international law, which may prove controversial for friends and/or opponents and which may compromise the Government's own negotiating position as a tense international situation develops (para 6).

18. For all of these reasons, the subject matter of CND's claim is non-justiciable and is wholly unsuited to a claim for judicial review.

NO DUTY TO GIVE REASONS

19. Further and in any event, the essence of CND's proposed claim is to require the Government to give reasons for its understanding of the legal position on the interpretation of SCR 1441. That is part of what was sought by CND in its letter before action [Bundle, e.g. p. 359E], and it would be the practical effect if permission were granted and these proceedings were to result in any declaration.

20. The conditions under which a public authority may come under a duty at law to give reasons are not satisfied in this case. It is well established that there is no general obligation to give reasons, and the particular factors which may in a particular case give rise to such an obligation are not present in the circumstances of this case: see, especially, *Stefan v GMC* [1999] 1 WLR 1293 (PC), 1300 and 1301G-1303H. This is in part because a universal requirement for reasons may "impose an undesirable legalism into areas where a high degree of informality is appropriate" (1300F). Unlike hearings before the Health Committee of the GMC which were at issue in *Stefan,* there are numerous and weighty grounds of "policy" and "public interest" (1303H) justifying no requirement to give reasons for the United Kingdom's view on the interpretation of SCR 1441 [Ricketts 1, paras 3 -6 and 8 - 10].

PREMATURE

21. Further and again in any event, there is at the present time no decision in relation to which reasons could be given. No decision has in fact been taken as to whether and when the armed forces of the United Kingdom might be deployed against Iraq. This is acknowledged by CND in the Detailed Statement of Grounds, albeit with equivocation (especially para 44). For that reason alone, this application for permission should be refused.

22. The furthest that the Secretary of State for Foreign and Commonwealth Affairs has judged it appropriate to go at this time is to state that the position of the United Kingdom Government must be reserved [House of Commons, 25 November, quoted at Ricketts 1, para 7]. No definitive view, either one way or the other, of the legal position under international law has been expressed. That reflects a considered position, which is judged to be in the national interest and in the interests of the conduct of the United Kingdom's international relations [Ricketts 1, para 8].

23. CND are therefore constrained to point to the wholly unexceptional and unsurprising statements made by the Government that the United Kingdom Government will act within international law [e.g. Detailed Statement of Grounds, para 28]. This is no more solid a foundation for the claim than would be a statement that the Government will act in accordance with domestic law. It cannot enable CND to overcome such a fundamental obstacle to its challenge as the absence of any decision (let alone any justiciable decision). The present case is quite different to any of the cases on which CND seek to rely (in particular, Detailed Statement of Grounds, para 29), which concerned decisions which had actually been taken, in the past, and in relation to which the decision maker stated that he had relied on particular legal advice. Here, no such decision has been taken, or indeed may ever need to be taken.

24. The courts will not grant declaratory relief in relation to a matter which is abstract and theoretical. The fact that the timetable for future decisions may prove to be a tight one does not render this application, at the present time, any less hypothetical, abstract or theoretical. The courts can, in appropriate cases, hear applications with great expedition (see, e.g. *R v Portsmouth Hospital, ex p. Glass* [1999] 2 FLR 905 where a declaration about how a patient should be treated if an emergency arose was refused, since it was not possible to know what would be the most appropriate treatment until the emergency occurred).

25. These proceedings do not concern specific facts which are already in existence. Rather they are premised upon conjecture and speculation by CND. See, for example, the unsupported (and contested) assertion at

108

Detailed Statement of Grounds, para 50(2) "although the government statements on the legality of attacking Iraq without a further UN Security Council Resolution are equivocal, they give a **strong indication** that the government is **minded** to attack without a further resolution" (emphasis added). Accordingly, CND cannot properly claim a declaration in relation to specific facts which are already in existence, and the basis upon which it seeks to found these proceedings is hypothetical, turning on facts and circumstances which have not yet occurred and may never occur at all (see *Zamir & Woolf, The Declaratory Judgment* (3rd ed.), 4.070, p.153). The formulation of a legal position with regard to a future Security Council resolution must be dependent upon the facts and circumstances prevailing at the time (for example, taking account of the nature of any material breach of SCR 1441 which may occur) [Ricketts 1, para 10].

26. Furthermore, there would be no public interest in the Court giving an advisory opinion on this hypothetical issue. For the reasons set out in the witness statement of Peter Ricketts, the public interest is entirely against the giving of any such opinion.

STANDING

27. A claimant for Judicial review must be able to satisfy the test of a "sufficient interest" in the subject matter of the proposed claim: section 31(3) of the Supreme Court Act 1981. This is a jurisdictional condition for the bringing of any application, and standing cannot be conferred by consent: *R v Secretary of State for Social Services, ex p. CPAG* [1990] 2 QB 540, 556E-F. Accordingly, the Court needs to address this jurisdictional condition, which is not purely a question of discretion, but rather a mixed decision of fact and law which the Court must decide on legal principles: *R v Secretary of State for the Environment, ex p. Rose Theatre Trust Co* [1990] 1 QB 504, 520C per Schiemann J. This is not a case in which it is not possible for the issue of standing to be addressed and determined at the permission stage; the Court has detailed submissions on all relevant factual and legal matters pertaining to standing.

28. Although the courts have in recent years taken a more generous approach to the test of sufficient interest, it does remain a hurdle which every claimant must surmount having regard to the particular circumstances and context of the challenge. The proposed Defendants do not doubt that CND has strongly held political views which it is of course entitled to ventilate to the public by all appropriate means. However, as is apparent from the witness statement of Carol Naughton, those political concerns focus upon the United Kingdom's nuclear weapons system, and more generally upon the peaceful resolution of

conflict [Naughton 1, para 1, Bundle p.360]. CND's concern is to prevent any use of force against Iraq, in particular involving Trident [Naughton 1, para 7, Bundle p.363]. Those are political concerns about the use of force, and in particular the use of nuclear weapons, and are self-evidently not a concern about whether, as a matter of international law, there would be a need for a second Security Council Resolution in the event of a material breach of SCR 1441. Merely to assert an interest, whether as an individual or a company, does not satisfy the sufficient interest test (see *Rose Theatre Trust Co* p.520E). Nor can such an interest be manufactured by entering into correspondence with a Secretary of State: *Rose Theatre Trust Co* p. 521H [c.f. Naughton 1, paras 3-6, Bundle p.361-363]. Accordingly, the proposed Defendants. submit that the Government is under no obligation to make a definitive statement of its legal position under international law to a private organisation such as CND, and that CND therefore lacks standing to bring this claim.

CONCLUSION

29. For all the reasons set out above, it is submitted that permission should be refused, alternatively the claim should be dismissed.

PHILIP SALES

JEMIMA STRATFORD

6th December 2002

[1] The Proposed First Defendant is not properly named as a Defendant. The Prime Minister is not an authorised Government Department within section 17 of the Crown Proceedings Act 1947

7. THE CND CASE PRESENTED TO THE HIGH COURT

****

Skeleton Argument of Rabinder Singh QC, Charlotte Kilroy, and Michael Fordham, 6 December 2002

IN THE ADMINISTRATIVE COURT   CO/5429/2002

R (CND) v Prime Minister and Secretaries of State

_____

CLAIMANT'S SKELETON ARGUMENT

_____

judicial review: permission/preliminary issue
Monday 9 December 2002

SUGGESTED PRE-READING (t/e: 2 hours)

(1) The skeleton arguments

(2) The grounds and statement of facts **(bundle tabs 1-3)**

(3) Security Council Press Release SC/7564 **(pp.71-75, 78-82)**

(4) Witness statement: Naughton **(pp. 360-412)**; Ricketts (lodged separately.)

THIS PRELIMINARY HEARING

1. There are before the Court: (1) the claimant's application for permission to seek judicial review; and (2) the invitation, made by the defendants, that the Court should dismiss the claim by a ruling, as a preliminary issue and without consideration of international law, that the subject-matter is necessarily non-justiciable.

2. The claimant submits that: (1) the Court should grant permission for judicial review, there being no clean knock-out blow; and (2) the Court should decline the invitation to dismiss the case. Matters should proceed, as the defendants indicated to Maurice Kay J at the directions hearing (29.11.02) that they otherwise would, namely with a further 7 days to consider the position and put together whatever case on international law they wish to put before the Court.

WHAT THE CLAIM IS ABOUT

3. The claimant has filed detailed grounds for judicial review **(tabs 1-2)**, to which attention is invited, whose contents are not repeated here. In essence:

    (1)   This claim for judicial review arises out of the prospect of military action by the United Kingdom against Iraq to enforce

United Nations Security Council Resolution 1441 (8.11.02) in the event of non-compliance by Iraq with its terms.

(2) The substantive question raised in the proceedings is this: whether Resolution 1441 authorises States to take military action in the event of non-compliance by Iraq with its terms. The consequence, if not, is that international law would require a further mandate from the Security Council, for military action for such non-compliance with the terms of the Resolution.

4. The claimant submits that:

(3) The question on which the Court would be ruling is an issue of law. Indeed, it is in essence a question of interpretation (of the Resolution). The argument would be legal argument.

(4) It is moreover a relevant question of law.

(5) As a relevant question of law, the case should not be dismissed without consideration of its legal merits, on grounds of a suggested justiciability bar.

(6) The identification of the requirements of international law are not a matter within the exclusive province of the Executive.

5. The claimant's argument on the substantive issue of international law is straightforward. It is set out in the grounds **(tab 1 para 13-16, tab 2 paras 51-88)**. The nature of the argument can be seen from these main points:

1) An aggressive war is an act contrary to the law of nations, and prohibited by peremptory norms of customary international law (*Nicaragua v United States*, [1986] ICJ Reports 14, at para 190) and by Article 2(4) of the UN Charter.

2) A war is an aggressive war unless it is conducted with lawful justification. Unless a war is authorized by the Security Council under Chapter VII of the UN Charter, or justified under Article 51 of the Charter it is unlawful.

3) Military action against Iraq is not authorized by Resolution 1441. Resolution 1441 sets out the obligations upon Iraq. It expressly deals with the question of enforcement (paragraph 11). It does not authorise States to use force. On the contrary, it provides that to the extent of any breach the matter would revert to the Security Council (paragraphs 4, 12).[1]

4) Resolution 1441 constitutes action under Chapter VII of the Charter of the United Nations. Chapter VII does not contain any authority for States to take military action for enforcement

of Security Council Resolutions. On the contrary: Article 2(4) contains a clear prohibition on use of force by States (which moreover reflects part of the jus cogens); Article 24 makes clear that force is a matter for the Security Council itself; and Article 51 shows that there is an exception, not for enforcement of Security Council Resolutions, but in special circumstances of self-defence.

Those points engage not foreign policy "debate", restricted to the political forum, but legal interpretation apt for consideration by a Court of law.

WHAT THE CLAIM IS NOT ABOUT

6. This claim for judicial review does not seek to raise any question as to whether it would be appropriate to seek a further mandate from the UN Security Council as a matter of (a) political judgment, (b) diplomatic function, or (c) foreign policy. Nor does this claim raise any question in which the Court is being asked to scrutinise an Executive decision, dealing directly with a matter of defence, on a ground relating to (i) its factual merits or (ii) its rationality. Nor does the claimant ask the Court for any remedy which would constrain the Executive in relation to any decision which it may take, whether as a matter of political judgment, diplomatic function or foreign affairs or at all, as to whether to take military action; or whether or how to deploy troops.

WHAT THE GOVERNMENT HAS SAID

7. The Government has made clear that it is contemplating military action against Iraq, in the event of Iraq's non-compliance with UN Security Council Resolutions, now Resolution 1441:

> *the action that we need to take is to ensure that the UN resolutions are properly implemented - that is the clear purpose.[2]*

> *we are not at the stage of taking decisions about military action. However, it is important to recognise that in the event of the UN's will not being complied with, we must be prepared to take that action.[3]*

> *As the UN process moves forward, so should our preparedness for military action in the event that the process fails.[4]*

> *NATO Allies stand united in their commitment to take effective action to assist and support the efforts of the UN to ensure full and immediate compliance by Iraq, without conditions or restrictions, with UNSCR 1441.[5]*

8. The Government has said that it regards as essential that any such action be taken having regard to and in accordance with international law:

we will always act in accordance with international law[6]

the issues before us come down to four...

The fourth question is whether even if Saddam is as great a threat as we say, it is justifiable to use force to deal with the threat. The short answer to that question is yes, provided force is a last resort and its use is consistent with international law.

Law, whether domestic or international, fundamentally depends for its legitimacy on the values its reflects. Law without values is no law at all. But while the moral legitimacy of any law will strengthen the natural consent for that law, there will always be some who reject or despise the values on which the law is based. Against them, the law has to be enforced, ultimately, by the force of arms. But the force which is used has itself to be consistent with the moral and legal framework it seeks to defend. Laws without force is no law. Force without law is no law.[7]

If there is military action, any participation in it by Her Majesty's Government would be strictly in accordance with our obligations in international law...[8]

I repeat, any decisions that we make in respect of military action will be made within the context of the body of international law...[9]

If force becomes necessary, any decisions made by Her Majesty's Government will be careful, proportionate and consistent with our obligations in international law.[10]

I can assure you any action we do take... in the context of Iraq... will continue to be justified under International law.[11]

It is to be noted that international law has featured in Government observations about Iraq[12] and in cross-party support[13].

9. The Government has recognised that there is an important question[14] of whether Resolution 1441 authorises the use of force by States in the event of non-compliance by Iraq with its terms, there being a legal interrelationship between the absence of a Security Council mandate and international law:

we have always made it clear that within international law we have to reserve our right to take military action, if that is required, within the existing charter and the existing body of

UN Security Council resolutions, if, for example, a subsequent resolution were to be vetoed.[15]

We have always made it clear that any action that we take will be taken within the context of each of our obligations in international law and the same applies to the United Nations. That remains our position... [T]he Security Council resolutions form part of international law but not the total corpus, and whether military action is justified in International law, with or without a second resolution, depends on the circumstances.[16]

[Asked:] If Iraq fails to comply and military action - the most serious of consequences - ensues, would that require a mandate from the UN ? Would this country support a coalition of nations undertaking that military action if such a mandate were not forthcoming ? Under what legal verification would that be possible ?

[Answer:] we must reserve the right, within our obligations under international law, to take military action if we deem that necessary, outwith a specific Security Council resolution being passed in the future.

I repeat that the UN charter, Security Council resolutions and customary international law are the basis of international law. They have to come together. Judgments about whether military action is necessary and justified in international law must be made on that totality.[17]

I want to... answer four key questions...

Thirdly, would there have to be a second Security Council resolution if military action proved necessary ?...

Resolution 1441 does not stipulate that there has to be a second Security Council resolution to authorise military action in the event of a further material breach by Iraq... [T]he preference of the Government in the event of any material breach is that there should be a second Security Council resolution authorising military action. However, the faith now being placed in the Security Council by all members of the United Nations, including the United States, requires the Council to show a corresponding level of responsibility. So far, it has done so and I believe that it will do so in the future, but we must reserve our position in the event that it does not.[18]

[asked:] many people think America hasn't got authorisation for war on Saddam Hussein without a new fresh mandate from the Security Council, is that your view ?

[answer:] I don't think that's necessarily the case no.[19]

> *[The Foreign Secretary] said that the Government did not regard it as necessary for a second resolution to be brought before the UN security council.*[20]

JUSTICIABILITY

10. The question of justiciability is dealt with in the grounds at tab 1 para 7-9, tab 2 paras 19-37. Justiciability goes to the separation of powers between the Executive and the Courts. In the present case, the question of justiciability will come to this: is the substantive issue in this claim for judicial review one which is within the exclusive province of the Executive (as say the defendants), or is it (as says the claimant) a relevant question of law proper for a ruling by the Court in the exercise of its supervisory   jurisdiction to ensure that the Executive does not take political decisions on the basis of an erroneous understanding of the law?

11. There is a more immediate question, on this initial hearing: is it appropriate to <u>compartmentalise</u> the questions of (i) justiciability and (ii) international law, so as to deal with the former on a blanket basis and isolated from an analysis of the issue of substance. As to this:

    (1)   The claimant submits that compartmentalisation is inappropriate. The response of the Court is linked to the particular context[21], and   will involve an analysis of <u>the nature of the issue,</u> as to whether it has <u>legal</u> relevance and merit. Justiciability cannot be approached in a vacuum. The law on justiciability has now reached a similar position to that which the law on standing reached long ago, it being undesirable to isolate standing from legality.[22]

    (2)   Given that the defendants seek to have the claim dismissed without consideration of international law, it would be appropriate for the Court to test the position by <u>assuming in the claimant's favour</u> that the claimant is right (a) that the international law question is relevant, and (b) as to the answer to the international law question. The defendants' suggested knock-out blow is <u>not</u> said to be: (a) that international law (justiciable where legally relevant) is irrelevant in this case; nor (b) that the claimant is plainly and obviously wrong about international law.

12. The claimant advances the following propositions, in support of its contention that this case ought not to be dismissed as non-justiciable, and certainly not without addressing and analysing the argument on international law:

International law

1)   The domestic Court has jurisdiction to rule on a relevant question as to what international law requires, that not being per se a matter within the exclusive province of the Executive. The question of international law must be one which is relevant to the position of the Executive in the particular case, over which the Court is exercising its supervisory jurisdiction.

    See eg. *R (on the application of Abbasi) v Secretary of State for Foreign and Commonwealth Affairs* **[2002] EWCA Civ 1598.**

2)   The prohibition on the use of force has the character of *jus cogens*, a peremptory norm of customary international law. It is a well established rule of English law that all rules of customary international law are part of the law of the land; and that among those rules of customary international law *jus cogens* enjoys a higher status as one of the fundamental standards of the international community. Violations of *jus cogens* therefore come under the court's supervisory jurisdiction.

    (see *Abbasi* at [28], [68]-[69]; *Oppenheim* at 56-57; *Trendtex Trading Corporation v Central Bank of Nigeria [1977] QB 529; Reg. v. Bow Street Magistrate, Ex p. Pinochet* (No. 3) [2000] 1 AC 147 at 198)

3)   International law is relevant to the Court's supervisory jurisdiction where the Executive has a stated intention to act by having regard to international law. The Court can appropriately assume the judicial function of ensuring that the Executive directs itself correctly as to what international law requires.

    See *R v Secretary of State for the Home Department, ex p Launder* [1997] 1 WLR 839, 867C-F (Lord Hope); *R v Director of Public Prosecutions, ex p Kebilene* [2000] 2 AC 326, 367E-H (Lord Steyn) 341 (Lord Bingham).

4)   The Court can properly express a view on international law, without there needing to be a statutory context under consideration; though, if there is, international law cannot assist if inconsistent with a clear domestic statutory provision

    See *Abbasi* at [57]; R v Lyons [2002] 3 WLR 1562 at [14] (Lord Bingham CJ), [28] (Lord Hoffman), [67] (Lord Hutton), [81] (Lord Hobhouse), [109] (Lord Millett).

<u>Justiciability</u>

1) Justiciability depends not on any general principle but on subject matter and suitability in the particular case.

See *Abbasi* at [85].

2) A case is not to be treated as non-justiciable simply because it relates to a sensitive `field of activity'. Thus, even Executive decisions dealing directly with matters of defence are not immune from judicial review, since that would be repugnant to the rule of law.

See *R (on the application of International Transport Roth GmbH) v Secretary of State for the Home Department* [2002] EWCA Civ 158 [2002] 3 WLR 344 at [85] (Laws LJ).

3) What matters is whether the particular issue is or is not one which lies within the exclusive province of the Executive.

See *Secretary of State for the Home Department v Rehman* [2001] UKHL 47 [2001] 3 WLR 877 at [54] (Lord Hoffmann).

4) Illustrative of a particular complaint not susceptible of judicial determination is the scrutiny of a defence-related decision on grounds relating to its factual merits.

See *Roth* at [85] (Laws LJ).

13. The Court is invited to reject the suggestion that there is in this case a justiciability bar which precludes the Court from analysing, and excuses the defendants from answering, the substantive question of law.

NATIONAL INTEREST

14. The defendants have now[23] suggested that the very act of speaking about what international law requires might involve disclosing material which would threaten the security of the State. That, however, betrays a misapprehension of what the issue is (and what it is not: paragraph 6 above). The issue is and remains whether Resolution 1441 authorises States to take military action in the event of non-compliance by Iraq with its terms or whether a further Security Council Resolution is needed. That is a question of interpretation of the Resolution within its legal context (Chapter VII of the Charter and customary international law).

15. In his witness statement of 5 December 2002, Peter Ricketts states that the disclosure of a definitive statement of the Government's legal position would be prejudicial to the national interest and to the conduct of the Government's foreign policy. He states that in international

relations issues of law, politics and diplomacy are closely bound up together, and that the assertion of arguments of international law by one state is in practice regarded by other states as a political act. The UK's international alliances could be damaged by the incautious assertion of arguments under international law which affect the position of those other states, and its success in negotiations prejudiced. Furthermore an adversary could plan on the basis of the legal 'bottom line'.

16. This is not a debate about international relations, it is a judicial adjudication on a question of legal interpretation. Moreover;

(1) The UK has an obligation both internationally and domestically to act in accordance with customary international law. There is no doubt that this obligation is justiciable in the international courts (see the *Nicaragua* case). In the ***Expenses case (1962) ICJ reports, 151*** the ICJ firmly rejected the suggestion that it could not interpret a provision of the UN Charter because the question put to it was intertwined with political questions. It stated: "*The court...cannot attribute a political character to a request which invites it to undertake an essentially judicial task, namely, the interpretation of a treaty provision.*"

(2) If international courts will consider a concrete legal question which nonetheless has political significance, there is no reason why a domestic court should be precluded from doing so on that ground alone (see ***R v Home Secretary ex parte Adan [2001] 2 AC 477***).

(3) It is clear that the Government regularly states what its understanding of international law and Resolution 1441 is (see Ambassador Greenstock's statements to the Press (**p63**), the Prime Minister's statements to the press (**p70B**), Mr Straw in Parliament (**pp259A-F**) and that it will comply with international law.

(4) If the Government is giving assurances to the British public that it will act in accordance with international law the British public is entitled to know what that means. The Government is effectively saying that it wants the option of acting unlawfully without the opprobrium of being seen to do so. This is not a valid ground on which a Court should judge an issue to be non-justiciable.

(5) The Government's argument is essentially one of timing. Once it takes action upon a breach of SCR 1441 then the question will be whether the action it took was compatible

with international law, and all the arguments about prejudice in Mr Rickett's witness statement would fall away. Is the Court to reject a claim on the grounds of non-justiciablity on the basis that it is prejudicial for a Government to discover that its proposed action is unlawful before the event has taken place, when that Government stated publicly that it would only act in accordance with international law?

17. The Claimant's application for a declaratory judgment does not in any way involve forecasting the future (Mr Ricketts paragraph 10 of his witness statement). The Claimant is not seeking to pre-empt any future decisions on whether the UK would be entitled to take action on the basis of Article 51 of the UN Charter, or for humanitarian reasons. The Claimant's application relates to Resolution 1441 and whether a further UN Security Council Resolution would be required to enforce against any breach of that resolution. That is a pure question of interpretation of the Resolution itself against the background of the UN Charter and customary international law. The meaning of the Resolution will not change even if the circumstances do.

PREMATURITY AND STANDING

18. If the defendants seek to take a point (and at this permission stage) in relation to the prospective nature of the claim or the question of sufficient interest, each is dealt within in detail in the grounds for judicial review: **tab 1 paras 10-11; tab 2 paras 38-50**. The claimant submits that, if and to the extent that the claim is "non-justiciable" then it will fail for that reason. Similarly, if the claimant is wrong as to the nature of the international law question and/or the answer to that question, the claim would for that reason be dismissed. If, however, the matter is justiciable and the claimant is right that there is a relevant question of international law on which it is correct, it would not be right for the claim to fail on some other ground relating to its timing or the identity of the claimant.

19. The case raises issues of very great importance, brought in the public interest. Although it is "prospective" in the sense that the defendants have said that no decision has been taken as to military action **(pp.98, 115, 270)**:

(1) The prospect of military action is and remains a real one: paragraph 7 above.

(2) The issue of international law, whether ruled on by the Court or even if left to the exclusive province of the Executive, would necessarily need to inform prospectively the decision whether to proceed with military action.

(3)   It cannot seriously be suggested that, if justiciable, it would be better for the issue to be resolved after military action has been taken.

20.   In fact, this would be a very good example of the Court appropriately using its "advisory" jurisdiction (*R v Secretary of State for the Home Department, ex p Mehari* [1994] QB 474, 491G-H (Laws LJ); *In re S (Hospital Patient: Court's Jurisdiction)* [1996] Fam 1, 18A (Sir Thomas Bingham MR)).

(1)   The issue is of public importance, serving a useful purpose in the public interest, is in sufficiently precise terms and the appropriate parties are before the Court: see *London Borough of Islington v Camp* 20th July 1999 unrep.; also *The Woolf Report, Access to Justice* (1996) at p.252.

(2)   An advisory declaration would mean that whatever political choices are made by Government, they would be made on an informed basis as to the law (favourable or adverse) and facing up to the legal implications: cf. (by way of analogy) *R v Secretary of State for the Home Department, ex p Simms* [2000] 2 AC 115, 131E-F (Lord Hoffmann).

CONCLUSION

21.   The Court is invited to decline the Government's invitation to dismiss this important case without consideration of the issue of international law, and to make directions for the further conduct of these proceedings.

RABINDER SINGH QC
MICHAEL FORDHAM
CHARLOTTE KILROY
6.12.02

IN THE ADMINISTRATIVE COURT
R (CND) v Prime Minister and Secretaries of State

CLAIMANT'S SKELETON ARGUMENT

Public Interest Lawyers
50-54 St Paul's Square, Birmingham B3 1QS
CND.SKE

FOOTNOTES

[1].   The travaux preparatoires include an unadopted draft which did provide **(p.401)** that "breach authorises member states to use all necessary means to restore international peace and security in the area".

2.   The Prime Minister to Parliament (24.9.02) **(p.113).**

3.   The Prime Minister to Parliament (24.9.02) **(p.115).**

4.   The Foreign Secretary to Parliament (25.11.02) **(p. 270).**

5.   NATO Prague Summit Statement on Iraq (21.11.02) **(P. 349)**.

6.   The Prime Minister to Parliament (24.9.02) **(p.110)**.

7.   The Foreign Secretary to Parliament (24.9.02) **(pp. 125, 131)**.

8.   The Foreign Secretary to Parliament (24.9.02) **(p.133)**.

9.   The Foreign Secretary to Parliament (7.11.02) **(p.246)**.

10. The Foreign Secretary to Parliament (25.11.02) **(p.270)**.

11. Letter from Ministry of Defence to claimant's solicitor (24.5.02) **(p.374)**.

12. The Prime Minister to Parliament (24.9.02): 'Iraq deserves to be led by someone who can abide by international law" **(P.106)**.

13. Mr Ancram to Parliament (24.9.02) (p.135): "We must act legally - the Conservative Party puts great store by the rule of law and will want to be assured throughout this process that international law is being pursued"; Mr Moore (25.11.02) (p.294): "the framework of international law must govern the whole debate, and the actions of our Government... "

14. See also: (24.9.02) Mr Duncan Smith and the Prime Minister **(pp.109-110)**, Mr Jenkin **(p.236)**; (7.11.02) Mr Ancram **(p.244)**, the Foreign Secretary **(pp.249-250)**; (on 25.11.02) the Foreign Secretary **(pp.273-275)**, Mr Ancram and the Foreign Secretary **(pp.281-282)**, Mr Llwyd (25.11.02) **(p.315)**.

15. The Foreign Secretary to Parliament (7.11.02) **(p.246)**.

16. The Foreign Secretary to Parliament (7.11.02) **(p.250)**.

17. The Foreign Secretary to Parliament (7.11.02) **(p.251)**.

18. The Foreign Secretary to Parliament (25.11.02) **(pp.263, 267)**.

19. Defence Secretary (Mr Hoon) on BBC's *On The Record* (10.11.02) **(p.352)**.

20   Press report (20.11.02) **(p.99)**.

21   *R v Secretary of State for the Home Department, ex p Daly* [2001] UKHL 26   [2001] 2AC 532 at [28] (Lord Steyn: "In law context is everything").

22   *R v IRC, ex p National Federation of Self-Employed* [1982] AC 617.

23   Cf. paragraph 9 above.

8. THE HIGH COURT JUDGEMENT

Judgment of Lord Justice Simon Brown, Mr Justice Maurice Kay and Mr Justice Richards, 17 December 2002

****

Neutral Citation No: [2002] EWHC 2777 (Admin)   Case No: CO/5429/2002

IN THE HIGH COURT OF JUSTICE

QUEEN'S BENCH DIVISION (DIVISIONAL COURT)

Royal Courts of Justice

Strand, London, WC2A 2LL

Date: 17th December 2002

Before:

THE RIGHT HONOURABLE LORD JUSTICE SIMON BROWN

THE HONOURABLE MR JUSTICE MAURICE KAY

and

THE HONOURABLE MR JUSTICE RICHARDS

....

Between

THE CAMPAIGN FOR NUCLEAR DISARMAMENT Applicant

- and -

(1) THE PRIME MINISTER OF THE UNITED KINGDOM Respondents

and

(2) THE SECRETARY OF STATE FOR FOREIGN & COMMONWEALTH AFFAIRS

and

(3) THE SECRETARY OF STATE FOR DEFENCE

- - - - - - - - - - - - - - - - - - - -

Rabinder Singh Esq, QC, Michael Fordham Esq & Ms Charlotte Kilroy
(instructed by **Public Interest Lawyers**) for the Applicant
Philip Sales Esq & Ms Jemima Stratford
(instructed by **The Treasury Solicitor**) for the Respondents
Hearing dates : 10th/11th December 2002

- - - - - - - - - - - - - - - - - - - -

JUDGMENT : APPROVED BY THE COURT FOR HANDING DOWN (SUBJECT TO EDITORIAL CORRECTIONS)

Lord Justice Simon Brown:

1. This application is nothing if not topical. Resolution 1441 was unanimously adopted by the United Nations Security Council on 8 November 2002. It affords Iraq "a final opportunity to comply with its disarmament obligations" (paragraph 2) and recalls that the Council "has repeatedly warned Iraq that it will face serious consequences as a result of its continued violations of its obligations" (paragraph 13). Just ten days ago, pursuant to paragraph 3, Iraq provided the United Nations' Monitoring Verification & Inspection Commission (UNMOVIC) and the International Atomic Energy Agency (IAEA) with a twelve thousand page dossier by way of a "declaration of all aspects of its programmes to develop chemical, biological and nuclear weapons". UNMOVIC and IAEA are presently engaged in their inspection activities. All this is well known, front-page and television news on a daily basis. It is a time of great international tension.

2. What the applicants, Campaign for Nuclear Disarmament (CND), seek by this judicial review application is solely declaratory relief, an advisory declaration as to the true meaning of Resolution 1441 and more particularly as to whether it authorises States to take military action in the event of non-compliance by Iraq with its terms. CND submit it does not. In short, the court is being invited to declare that the UK Government would be acting in breach of international law were it to take military action against Iraq without a further Resolution. It is, to say the least, a novel and ambitious claim.

3. Before coming to examine it let me first set it in the context of certain public statements made by the defendants upon which the applicants seek to rely. Although many such are to be found in the documents before us, I shall quote just three, each made by the Foreign Secretary, the second defendant:

    i. **7 November 2002 (the day before Resolution 1441 was adopted), in the House of Commons:**

        "I do not want to anticipate what will happen if there is a breach, except to say that although we would much prefer decisions to be taken within the Security Council, we have always made it clear that within international law we have to reserve our right to take military action, if that is required, within the existing Charter and the existing body of UN Security Council resolutions if, for example, a subsequent resolution were to be vetoed. However, I do not believe it will come to that."

ii.   **10 November 2002, when interviewed on BBC Radio 4**:

"Well, I think it's pretty obvious what 'serious consequences' means. Of course there were some negotiations over the text, but the United States and the United Kingdom would not have voted for this text, indeed sponsored the text, had we not been satisfied that it spelt out a very clear set of ultimata to Saddam Hussein, gave the inspectors the best possible powers and also spelt out at the end of the resolution what would happen if Saddam Hussein did not cooperate. It's all there. It's very clear and, yes, military action is bound to follow if Saddam Hussein does not cooperate fully with the terms of this resolution."

iii.   **25 November 2002, in the House of Commons**:

"I should make it clear to the House, as I did on 7 November, that the preference of the British Government, in the event of a material breach, is that there should be a second Resolution authorising military action. The faith now being placed in the Security Council by all members of the United Nations, including the US, requires the Council to show a corresponding level of responsibility. So far it has more than done so. I believe it will do so in the future. But we must reserve our position in the event that it does not."

4.   As was indicated in the first of those statements and as, indeed, has repeatedly been stated by the ministers throughout the whole course of events, the government intends only to take action which is justified by international law. As the first defendant said in Parliament on 24 September 2002:

"We will always act in accordance with international law."

5.   There is no reason to doubt the government's good faith in this commitment and I do not understand the applicants to question it. On the contrary, it forms the first plank of their argument for the declaration sought. What Mr Rabinder Singh QC submits is that, the government having clearly stated that it would not wish to take military action save in accordance with international law, "there is a great public interest in ensuring that the government is adequately informed on this key question of law; the government should have the benefit of judicial guidance as to what the law is". I take this from the applicant's written reply. In the same passage "CND makes it clear that it does not invite the court to seek to influence the policy decisions of the government in this area".

6.   The applicant's argument would appear to suggest that government's need of the court's assistance in understanding the true position in

international law is evident from two things: first, CND's contention that without a second Security Council resolution military action against Iraq would be unlawful; secondly, the government's apparent belief to the contrary evidenced by the second of the Foreign Secretary's statements set out above (the evidential high-water mark of the applicant's case that the defendants have misdirected themselves in law on the question), and perhaps also by the third of those statements in which, by "reserv[ing]" the government's position in the event that no second resolution is adopted, Mr Straw is said to have implied that the UK government would regard itself nevertheless as able to take military action. At the very least, it appears to contemplate that possibility.

7.   Essentially, therefore, it is CND's case that they are bringing this application solely to ensure that government do not at some future date embark upon military action against Iraq in the mistaken belief that it is lawful to do so when in fact it is not. Given CND's avowed purpose, which is to campaign against war and in favour of the peaceful resolution of conflict, some might think this disingenuous. Such suspicions might be sharpened by seeing it asserted in CND's skeleton argument that "the Government is effectively saying that it wants the option of acting unlawfully without the opprobrium of being seen to do so". For present purposes, however, I propose to accept it at face value. The critical question nevertheless remains whether, even assuming this to be so, the claim is one which the court should properly entertain and determine. That is the issue presently before us. Pursuant to an order made by Maurice Kay J on 29 November 2002, the application has been confined initially to the determination of preliminary issues in the way of justiciability, prematurity and standing - everything, in short, save for the substantive point of international law upon which the applicants ultimately seek the court's ruling.

8.   Before, however, coming to these preliminary issues, it is I think necessary to sketch in at least the framework of the argument which CND wish to advance on the substantive question. For this purpose I must set out three further paragraphs of Resolution 1441. By these paragraphs the Security Council:

> "4. Decides that false statements or omissions in the declarations submitted by Iraq pursuant to this resolution and failure by Iraq at any time to comply with, and cooperate fully in the implementation of, this resolution shall constitute a further material breach of Iraq's obligations and will be reported to the Council for assessment in accordance with paragraphs 11 and 12 below;
>
> ...11. Directs the Executive Chairman of UNMOVIC and the

Director-General of the IAEA to report immediately to the Council any interference by Iraq with inspection activities, as well as any failure by Iraq to comply with its disarmament obligations, including its obligations regarding inspections under this resolution;

12. Decides to convene immediately upon receipt of a report in accordance with paragraphs 4 or 11 above, in order to consider the situation and the need for full compliance with all of the relevant Council resolutions in order to secure international peace and security."

9.   Following the adoption of Resolution 1441, public statements were made by a number of the ambassadors to the United Nations from the Member States of the Security Council. The UK's ambassador stated:

"There is no 'automaticity' in this Resolution. If there is a further Iraqi breach of its disarmament obligations, the matter will return to the Council for discussion as required in operational paragraph 12."

10.   CND point out that an earlier draft of the resolution had provided not merely that non-compliance with its terms should constitute a further material breach of Iraq's obligations but also "that such breach authorises Member States to use all necessary means to restore international peace and security in the area". The phrase "all necessary means" is widely recognised to encompass the use of force and indeed this form of words is to be found in Resolution 678 of 29 November 1990 by which Member States were authorised to act following Iraq's invasion of Kuwait. The omission of that clause from Resolution 1441 as adopted is, suggest CND, striking and significant. That consideration, they submit, coupled with ambassadorial statements exemplified by that made by the UK ambassador and, most importantly of all, the express text of the resolution by which any breaches must be reported back to the Council for it to deal with as it may then think appropriate, makes good their contention that breach of the resolution would not of itself authorise the taking of military action. Their case on the true construction of the resolution, they submit, is not merely arguable but strong. They further submit that it raises a sharp-edged question of law involving no considerations of policy, no disputed areas of fact, no consideration of the developing international situation. It is thus an issue upon which the court can and should decide. Such, in a nutshell, is the applicant's contention.

11.   The defendants assert to the contrary that there are compelling reasons for the court not to embark upon such an exercise, prominent amongst them considerations of the national interest. It is in this connection that

there is before the court a statement dated 5 December 2002 made by Mr Ricketts, Director General for Political Affairs at the Foreign and Commonwealth Office, who draws upon 28 years' experience closely involved in the United Kingdom's conduct of its international relations and diplomatic negotiations with foreign States. I must set out the bulk of this statement in full:

> "3. The claimants have asked that the Government explain its understanding of the legal position with regard to the interpretation of Security Council Resolution 1441 (2002). In the judgment of the Secretary of State and the Foreign & Commonwealth Office, and in my own opinion, however, it would be prejudicial to the national interest and to the conduct of the Government's foreign policy if the Government were to be constrained to make a definitive statement of its legal position under international law in relation to issues concerning the international relations of the United Kingdom. The short point is that it is an unavoidable feature of the conduct of international relations that issues of law, politics and diplomacy are usually closely bound up together. The assertion of arguments of international law by one state is in practice regarded by other states as a political act, and they react accordingly. The UK's international alliances could be damaged by the incautious assertion of arguments under international law which affect the position of those other states.

> 4.   This is especially true in a situation which (like the present situation covered by resolution 1441) is sensitive and where tension is high on all sides: the assertion of arguments of international law by one state which are unpalatable to other states may have the effect of increasing tension and diminishing the possibilities for a diplomatic (and, it is hoped, peaceful) solution. It is also especially true where the issue of international law to be considered is an issue which (like the interpretation of resolution 1441) affects not just the United Kingdom, but many other states as well, who will have their own strongly held views about the matter. It is frequently important for the successful conduct of international affairs that matters should not be reduced to simple black and white, but should be left as shades of grey and open for diplomatic negotiation. Questions of international law often remain at large and may form part of the wider debate between and within states.

5. Further, there are many and obvious examples of situations where the disclosure of a legal position on the part of the Government would be prejudicial to the national interest, as tending to indicate to other states the practical constraints affecting the Government. To disclose the Government's understanding of the legal position under international law of an international negotiation (eg of an amendment to a treaty, or of a resolution) could plainly be prejudicial to the success of the Government in that negotiation – as a practical indication of the constraints under which the Government may understand itself to be operating, and its legal "bottom line". Where an international issue involves the possible use of force by the Government, the advance discussion of legal advice as to the legality or otherwise of the use of force in a variety of possible circumstances could be of immense value to the potential adversary, allowing it to plan and adopt positions contrary to the interests of this country with greater assurance than would otherwise be the case.

6. The practical experience of the Foreign & Commonwealth Office shows, therefore, that the greatest care should be exercised and sensitive diplomatic judgment be brought to bear before the Government commits itself to supporting arguments in international law, which may prove controversial for friends and/or opponents and which may compromise the Government's own negotiating position as a tense international situation develops."

12. Having then set out the Foreign Secretary's statement in the House of Commons on 25 November 2002 (see paragraph 3(iii) above), Mr Ricketts continues:

8. That statement is a considered position. The judgment of the Secretary of State and of the Foreign & Commonwealth Office is that, in this sensitive area and at this time, it would be detrimental to the national interest and the conduct of this country's international relations for the Government to go further or to commit itself to any more definitive view. The question whether the Government's views on the legal position on this issue should be further disclosed is a political issue, a decision on which would have consequences for our international relations. Any indication of the constraints (including legal constraints) which may affect decisions by an international coalition to use force to secure Iraqi compliance with its obligations regarding weapons of mass destruction could well be detrimental to achieving that objective.

9. Further, to make public the Government's detailed understanding of the legal position on the interpretation of SCR 1441(2002) in advance of any future negotiation in the Security Council of a further resolution could well be detrimental to the success of that negotiation.

10. It is also clear that the formulation of a legal position with regard to a future Security Council resolution must be dependent upon the facts and the circumstances prevailing at the time. To indicate now whether it is the Government's view that a resolution is or is not necessary, other than in abstract terms, would not be possible in view of the impracticability of forecasting the developing situation in detail, and would not be helpful in terms of arriving at a resolution of the situation in the interests of the United Kingdom. Thus, in the House of Commons on 25 November, the Foreign Secretary stated:

'Paragraph 4 [of Security Council resolution 1441] therefore defines in general terms what a material breach will consist of. As with any definition of that type, it is never possible to give an exhaustive list of all conceivable behaviours that it covers. That judgement has to be made against the real circumstances that arise'"

13. I shall have to return later to the main thrust of that statement, Mr Ricketts's strongly expressed view that "it would be prejudicial to the national interest and the conduct of the government's foreign policy if the government were to be constrained to make a definitive statement of its legal position under international law", for the various reasons which he then explains. For the moment I pause only to note the contention in paragraph 10 of the statement that the substantive issue sought to be raised here is not the clear-cut question of construction suggested by CND but rather is fact-sensitive and dependent upon the developing international situation. Mr Sales argues that the developing facts could become relevant in two main ways. First, the nature and extent of any non-compliance could affect the question whether article 51 of the United Nations Charter (the self-defence provision) provided an alternative basis of authorisation for military action. Secondly, the reaction of states to the developing situation hereafter - how in future they act and what they say with regard to the necessity or otherwise for a second resolution - may well, by virtue of article 31.3(b) of the Vienna Convention on the Interpretation of Treaties, of itself affect the true interpretation under international law of Resolution 1441.

14. Persuasive though for my part I find Mr Sales' arguments on these points, I am content for present purposes to assume in CND's favour that the point of international law upon which they wish this court to pronounce is indeed capable of resolution without reference to the developing situation, without indeed there being any need for factual judgment at all. Furthermore, given the nature of this preliminary hearing, I shall naturally assume CND's case on the true construction of Resolution 1441 to be at the very least a properly arguable one.

15. I come, therefore, to the preliminary issues now before us: justiciability, prematurity and standing. The principal of these, of course, is justiciability although the present question might perhaps best be formulated simply thus: should the court in its discretion entertain this substantive application? It is not, of course, a challenge: no decision is impugned, neither an existing decision nor even a prospective decision. (CND must inevitably recognise that any future decision to take military action would plainly be beyond the court's purview). It is nakedly an application for an advisory declaration. The court's jurisdiction to grant relief in this form, rarely though it is exercised, cannot be doubted. Should it, however, be exercised here? That is the crucial question for determination on this preliminary hearing.

16. I have already indicated the essential basis upon which Mr Singh invites us to hear and determine this issue of international law. It involves, he says, a pure question of interpretation and it is, he submits, of the first importance that the court should resolve it lest the UK government, contrary to its stated intentions, embark upon unlawful military action through an erroneous understanding of the true legal position. Let me now set out the argument in a little more detail.

17. Its starting point, as I understand it, is that the prohibition on the unlawful use of force is a peremptory norm of customary international law and as such part of the common law of England in the absence of any contrary statutory duty. The use of force is unlawful unless authorised. Non-compliance with Resolution 1441 would not of itself provide such authorisation. An application, therefore, which is designed to avert a possible breach of a peremptory norm of customary international law - more, a norm with the character of *jus cogens*, thereby enjoying a higher status as one of the fundamental standards of the international community - falls within the court's common law supervisory jurisdiction.

18. Mr Singh next submits that the court's jurisdiction is not to be regarded as ousted by the nature of the context within which this

issue of law arises for decision, that of threatened military action. A case is not to be treated as non-justiciable simply because it relates to a sensitive field of executive action. There are no longer any no-go areas for the courts whether on the ground that the source of the power being exercised is the prerogative or because it is being exercised in relation to a particularly sensitive part of public administration, here the defence of the realm. Lord Roskill's list of "excluded categories" - certain areas of decision making under prerogative power, namely "those relating to the making of treaties, the defence of the realm, the prerogative of mercy, the grant of honours, the dissolution of Parliament and the appointment of ministers", all said to be beyond the reach of judicial review - see *CCSU -v- Minister for Civil Service* [1985] AC 374, 418 - now lies in tatters. One by one the barriers have fallen: the immunity from review of the exercise of prerogative power in *CCSU* itself; the refusal of a passport in *R -v- Secretary of State for Foreign & Commonwealth Affairs, ex parte Everett* [1989] QB 811; the prerogative of mercy in *R -v- Secretary of State for the Home Department, ex parte Bentley* [1994] QB 349.

19. In short, the class of case of itself provides no bar. What matters, submits Mr Singh, is whether the particular issue sought to be litigated is or is not one lying within the exclusive province of the Executive. In this regard he points to Lord Hoffmann's speech in *Home Secretary -v- Rehman* [2001] 3 WLR 877, 895:

> "It is important neither to blur nor to exaggerate the area of responsibility entrusted to the executive. The precise boundaries were analysed by Lord Scarman, by reference to *Chandler -v- DPP* in [1964] AC 763 in his speech in *CCSU -v- Minister for the Civil Service* [1985] AC 734, 406. His analysis shows that the Commission [SIAC] serves at least three important functions which were shown to be necessary by the decision in *Chahal*. First, the factual basis for the executive's opinion that deportation would be in the interests of national security must be established by evidence. It is therefore open to the Commission to say that there was no factual basis for the Home Secretary's opinion that Mr Rehman was actively supporting terrorism in Kashmir. In this respect the Commission's ability to differ from the Home Secretary's evaluation may be limited, as I shall explain, by considerations inherent in an appellate process but not by the principle of the separation of powers. The effect of the latter principle is only, subject to the next point, to prevent the Commission from saying that although the Home Secretary's opinion that Mr

Rehman was actively supporting terrorism in Kashmir had a proper factual basis, it does not accept that this was contrary to the interests of national security. Secondly, the Commission may reject the Home Secretary's opinion on the ground that it was 'one which no reasonable minister advising the Crown could in the circumstances reasonably have held'. Thirdly, an appeal to the Commission may turn upon issues which at no point lie within the exclusive province of the executive. A good example is the question, which arose in *Chahal* itself, as to whether deporting someone would infringe his rights under Article 3 of the Convention because there was a substantial risk that he would suffer torture or inhuman or degrading treatment. The European jurisprudence makes it clear that whether the deportation is in the interests of national security is irrelevant to rights under Article 3. If there is a danger of torture, the government must find some other way of dealing with a threat to national security. Whether a sufficient risk exists is a question of evaluation and prediction based on evidence. In answering such a question, the executive enjoys no constitutional prerogative." (paragraph 54)

20. There, submits Mr Singh, in the third of SIAC's functions, is an illustration of where the courts can legitimately overturn an executive decision even in the field of national security.

21. Mr Singh further relies upon passages in Laws LJ's judgment in *Marchiori -v- The Environment Agency & Others* [2002] EWCA Civ 03, notably the following:

"38. [I]t seems to me, first, to be plain that the law of England will not contemplate what may be called a merits review of any honest decision of government on matters of national defence policy. Without going into other cases which a full discussion might require, I consider that there is more than one reason for this. The first, and most obvious, is that the court is unequipped to judge such merits or demerits. The second touches more closely the relationship between the elected and unelected arms of government. The graver a matter of State and the more widespread its possible effects, the more respect will be given, within the framework of the constitution, to the democracy to decide its outcome. The defence of the realm, which is the Crown's first duty, is the paradigm of so grave a matter. Potentially such a thing touches the security of everyone; and everyone will look to the government they have elected for wise and effective decisions. Of course they may or may not be satisfied, and their satisfaction or otherwise will sound in the ballot-box. There is, and cannot be, any expectation that the unelected judiciary will play any role in such questions, remotely comparable to that of government. ...

39. I recognise that the notion of so grave a matter of State lacks sharp edges. But it is now a commonplace that the intensity of judicial review depends on the context (see for example *Daly* [2001] 2 WLR 1622 per Lord Steyn at paragraph 28). One context will shade into another; there is for instance a distinction between a deportation decision affecting a specific individual (as in *Rehman*) and a decision of defence policy (such as *Trident*), though both involve matters of national security.

40. Secondly, however, this primacy which the common law accords to elected government in matters of defence is by no means the whole story. Democracy itself requires that all public power be lawfully conferred and exercised, and of this the courts are the surety. No matter how grave the policy issues involved, the courts will be alert to see that no use of power exceeds its proper constitutional bounds. There is no conflict between this and the fact that upon questions of national defence, the courts will recognise that they are in no position to set limits upon the lawful exercise of discretionary power in the name of reasonableness. ..."

22. It is the applicants' argument, founded on these and similar dicta in other recent judgments - most notably in *Abbasi -v- Secretary of State for Foreign & Commonwealth Affairs* [2002] EWCA Civ 1598 - that no longer are there any forbidden areas of executive action into which the courts simply cannot look; there are only aspects of decision making which the court must necessarily accept lie properly and solely with the executive, for example questions of policy and the substantive merits of factual decisions in sensitive fields like those of national security, defence and foreign relations. These are fields in which "the court is unequipped to judge such merits or demerits" and where in any event respect is properly due to the democratically elected government which is answerable politically for its actions. This case, however, runs the applicants' argument, raises no such considerations. There are no issues which CND seek to have decided here which touch on policy or the merits of any decision. Rather they seek a ruling on a pure point of law in the field of customary international law which is itself part of English common law. The courts should not refuse this invitation. They cannot justifiably accord to the executive the exclusive right to determine this

question; on the contrary, it is a question altogether more appropriate for decision by the court in the exercise of its conventional supervisory jurisdiction: to ensure that those exercising public power have not erred in law in the classic sense of misunderstanding their legal powers.

23. Skilfully and resourcefully though this argument was advanced it is clearly not without its difficulties. The first is its invocation of the principle that the common law encompasses also customary international law. Correct although this undoubtedly is, I have difficulty in understanding how it avails the applicants here. To engage in war without lawful justification is certainly contrary to the law of nations. The issue which the applicants seek to have determined here, however, is whether in the circumstances postulated war *would* be unlawful and that, of course, involves the interpretation of Resolution 1441 itself, a specific international treaty which clearly is *not* part of our domestic law. Ordinarily speaking, English courts will not rule upon the true meaning and effect of international instruments which apply only at the level of international law - see, most recently, *R -v- Lyons* [2002] 3 WLR 1562.

24. Recognising this difficulty, as many of Mr Singh's submissions appear to do, the applicants seek to distinguish *Lyons* and point to other recent case law illustrating the court's preparedness at least in certain circumstances to rule upon the State's obligations under international law. Pressed as to which authorities come closest to supporting the applicants' submission that the court should assume the right to rule upon this issue of international law, Mr Singh relies most heavily on two: *R -v- Home Secretary, ex parte Adan* [2001] 2 AC 477 and *Abbasi*. Let me consider in turn each of these undoubtedly important cases.

25. A central issue raised in *Adan* was whether the courts of this country should entertain a contention that the courts of France and Germany are misapplying the Refugee Convention. The United Kingdom takes the view that the Convention extends protection to asylum seekers in fear of non-State persecution if for any reason the State cannot protect them against it. France and Germany interpret the Convention differently, more narrowly. The House of Lords held that the Convention has one autonomous meaning, namely that adopted by the United Kingdom. In so ruling, their Lordships rejected an argument for the Secretary of State based on the principle of comity, the contention that Parliament could not have intended either the Secretary of State or the courts of this country to have to make a decision that an action by a foreign government or a ruling by a foreign court was wrong in law. Their Lordships were concerned, as they explained, with the United Kingdom's obligation under the Convention as interpreted by the

United Kingdom and with the Secretary of State's obligation under the Asylum and Immigration Act 1996 pursuant to which he issued the relevant certificates. As Lord Steyn put it at p518:

"[C]ounsel for the Secretary of State raised a matter which did cause me concern at one stage, namely whether the view I have adopted contains an implicit criticism of the judicial departments of Germany and France. I certainly intend no criticism of the interpretations adopted in good faith in Germany and France. Unanimity on all perplexing problems created by multilateral treaties is unachievable. National courts can only do their best to minimise their disagreements. But ultimately they have no choice but to apply what they consider to be the autonomous meaning. Here the difference is fundamental and cannot be overcome by a form of words. The House is bound to take into account the obligations of the United Kingdom government and to apply the terms of ... the 1996 Act."

26. Lord Phillips MR was later to say in *Abbasi* at paragraph 57:

"Although the statutory context in which *Adan* was decided was highly material, the passage from Lord Cross's speech in *Cattermole* supports the view that, albeit that caution must be exercised by this court when faced with an allegation that a foreign state is in breach of its international obligations, this court does not need the statutory context in order to be free to express a view in relation to what it conceives to be a clear breach of international law, particularly in the context of human rights."

27. *Oppenheim -v- Cattermole* [1976] AC 249 (the other case to which Lord Phillips was there referring) raised the issue whether a decree passed in Germany in 1941, depriving Jews who had emigrated from Germany of their citizenship, should be recognised by the English court. The House of Lords concluded not, Lord Cross saying:

"To my mind a law of this sort constitutes so grave an infringement of human rights that the courts of this country ought to refuse to recognise this as a law at all."

28. *Abbasi* itself concerned a challenge by a British citizen captured by United States forces in Afghanistan and held in Guantanamo Bay with regard to the exercise of the Foreign Secretary's powers of intervention on behalf of British citizens abroad. Two central issues were identified: first, whether the English court will examine the legitimacy of action taken by a foreign sovereign state; secondly, whether the English court will adjudicate upon actions taken by the executive in the conduct of foreign affairs. There is much that is illuminating of both those issues to

be found in the court's judgment. By way of citation, however, I shall confine myself to the court's summary in paragraph 106 of its views as to what the authorities establish and its main reasons expressed in paragraph 107 for rejecting the application:

"106. ...

(i)   It is not an answer to a claim for judicial review to say that the source of the power of the Foreign Office is the prerogative. It is the subject matter that is determinative.

(ii)   Despite extensive citation of authority there is nothing which supports the imposition of an enforceable duty to protect the citizen. The ECHR does not impose any such duty. Its incorporation into the municipal law cannot therefore found a sound basis on which to reconsider the authorities binding on this court.

(iii)   However the Foreign Office has discretion whether to exercise the right, which it undoubtedly has, to protect British citizens. It has indicated in the ways explained what a British citizen may expect of it. The expectations are limited and the discretion is a very wide one but there is no reason why its decision or inaction should not be reviewable if it can be shown that the same were irrational or contrary to legitimate expectations. But the court cannot enter the forbidden areas, including decisions affecting foreign policy.

(iv)   It is highly likely that any decision of the Foreign & Commonwealth Office, as to whether to make representations on a diplomatic level, will be intimately connected with decisions relating to this country's foreign policy, but an obligation to consider the position of a particular British citizen and consider the extent to which some action might be taken on his behalf, would seem unlikely itself to impinge on any forbidden area.

(v)   The extent to which it may be possible to require more than that the Foreign Secretary give due consideration to a request for assistance will depend on the facts of the particular case. ...

107. We have made clear our deep concerns that, in apparent contravention of fundamental principles of law, Mr Abbasi may be subject to indefinite detention in territory in which the United States has exclusive control with no opportunity to challenge the legitimacy of his detention before any court or tribunal. However, there are a number of reasons why we consider that the applicant's claim for relief must be rejected:

(i)   It is quite clear from Mr Fry's evidence that the Foreign & Commonwealth Office have considered Mr Abbasi's request for assistance. He has also disclosed that the British detainees are the subject of discussions between this country and the United States both at Secretary of State and lower official levels. We do not consider that Mr Abbasi could reasonably expect more than this. In particular, if the Foreign & Commonwealth Office were to make any statement as to its view of the legality of the detention of the British prisoners, or any statement as to the nature of discussions held with United States officials, this might well undermine those discussions.

(ii)   On no view would it be appropriate to order the Secretary of State to make any specific representations to the United States, even in the face of what appears to be a clear breach of a fundamental human right, as it is obvious that this would have an impact on the conduct of foreign policy, and an impact on such policy at a particularly delicate time."

29.   The "apparent contravention of fundamental principles of law" (paragraph 107) and "clear breach of a fundamental human right" (paragraph 107(ii)) are a reference to the undisputed fact that Mr Abbasi was being denied access to a court to challenge the legality of his detention. The Court of Appeal carefully refrained from investigating, let alone expressing a view on, the legality of the detention itself; that is clearly apparent from the judgment as a whole, not least the final sentence of paragraph 107(i). That notwithstanding, it is Mr Singh's submission that the Court of Appeal can there be seen to have been prepared to state its view on an issue of international law in a plainly sensitive area, namely the US administration's denial to detainees of any right akin to *habeas corpus*.

30.   Before coming to consider the extent to which these authorities on analysis truly assist the applicants, it is convenient first to note the main passages in Lord Hoffmann's speech in *Lyons* on which Mr Sales relies in response to this part of CND's argument and the way in which Mr Singh for his part suggests that *Lyons* can be distinguished.

31.   The appellants in *Lyons*, it will be remembered, were seeking to overturn their convictions, secured before the Human Rights Act 1998 came into force, in reliance on a ruling by the ECHR that the admission of certain statements against them had infringed their right to a fair trial under article 6. The following passages in Lord Hoffmann's speech are those most relevant to the present application:

> "27. ... [T]he Convention is an international treaty and the ECHR is an international court with jurisdiction under

international law to interpret and apply it. But the question of whether the appellants' convictions were unsafe is a matter of English law. And it is firmly established that international treaties do not form part of English law and that English courts have no jurisdiction to interpret or apply them: *J H Rayner (Mincing Lane) Limited -v- Department of Trade and Industry* [1990] 2 AC 418 (the *International Tin Council* case). Parliament may pass a law which mirrors the terms of the treaty and in this sense incorporates the treaty into English law. But even then, the metaphor of incorporation may be misleading. It is not the treaty but the statute which forms part of English law. And English courts will not (unless the statute expressly so provides) be bound to give effect to interpretations of the treaty by an international court, even though the United Kingdom is bound by international law to do so. ...

40. The argument that the courts are an organ of state and therefore obliged to give effect to the state's international obligations is in my opinion a fallacy. If the proposition were true, it would completely undermine the principle that the courts apply domestic law and not international treaties. There would be no reason to confine it to secondary obligations arising from breaches of the treaty. The truth of the matter is that, in the present context, to describe the courts as an organ of the state is significant only in international law. International law does not normally take account of the internal distribution of powers within a state. It is the duty of the state to comply with international law, whatever may be the organs which have the power to do so. And likewise, a treaty may be infringed by the actions of the Crown, Parliament or the courts. From the point of view of international law, it ordinarily does not matter. In domestic law, however, the position is very different. The domestic constitution is based upon the separation of powers. In domestic law the courts are obliged to give effect to the law as enacted by Parliament. This obligation is entirely unaffected by international law."

32. The applicants seek to distinguish that authority on two bases: first, they submit that the appellants there had nothing but the treaty to rely upon, the Convention at the relevant time not having been incorporated into English law; here by contrast the applicants assert that their claim for a declaration is under customary international law and therefore justiciable at common law. Secondly, it is suggested that the appellants

in *Lyons* were in any event confronted by an English statute precluding their success unless the convictions were found to be unsafe as a matter of English law, whereas here no such statute stands in the applicants' path.

33. Before concluding this summary of the applicants' case there are just two further authorities to which I should briefly refer, *R -v- Home Secretary ex parte Launder*[1997] 1 WLR 839 and *R -v- Director of Public Prosecutions ex parte Kebilene* [2000] 2 AC 326. Each involved a challenge to an executive decision taken under English law - in *Launder* a decision to extradite, in *Kebilene* a decision to prosecute - at a time prior to the incorporation of ECHR. The decision in each case had been taken by reference to an understanding of the UK's international law obligations under the Convention. A single citation from Lord Steyn's speech in *Kebilene* (itself referring to Lord Hope's speech in *Launder*) sufficiently encapsulates the principle for which Mr Singh cited these authorities and on which he seeks to rely:

> "Lord Bingham of Cornhill CJ [in the Divisional Court below] pointed out that in the present case the Director wished to know where he stood on the issue of compatibility of the legislation. The Director sought and relied on legal advice on that issue. Lord Bingham said that if the advice was wrong, the Director should have the opportunity to reconsider the confirmation of his advice on a sound legal basis. As Lord Bingham observed '... this approach is consistent with the judgment of Lord Hope [in *Launder* at p867]:
>
> 'If the applicant is to have an effective remedy against a decision [on extradition] which is flawed because the decision-maker has misdirected himself on the Convention which he himself took into account, it must surely be right to examine the substance of the argument'
>
> I respectfully agree. There was no infringement of the principle of Parliamentary sovereignty."

34. In both those cases, submits Mr Singh, one finds the court investigating and reaching a conclusion on the position under international law so as to ensure that the executive decision maker has not misunderstood it and thereby misdirected himself in law - or, it is perhaps more accurate to say, taken account of an immaterial consideration. So too, he contends, should the court in the present case assume and exercise jurisdiction to guard against a comparable misunderstanding by government as to the legal effect of Resolution 1441.

35. I have, I hope, in the preceding pages fairly summarised the applicants' arguments and the principal authorities upon which they rely. The

defendants' arguments I propose to deal with substantially more shortly. This is not because they lacked anything in the way of thoroughness, but rather because to my mind there are really only two of them which need to be considered, each, as I believe, destructive of central aspects of the applicants' case and in combination fatal to its success. The first goes to the court's jurisdiction to rule on matters of international law unless in some way they are properly related to the court's determination of some domestic law right or interest. The second focuses on Mr Ricketts's statement and the sound reasons of national interest which he gives as to why the court should not require the government publicly to declare its definitive view of the position in international law and, by the same token, why the court for its part should not embark upon the same exercise. Both arguments I find compelling. Let me take them in turn.

36. Should the court declare the meaning of an international instrument operating purely on the plane of international law? In my judgment the answer is plainly no. All of the cases relied upon by the applicants in which the court has pronounced upon some issue of international law are cases where it has been necessary to do so in order to determine rights and obligations under domestic law. In *Adan*, as has been seen, the English courts felt bound to consider the position under the Convention to determine whether the Secretary of State had acted properly in issuing certificates under the relevant statute. They had, indeed, "no choice but to apply what they considered to be [the Convention's] autonomous meaning" (per Lord Steyn - see paragraph 25 above). In *Oppenheim -v- Cattermole* a view had to be taken upon the legality of the Nazi decree to decide whether or not "to recognise this as a law at all" (per Lord Cross - see paragraph 27 above). True it is that in *Abbasi* the court recognised the breach of fundamental human rights constituted by the denial to all detainees of access to a court to challenge the legality of their detention. But as already pointed out the court carefully refrained from considering the legality of the detention itself and throughout it was concerned solely with Mr Abbasi's rights under domestic law, namely his right to have the Foreign Secretary properly exercise his discretion whether, and if so how, to assist the applicant as a British citizen. *Abbasi*, indeed, so far from affording support to the applicants' argument, in my judgment tends rather to undermine it. *Launder* and *Kebilene* likewise were cases in which the courts were prepared to examine the position under an international convention but only in the context of reviewing the legality of a decision under domestic law. As Mr Sales points out, there is in the present case no point of reference in domestic law to which the international law issue can be said to go; there is nothing here

susceptible of challenge in the way of the determination of rights, interests or duties under domestic law to draw the court into the field of international law. Laws LJ's dictum in paragraph 40 of his judgment in *Marchiori* (see paragraph 21 above) that "democracy itself requires that all public power be lawfully conferred and exercised, and of this the courts are the surety", contrary to Mr Singh's submission, is not in point here: the domestic courts are the surety for the lawful exercise of public power only with regard to domestic law; they are not charged with policing the United Kingdom's conduct on the international plane. That is for the International Court of Justice. Mr Singh was quite unable to point to any case in which the domestic courts have ruled on a matter of international law in no way bearing on to the application of domestic law.

37. *Lyons*, again contrary to Mr Singh's submission, is in my judgment indistinguishable in principle from the present case. The courts there refused to take account of the State's duty in international law since it did not properly sound in domestic law. No more does it here. The absence of any relevant statutory provision here is nothing to the point. Nor, as I sought to explain in paragraph 23 above, can the applicants escape the rule which *Lyons* exemplifies by seeking to invoke the principle of customary international law. What is sought here is a ruling on the interpretation of an international instrument, no more and no less. It is one thing, as in cases like *Kebilene* and *Launder*, for our courts to consider the application of an international treaty by reference to the facts of an individual case. (That, indeed, would have been the position in *Lyons* itself had the courts been prepared to undertake the exercise.) It is quite another thing to pronounce generally upon a treaty's true interpretation and effect. There is no distinction between the position of the United Kingdom and that of all other States to whom Resolution 1441 applies. Why should the English courts presume to give an authoritative ruling on its meaning? Plainly such a ruling would not bind other States. How could our assumption of jurisdiction here be regarded around the world as anything other than an exorbitant arrogation of adjudicative power?

38. The general rule is that, in the interests of comity, domestic courts do not rule on questions of international law which affect foreign sovereign states. As Diplock LJ said in *Buck -v- Attorney-General* [1965] Chancery 745, 770:

> "For the English court to pronounce upon the validity of a law of a foreign sovereign state within its own territory, so that the validity of that law became the *res* of the *res judicata* in the suit, would be to assert jurisdiction over the internal affairs of

that state. That would be a breach of the rules of comity. In my view, this court has no jurisdiction so to do."

39. Twenty years later, Lord Diplock (as he had by then become) returned to the theme in *British Airways -v- Laker Airways* [1985] AC 58, 85: "The interpretation of treaties to which the United Kingdom is a party but the terms of which have not either expressly or by reference been incorporated in English domestic law by legislation is not a matter which falls within the interpretative jurisdiction of an English court of law."

40. I would notice too in this connection the reference in paragraph 57 of the court's judgment in *Abbasi* to the court exercising caution when faced with an allegation that a foreign state is in breach of international law - see paragraph 26 above. Whilst the statutory context within which *Adan* was decided necessarily defeated the Crown's case on comity there, plainly that is not so here. Here there is simply no foothold in domestic law for any ruling to be given on international law. There would need to be compelling reason for the court to take the unprecedented step of assuming jurisdiction here and no good reason not to. In fact, however, the opposite is the case. I turn to the second of Mr Sales's main arguments.

41. Mr Ricketts's statement attests to two specific reasons why it would be damaging to the national interest for the government to commit itself publicly to a definitive view of the legal effect of Resolution 1441 and to parade its arguments in support. First, it would adversely affect the conduct of our international relations with regard to the Iraq situation. Secondly, it would tie the United Kingdom's hands if and when it has to re-enter the negotiating chamber. I have already set out the statement in paragraphs 11 and 12 above and shall not attempt a paraphrase. Mr Ricketts's assertions, I have to say, appear to me not merely persuasive but in large part self-evident. Much the same thinking plainly informs the Court of Appeal's observation in the last sentence of paragraph 107 (i) of the judgment in *Abbasi* as to the risk of discussions between States being undermined. Whatever particular position the government were to adopt, how could it fail to antagonise some at least of our international colleagues? Were the government, for example, to accept and assert publicly the interpretation of the resolution contended for by CND, how could that not (a) damage our relations with, say, the USA who may well take a different view of its effect, and (b) give comfort to the Iraqis? If, at some future date, following a report under paragraphs 4 and/or 11 of the resolution, the Security Council were to consider the matter afresh under paragraph 12, how could the United Kingdom, assuming it were to negotiate for a second resolution, not be

disadvantaged in that negotiation if it admitted that States would otherwise be powerless to act?

42. All this surely is obvious. It is hardly surprising that the Foreign Secretary expressed himself as he did on 25 November 2002 (see paragraph 3(iii) above), carefully avoiding committing the government to a view, that statement being, as Mr Ricketts observes, "a considered position". Even, however, were all this not obvious, we would at the very least be bound to recognise Mr Ricketts's experience and expertise in these matters and that the executive is better placed than the court to make these assessments of the national interest with regard to the conduct of foreign relations in the field of national security and defence. We could not properly reject Mr Ricketts's views unless we thought them plainly wrong. Lord Steyn in *Rehman*, albeit finding it "well established in the case law that issues of national security do not fall beyond the competence of the courts", then added:

> "It is, however, self-evidently right that national courts must give great weight to the views of the executive on matters of national security."

43. Mr Ricketts's statement, of course, is directed rather to the reasons why the government for its part should not be required to state its position on the meaning of Resolution 1441 than to why the court should not grant an advisory declaration on the point. Clearly, however, the one follows from the other. The logic is inescapable. On the international plane, as a matter of practical international politics, other States do not make nice distinctions between legal assertions by government and declarations of law by national courts. But, that aside, any declaration by the court would as a matter of practical reality embarrass the government no less than were it to state a definitive view itself. By constitutional convention the government will always comply with decisions of the court. Whatever the court were to declare the instrument to mean, the government could not ignore that ruling or assert some different meaning in its dealings with other States. And, indeed, the objections go further still. Were the court even to embark upon a hearing of the substantive issue the government would be placed in an impossible position. In practice it would be forced to adopt and argue its position before the court, the very thing that Mr Ricketts indicates would damage the conduct of our international relations. The objection, in short, is not merely to the court ever granting an advisory declaration, but in addition to the court even embarking on the argument.

44. If follows from all this that in my judgment strong reasons exist for the court to reject CND's application at this preliminary stage without ever proceeding to the hearing of the substantive issue. As already indicated,

even assuming we had jurisdiction to decide the question of international law upon which our ruling is sought, there would need to be compelling reason to do so. The reason advanced by CND is, as stated, to guard against the United Kingdom going to war under a mistake of law. How real a risk is that, however? I am bound to say that for my part I think it no more than fanciful. Plainly the government has access to the best advice not only from law officers but also from a number of distinguished specialists in the field. Why should it be thought that the advice obtained is likely to be wrong? CND's answer to that is that various statements made by ministers most notably the Foreign Secretary's statement on 10 November 2002 that "military action is bound to follow" if the terms of Resolution 1441 are breached (see paragraph 3(ii) above) suggest that the government believes no second resolution to be necessary and that this is wrong. I find this argument unconvincing. Quite apart from the fact that it begs the question as to the true interpretation of Resolution 1441, I can find in the ministerial statements nothing to indicate the government's actual view. We simply do not know it.

45. How, then, does Mr Singh seek to meet the argument that any declaration here could be damaging to the national interest. What he submits is that the only proper course for government to take is to conduct its international relations openly in accordance with whatever advice it has received. Government should not, he submits, dissemble or bluff in its negotiations with other States. This appears to me to represent a singularly utopian view of international affairs. For my part I cannot accept it. The plain fact is that even to argue the substantive issue here, let alone to decide it, would be contrary to the national interest.

46. I should say just a word or two at this stage about advisory declarations. These, valuable tools though they can be in the exercise of the court's supervisory jurisdiction, should be sparingly used. Their essential purposes are, first, to reduce the danger of administrative activities being declared illegal retrospectively, and, secondly, to assist public authorities by giving advice on legal questions which is then binding on all see Zamir & Woolf: The Declaratory Judgment, 3rd Edition, 2002 at p143. To make such a declaration here, however, would risk giving them a bad name. The jurisdiction is being invoked for wholly impermissible reasons.

47. I would state my conclusions in summary form as follows:

   i.   The court has no jurisdiction to declare the true interpretation of an international instrument which has not been incorporated into English domestic law and which it is unnecessary to interpret for the purposes of determining a person's rights or duties under domestic law. That is the position here.

ii. The court will in any event decline to embark upon the determination of an issue if to do so would be damaging to the public interest in the field of international relations, national security or defence. That too is the position here. Whether as a matter of juridical theory such judicial abstinence is properly to be regarded as a matter of discretion or a matter of jurisdiction seems to me for present purposes immaterial. Either way I regard the substantive question raised by this application to be non-justiciable.

iii. Even were this claim not barred by either of the above considerations, I would still reject it on the ground that advisory declarations should not be made save for demonstrably good reason. Here there is none. There is no sound basis for believing the government to have been wrongly advised as to the true position in international law. Nor, in any event, could there be any question here of declaring illegal whatever decision or action may hereafter be taken in the light of the United Kingdom's understanding of its position in international law.

iv. Although in the ordinary way such fundamental objections to the very nature of the claim would strongly militate against permission being granted to advance it, because of the obvious importance of the issues before us and the skill and cogency of Mr Singh's arguments, I myself would propose that we grant permission and then, for the reasons given, dismiss the substantive claim. This, one notes, was the course adopted by the Court of Appeal in *Abbasi*. Frankly, it matters little which of the two routes is taken; these days the possibilities of appeal are the same in either case. Of one thing, however, I am sure: this application must fail and be dismissed at this preliminary stage.

48. By way of footnote I add just these brief comments on prematurity and standing, the other two issues separated out for consideration at this preliminary stage. Were the applicants' claim for an advisory declaration, contrary to my clear conclusions, a sound one, it could not sensibly be regarded as premature. On the contrary to postpone it would be to defeat its very purpose. As for standing, again, were the court to regard it an appropriate exercise of its jurisdiction to advise government as it is here invited to do, it would hardly be right to withhold that advice by reference to some suggested deficiency in CND's interest in the matter.

Mr Justice Maurice Kay :

49. I agree. The procedural position in this case is a little obscure but, although there is no challenge to an existing decision and the only remedy sought is a declaration of an advisory nature, the proceedings are wholly public law based and were properly commenced under Part 54. In these circumstances, they can only proceed with permission. The initial hurdle is in the preliminary issues which we have considered. Although the case for CND has been formulated and presented with coherence and intelligence it is, for the reasons given by Simon Brown LJ, fatally flawed. Nevertheless, because it is an unusual case relating to matters of great public importance I take the view that the appropriate course, and the expedient one in the light of the directions that were given on 29 November, is to grant permission but to dismiss the application.

50. I propose to add a few observations about the conceptual basis of this decision. In the course of submissions there was some debate over whether any obstacle in the way of CND's application is properly categorised as one of jurisdiction, justiciability or discretion. It is clear from *Council of Civil Service Unions v. Minister for the Civil Service* [1985] AC 374 that the controlling factor in considering whether a particular exercise or, for present purposes, prospective exercise of prerogative power is susceptible to judicial review is "not its source but its subject matter" (Lord Scarman, at p 407). It is also clear from that milestone authority that there are subject matters which are, in the language of Lord Phillips of Worth Matravers MR in *Abbasi*, "forbidden areas" (para 106(iii)). The first reason why the present application must fail is that its subject matter is one of those forbidden areas. In my judgment this is not because of an exercise of judicial discretion. It is a matter of principle. If it were purely a matter of discretion there would be circumstances in which the discretion could only be exercised after full consideration of the substantive case. It is because it is a matter of principle that I feel able to dismiss the present application on a preliminary issue without full consideration of the substantive case. In the *CCSU* case (at p 398) Lord Fraser spoke of "many of the most important prerogative powers concerned with control of the armed forces and with foreign policy and with matters which are unsuitable for discussion or review in the Law Court."

In my judgment, this is most appropriately characterised as justiciability. If authority were required for this proposition it is to be found in the *CCSU* case, *R v. Foreign Secretary, ex parte Everett* [1989] 1 QB 811 (per Taylor LJ at p. 820) and *R v. Criminal Injuries Compensation Board, ex parte P* [1995] 1 All ER 870, at pp 879882, per Neil LJ, who explained the difference between jurisdiction and justiciability in this context. I readily accept that the ambit of the "forbidden areas" is not immutable and that cases such as *Everett* and *Bentley* [2001] 1 Cr App 307 CA illustrate how the areas identified by Lord Roskill in the *CCSU* case have been reduced. However, the authorities provide no hint of retreat in relation to the subject matter of the present case. This is hardly surprising. Foreign policy and the deployment of the armed forces remain non-justiciable. That is the first basis upon which I would refuse the present application. I would also refuse it on the other grounds to which Simon Brown LJ has referred and for the same reasons given by him. I agree that the "international law" ground is more appropriately categorised as going to jurisdiction rather than justiciability.

Notwithstanding the erudition with which it was advanced, this is an unsustainable challenge.

Mr Justice Richards:

51.	I agree with both judgments. Although I accept that permission should be granted because of the importance of the matters raised, in my view the claim should not be allowed to proceed beyond the preliminary issues since it would be wholly inappropriate to entertain the substantive issues and the court would not countenance the grant of the declaration sought. I would summarise my reasons as follows.

52.	CND seeks an "advisory" declaration, before any decision is taken on the use of armed force against Iraq and with a view to "informing" the Government on the correct interpretation of Resolution 1441 as an input into any decision that may be taken. There are undoubtedly cases where it may be appropriate for the court to entertain a claim for a declaration in advance of a decision or even where there is no decision in prospect. In *London Borough of Islington v. Camp* (20 July 1999, unreported), on which CND relies, I examined some of the relevant authorities and principles and agreed to entertain a claim for purely declaratory relief, though expressly avoiding the expression "advisory opinion". As the judgment made clear, however, the circumstances of the case were highly unusual and it was in the public interest to entertain the claim. The jurisdiction remains one to be exercised only in exceptional circumstances. The circumstances of the present case, far from justifying that exceptional course, tell very strongly against doing so.

53.	The issue on which CND seeks a ruling is one on which the Government has deliberately refrained from expressing any concluded or definitive view. Its considered position, as set out in the Foreign Secretary's statement to Parliament on 25 November 2002, is to reserve its position in the event that there is a material breach of Resolution

1441 and the Security Council does not adopt a further resolution authorising military action. I do not accept that, merely because the Government has not ruled out the use of force without a further resolution, there is an inconsistency between its considered position and what CND contends to be the correct interpretation of Resolution 1441. The considered position simply avoids any direction of law one way or the other. Thus no misdirection in law would be established even if CND's interpretation of Resolution 1441 were upheld. Nor does the Foreign Secretary's radio interview on 10 November 2002, described as the evidential high watermark of CND's case, involve any direction in law as to the interpretation of Resolution 1441. Again it leaves the matter open.

54.   The very fact that the Government has refrained from committing itself to a position on the interpretation of Resolution 1441 militates against entertaining the present claim. No doubt the Government has access to expert legal advice and is able to form a reasoned judgment on the legal issue. It does not seek or need advice from the court. There is no obvious reason why the court should "inform" it or force a ruling upon it.

55.   The case against intervention becomes overwhelmingly strong once account is taken of the actual reasons for the Government's stance, as set out in the witness statement of Mr Ricketts. I refer in particular to the Government's judgment that "in this sensitive area and at this time, it would be detrimental to the national interest and the conduct of this country's international relations for the Government to go further or to commit itself to any more definitive view". The court must plainly respect and give weight to that judgment (cf. *Home Secretary v. Rehman* [2001] 3 WLR 877 at paras 26, 31, 5354). It follows, in my view, that to entertain the present claim would inevitably be to act contrary to the national interest. If the Government played an active part in the substantive proceedings, it would necessarily be drawn beyond its considered position. If it played no such part, its position would nonetheless be compromised by any judgment of the court. It could not ignore that judgment without giving rise to an unprecedented situation and risking strain to the established constitutional relationship between courts and executive. In any event I think it obvious that a judgment of the court would be liable to cause damage of the same kind as, on the evidence before the court, would be liable to be caused by a definitive statement of the legal position by the Government itself. I accept that other states are not likely to draw a clear distinction between the Government and a national court and that it would be very difficult for the Government in practice to dissociate its own position from the judgment of the court.

56. In marked contrast, therefore, with the case of *London Borough of Islington v. Camp*, there are strong public interest grounds why the court should not exercise its discretion to entertain the present claim or consider the grant of declaratory relief.

57. I have dealt with the matter so far solely in terms of discretionary considerations. I can add a number of other points also going to the court's discretion. In my view, even if this court were otherwise free to do so, it would be undesirable for it to rule on the interpretation of Resolution 1441 as an abstract legal question in advance of any decision and in circumstances where any difference of view over the correct interpretation of that instrument might not be of any relevance at the end of the day. In practice the point may not arise at all. If it does arise, it will arise against a particular factual background and in circumstances where the position adopted by other states may also be relevant and other rules of international law may also be in play. I recognise the force of CND's point that if one waits for a decision it will be too late to raise the issue in the national court; but even leaving aside the inappropriateness of entertaining such a claim when any ultimate decision would be unreviewable (see below), I consider there to be real objections to examining a question of this kind in isolation and on a contingent basis.

58. For those reasons I am satisfied that the claim should be rejected on discretionary grounds. Far from justifying the exceptional exercise of the court's jurisdiction to grant an advisory declaration, the circumstances make such a course inappropriate and contrary to the public interest.

59. I am also satisfied, however, that the objections to the claim go deeper than that. First, the claim would take the court into areas of foreign affairs and defence which are the exclusive responsibility of the executive Government areas that the court in *R (on the application of Abbasi) v. Secretary of State for Foreign and Commonwealth Affairs* [2002] EWCA Civ 1598 described at paragraph 106(iii) as "forbidden areas". Of course, the field of activity alone does not determine whether something falls within a forbidden area: "justiciability depends, not on general principle, but on subject matter and suitability in the particular case" (*Abbasi*, paragraph 85). In the course of his excellent submissions, Mr Rabinder Singh QC took us through the case law of the last 20 years to show the evolution of the courts' approach to that question and how far the courts have gone in identifying matters that can properly be the subject of judicial determination even though they fall within fields of activity once thought to be immune from review. He submitted that the subject matter of the present claim was one plainly suitable for judicial

determination, namely a clinical point of law, and that to leave it within the exclusive province of the executive would be contrary to the rule of law. But that neat attempt to isolate a purely judicial issue ignores two important features of the present case:

i.   According to Mr Ricketts's evidence, the assertion of arguments of international law is part and parcel of the conduct of international relations; it is frequently important for the successful conduct of international affairs that matters should not be reduced to simple black and white, but should be left as shades of grey and open for diplomatic negotiation; and in relation specifically to Resolution 1441 it would be detrimental to the conduct of this country's international relations for the Government to go further than its considered position. In the face of that evidence, it seems to me clear that the legal issue cannot in practice be divorced from the conduct of international relations and that by entertaining the present claim and ruling on the interpretation of Resolution 1441 the court would be interfering with, indeed damaging, the Government's conduct of international relations. That would be to enter a forbidden area. The situation is closely analogous to that considered in Abbasi at paragraph 107(i), where the court evidently thought it impermissible to require the FCO to make statements that might undermine discussions held with US officials.

ii.   A plain purpose of the present claim is to discourage or inhibit the Government from using armed force against Iraq without a further Security Council resolution. Thus the claim is an attempt to limit the Government's freedom of movement in relation to the actual use of military force as well as in relation to the exercise of diplomatic pressure in advance. That takes it squarely into the fields of foreign affairs and defence. In my view it is unthinkable that the national courts would entertain a challenge to a Government decision to declare war or to authorise the use of armed force against a third country. That is a classic example of a non-justiciable decision. I reject Mr Singh's submission that it would be permissible in principle to isolate and rule upon legal issues e.g. as to whether the decision was taken in breach of international law. The nature and subject matter of such a decision require it to be treated as an indivisible whole rather than breaking it down into legal, political, military and other components and viewing those components in isolation for the purpose of determining whether they are suited to judicial determination. The same objections of principle apply to an attempt to isolate in advance a potential legal component of a possible future decision with a view to limiting the Government's freedom of movement when taking the decision itself.

60. In the course of argument I suggested that justiciability might be an aspect of discretion. The contrast drawn was with the court's jurisdiction. Whilst I adhere to the view that justiciability is not a jurisdictional concept, it seems to me on reflection that it engages rules of law rather than purely discretionary considerations. They are rules that, in this context at least, the courts have imposed upon themselves in recognition of the limits of judicial expertise and of the proper demarcation between the role of the courts and the responsibilities of the executive under our constitutional settlement. The objections on grounds of non-justiciability therefore provide a separate and additional reason for declining to entertain the claim.

61. A further objection to the claim is that it asks the national court to declare the meaning and effect of an instrument of international law. The objection can be analysed in this way:

i.   The basic rule is that international treaties do not form part of domestic law and that the national courts have no jurisdiction to interpret or apply them (see e.g. *R v. Lyons* [2002] 3 WLR 1562 at paras 27 and 39). The same basic rule must in my view apply to an instrument such as Resolution 1441 which has been made under an international treaty and has been negotiated in the same way as a treaty.

ii.   Mr Singh sought to avoid the application of that rule by contending first that this case involves a principle of customary international law (indeed, a principle having the status of "jus cogens") prohibiting the unauthorised use of force and that customary international law forms part of domestic law. It seems to me, however, that recourse to customary international law cannot assist the claimant since what is directly in issue is not a principle of customary international law but the meaning and effect of Resolution 1441, an international instrument not forming part of customary international law.

iii. By way of exception to the basic rule, situations arise where the national courts have to adjudicate upon the interpretation of international treaties e.g. in determining private rights and obligations under domestic law and/or where statute requires decisions to be taken in accordance with an international treaty; and in human rights cases there may be a wider exception. Those examples feature in the discussion in *Abbasi* at paras 5157. None of them applies here.

iv.   A further exception can arise where a decision maker has expressly taken into account an international treaty and the court thinks it appropriate to examine the correctness of the self direction or advice on which the decision is based: see *R v. Secretary of State for the Home Department, ex parte Launder* [1997] 1 WLR 839, 867CF and *R v. Director of Public Prosecutions, ex parte Kebilene* [2000] 2 AC 326, 341 and 367EH, both of them cases where the court was willing to have regard to the European Convention on Human Rights prior to the Human Rights Act 1998 coming into force. Again, however, that is not this case. General statements by the Government that it will act in accordance with international law do not amount to a direction in law and the Government has in practice studiously avoided any direction on the interpretation of Resolution 1441.

v.   There may be other exceptional cases where the court can properly rule on the interpretation of an international instrument, but none has been shown to be applicable here.

vi.   Thus the case falls foul of the basic rule against the interpretation of international treaties by the national court.

62.   I am less certain about the strength of the objections advanced by reference to the implications of a ruling for other states:

i.   A declaration as to the meaning and effect of Resolution 1441 would certainly be of general application, in the sense that it would purport to interpret the resolution as a matter of international law. Mr Sales submitted that the court would thereby be ruling on the obligations of foreign states under an international instrument, which it does not have jurisdiction to do. He cited *British Airways v. Laker Airways* [1985] AC 58 at 8586, where, in the context of a dispute between the UK and US Governments about the latter's compliance with its treaty obligations, Diplock LJ observed that "[t]he interpretation of treaties to which the United Kingdom is a party but the terms of which have not either expressly or by reference been incorporated in English domestic law by legislation is not a matter that falls within the interpretative jurisdiction of an English court of law". On the face of it, this is simply an expression of the basic rule concerning the court's jurisdiction to interpret international treaties, which I have covered already. I doubt whether it supports the additional objection advanced by Mr Sales or whether a declaration on the meaning and effect of Resolution 1441 would amount to a ruling on the obligations of foreign states.

ii.   This leads into the related subject of comity upon which Mr Sales also relied. As to that, I doubt whether a ruling by the national court on Resolution 1441 would itself involve any express or implied criticism of other states. On the other hand, it might cause other states the same kind of problem as it would cause the UK Government in terms of international negotiating position. It might also be used in support of criticism of a state which took action on a basis inconsistent with the ruling. Thus I do not think that one can dismiss the argument on comity, though the weight properly to be given to it is hard to assess.

iii.   The simple point, as it seems to me, is that the court should steer away from these areas of potential difficulty in relation to other states unless there are compelling reasons to confront them. There are no such reasons in this case.

63.   In the light of my conclusions on the main issues I do not think it necessary to deal with standing.

64.   For those reasons I would grant permission but dismiss the claim on the basis of the preliminary issues.

154

PART III
THE BBC'S SHADOW "JUDICIAL REVIEW" BY THE "TODAY" PROGRAMME
9. Adjudication of Professor Vaughan Lowe, 19 December 2002

INTRODUCTION

Scope of the hearing

1. The purpose of this hearing has been to consider the question of the legality under international law of any possible military action that might be taken against Iraq in the coming months.

2. In order to give the clearest possible presentation of the legal issues involved, the hearing was organised on the pattern of proceedings before an international court. Legal arguments were presented from two perspectives. One corresponds to the view that one might expect to be taken by States that consider that the only possible legal basis for any military action against Iraq is a specific authorisation that might be given by the Security Council at some time in the future. The other perspective corresponds to the view that one might expect to be taken by States that consider that as a matter of international law the United States, assisted by other States such as the United Kingdom, already has the legal right to take action against Iraq, without the need for any further authorisation from the Security Council.

3. It must be made clear that the arguments advanced on either side do not represent the official positions of any of the States concerned. All involved in this exercise have tried to give as full and fair an account as possible of the arguments that could be made out for either side. It is, however, quite possible that the States concerned would not wish to advance some of these arguments, and possible also that they might frame some arguments differently or even advance some entirely different arguments.

4. It must also be stressed that no legal analysis can be detached from the facts. Again, all involved have tried to take into account all publicly available facts as of the date of the hearing. If new facts emerge, or new light is cast on existing facts, the analysis here would have to be reconsidered.

The Question is not whether or not to strike, but lawfulness of unilateral action

5. It is important to emphasise four points at the outset. First, it is accepted by both sides that if the Security Council were to direct that military action be taken against Iraq, such action would be lawful. The right of

the Security Council itself to decide upon military action against Iraq is not in doubt it is the right of individual States such as the United States and the United Kingdom to take action unilaterally, without any further express Security Council authorisation, that is in issue.

6. The second point is that the question that is being addressed is whether or not there is a need for further Security Council authorisation in order for it to be lawful for the United States and the United Kingdom to take military action against Iraq. The question is not whether or not there should be such military action. If there is a legal right to take such action, moral or political considerations might lead to the conclusion that it would be wrong or inadvisable to exercise that right. Conversely, even if there is no legal right to take such action, moral or political imperatives might lead to the conclusion that the action must be taken anyway, despite the fact that it would amount to a violation of international law.

7. That said, the question of the legality of any action against Iraq remains a matter of very great importance. The importance of the legal position has been emphasised repeatedly by politicians in many States; and rightly. If action is taken and that action is unlawful, it will undermine respect for the law and for the United Nations. Regional superpowers and others would doubtless see the action as a precedent permitting the use of military force by any State that considers that the public good or some higher justifies it in forcibly imposing policies on other States. The corrosive effects of unlawful action continue for many years, and are difficult to reverse. Conversely, if action is taken and that action is in accordance with international law, the action will tend to strengthen the Rule of Law, and to indicate that States cannot violate international law with impunity. In other words, those who must decide whether or not to take military action against Iraq must consider not only the moral, political, economic and other policy arguments, but also the legality of the action. If a course of action is proposed that would be unlawful, it must be asked whether the advantages of taking such action outweigh the disadvantages that would flow from the consequent weakening of international law.

The role of counsel

8. The third point concerns the role of counsel. These arguments have been presented by two prominent international lawyers. The case against the legality of unilateral action was argued by Nicholas Grief, international law professor at Bournemouth University and a barrister practising from 3 Paper Buildings. The case for the legality of unilateral action was argued by Professor Tony Aust, Deputy Director of the British Institute of International and Comparative Law and visiting professor at

University College London. In the great tradition of the English Bar, each of them has been asked to put forward not their own personal views, but the best argument that can be made out on behalf of a hypothetical client -a hypothetical State that might submit the legality of unilateral action against Iraq to an international court, and a State that might be called upon to defend such a case. The arguments that they put forward do not necessarily represent the views of any particular State, or of any organization with which they are or have been associated.

9.   Given the natural concern with the role of the United Kingdom in the events in Iraq, the question put before this hearing is framed in terms of the United Kingdom's right to act; but that way of framing the question has been adopted for clarity only, and must not obscure the fact that we have all approached the issue in general terms, asking whether any State has a right to take unilateral military action against Iraq.

10. I, also a professor of international law and practising barrister, am asked to play the role of an international court, and to summarize the arguments on each side and identify the central issues. In a real court, the verdict is the bottom line, and usually the main focus of interest. That is, I hope, not so here. The aim of all of us has been to give the clearest and most accurate summary of the arguments on either side of this serious and profoundly important controversy. I have reached my own personal view as to the proper decision on these questions, and will give it and explain it in due course; but it will necessarily be a personal, though informed, view.

A question of international, not English, law

11. The question is to be answered on the basis of international law that is, the body of laws that bind States in their relations with one another. All States accept that they are bound by international law, although there may be deep disagreement over what the law requires or permits States to do -exactly as there are disagreement over English law.

12. That brings me to the third preliminary point. Even if the unilateral use of military force against Iraq were to be a breach of international law, it would not follow that the British Government would be in breach of the law of the United Kingdom English Law or Scots law and so on. This is because of the constitutional relationship between the Government and the courts in this country. Curious as it may seem, more than three centuries after the Civil War which is commonly considered to have established that the Crown is subject to the Law and that Parliament is supreme, large areas of the conduct of foreign relations remain within what we still call the Royal or Crown Prerogative. That is to say, they are matters for the Executive - the Government - to decide, and not for Parliament or for the courts. While measures that change the legal rights

and duties of citizens in the United Kingdom need to be enacted by the full procedure of three readings in the House of Commons and House of Lords followed by the formal giving of the Royal Assent, the Government has the power to decide to take the United Kingdom to war, without the duty even of consulting Parliament, and the courts have no power to interfere with that decision.

13. Accordingly, even if a Government decision to use force against Iraq were clearly in breach of international law, it is very improbable indeed that any English or Scots court would order the Government to reconsider, let alone reverse, that decision. The courts would be very likely either to decide that they should not become involved in issues of this kind - that is, that the issues are non-justiciable - or to defer to the views of the Government.

The Application

14. In order to keep a sharp focus on the issues, the hearing followed the conventions of a judicial procedure. Accordingly, the starting point of the hearing was the application made by Professor Grief for a declaration that

> "Under present circumstances it would be contrary to international law for the United Kingdom to engage in military action against Iraq, or assist any other State in taking such action, unless it was expressly authorised to do so by the United Nations Security Council."

It is the specific terms of that request which are the focus of our discussion.

15. The arguments in favour of the granting of a declaration - in other words, the arguments against unilateral action against Iraq, were put by Professor Grief. The arguments on the other side were put by Professor Aust.

The common ground

16. There is a good deal of common ground between the two sides. While each side might describe this common ground slightly differently, I think that I can fairly summarise the generally-accepted position, shared by both sides, as follows.

17. Iraq, the United Kingdom, and the United States, and indeed all of the States primarily concerned, are members of the United Nations. They have all therefore chosen to bind themselves as a matter of international law by the provisions of the United Nations Charter. The Charter does not absolutely prohibit the use of force in international relations it does, however, regulate it.

18. The basic principle enshrined in the Charter is that the use of armed force by States is forbidden. The Charter provides for the lawful use of force in only two circumstances. First, force may be used by or with the authority of the Security Council to safeguard the interests of the international community. When the Charter was drafted, fifty years ago, it was intended that the Security Council should have its own United Nations forces at its disposal; but that plan was never realised and the Council proceeds instead by authorising States to take action in the name of the United Nations and subject to its overall control.

19. Decisions to authorise the use of force are taken by the Security Council; and it is necessary that any State that considers that force should be used in this way should convince a majority of the fifteen men and women who represent the States that the international community has elected onto the Security Council of the wisdom of that action. The majority in the Security Council must include all of the five permanent members of the Security Council - China, France, Russia, the United Kingdom, the United States of America.

20. The Security Council necessarily reaches its decisions only after the careful deliberation that is necessary in respect of such overwhelmingly important issues. The Charter is, however, realistic in recognising that sometimes States are not able to wait for a final decision from the Security Council before resorting to the use of force. That is why there is a second circumstance in which force may be used lawfully under the Charter. If any State, or group of States, is the victim of an armed attack, then that State or States has the right to use force to defend itself until such time as the Security Council has been able to take appropriate action.

21. These are not matters of policy. These are binding rules to which the States Members of the United Nations have solemnly committed themselves by ratifying the Charter. These rules cannot be disregarded by any State without it repudiating the obligations of United Nations membership.

22. In the present circumstances there are, therefore, only two possible legal bases upon which a right to use military force against Iraq might be asserted.The first is the undisputed right to self-defence under Article 51 of the Charter; and the second is that the Security Council, acting under Chapter VII of the Charter, has already provided the necessary degree of authorisation for such action.

23. It is necessary now to examine in a little more detail the way in which these principles are secured in the provisions of the United Nations Charter.

The prohibition on the threat or use of force

24. The basic rule is set out in Article 2(4) of the UN Charter, which stipulates that "all members shall refrain in their international relations from the threat or use of force against the territorial integrity or political independence of any State, or in any other manner inconsistent with the purposes of the United Nations."

25. That provision embodies the deliberate decision of the international community to move beyond the provisions that had been included in the Covenant of the League of Nations, which imposed no more than a cooling off period before States were entitled to resort to war. It also reflects a decision, which was set out in the 1925 Pact of Paris, to move beyond the prohibition on recourse to war for the solution of international controversies and as an instrument of international policies of states in their relations with one another. 'War' has, or had, a technical definition; and not all uses of force were on a scale or of a nature that amounted to war; but the UN Charter decided to use the much wider terms and prohibit the threat or use of 'force'.

26. The League Covenant and the Paris Pact were themselves reactions to the appalling horrors of the First World War. They were clear statements that the scale of suffering and damage resulting from modern warfare made it intolerable that warfare should be employed except in the most exceptional circumstances. That conviction hardened with the experiences of the Second World War and the first sight of the destructive potential of weapons of mass destruction. Since 1945 the prohibition of the unilateral use of force by States has been a cornerstone of the international system.

27. The basic prohibition in Article 2(4) of the Charter has been reaffirmed many times, notably in instruments such as the General Assembly's 1970 Declaration on Principles of International Law (GA Res. 2625 (XXV)), and in the decision of the International Court of Justice in the Nicaragua (Merits) case (ICJ Reports 1986, p. 14).

28. The prohibition in Article 2(4) of the Charter actually refers not to "the threat or use of force" but to "the threat or use of force against the territorial integrity or political independence of any State, or in any other manner inconsistent with the Purposes of the United Nations." It has sometimes argued that force that is not directed against the territorial integrity or political independence of any State, and which is used in a manner "consistent with the purposes of the United Nations" is permissible.

29. Professor Aust did not seek to rely upon any such narrow interpretation of Article 2(4); but it may be helpful for the sake of completeness, to

say that both the drafting history of Article 2(4) and its subsequent interpretation at the hands of States make clear that the provision was intended to impose a comprehensive prohibition on the threat or use of armed force in international relations. The reference to the threat or use of force "against the territorial integrity or political independence of any State" was not intended to limit the scope of the prohibition see B. Simma (ed.), The Charter of the United Nations (2d ed. 2002), pp. 123-124.

The power of the Security Council to decide to use force 30. The qualifications to the basic prohibition on the use of force in Article 2(4) are found later in the UN Charter.

31. First, Chapter VII of the Charter empowers the Security Council to take action with respect to threats to peace, breaches of the peace and acts of aggression. In particular, Article 42 empowers the Security Council to take such action, including the use of force, as may be necessary to maintain or restore international peace or security. Those powers may be exercised either by the establishment of United Nations forces, or by the authorisation of one or more member states to take forcible action on behalf of the United Nations.

32. The question whether the Security Council has, in its existing resolutions in relation to Iraq, already provided sufficient authorisation to justify military action by the United States and the United Kingdom in the event of a further material breach by Iraq of its international obligations, is clearly central to the question before us. Indeed, the arguments presented by Professor Grief and Professor Aust made clear that it is on this question that the main difference between them rests. That being the case, it will be convenient to clear the way for the main discussion by dealing next with second exception the right to use force in self defence.

The right of self-defence

33. The right to self-defence, is set out in Article 51 of the Charter. That provides that "nothing in the present Charter shall impair the inherent right of individual or collective self-defence if an armed attack occurs against a Member of the United Nations, until the Security Council has taken measures necessary to maintain international peace and security."

34. Professor Aust did not argue that Article 51 provided a justification for unilateral military action against Iraq at the present moment. On the facts as they stand, that seems to me to be right. There is no suggestion that the United States or the United Kingdom is currently the victim of an armed attack by Iraq; and they plainly cannot rely upon an argument that they need to use force to defend themselves against any such attack.

Nor is there any evidence of an imminent attack from Iraq, of the kind which might be argued to leave the intended target no other possible option but to use immediate force to ward off the threat.

35. Nor can the United Kingdom or the United States at present invoke the right of collective self-defence. In 1990, Kuwait was the victim of an armed attack by Iraq. There was no doubt that Kuwait was entitled to use force to defend itself, and to seek the assistance of other States in doing so, in exercise of the right of collective self-defence recognized in Article 51 of the Charter. It did so, seeking the support of the United States and others at a very early stage. But again, there is no suggestion that any other State is currently the victim of an armed attack by Iraq.

36. One sometimes sees statements that link in a single proposition the threat posed by Iraq and the threat posed by Al Qaeda. Al Qaeda has indeed mounted armed attacks on the United States and other "western" targets; and it might be suggested that there is therefore an "armed attack" that triggers the right of self defence under Article 51. The implication is that in acting to remove the continuing threat from Al Qaeda the United States may need to take action against Iraq. The short answer to any such argument is that on the facts as they have been made known up to the present, it is no part of the official position of the British Government that there is any such link between Al Qaeda and Iraq.

37. No such link was posited in either of the 'dossiers' on Iraq published in the autumn of 2002 by the Government see Iraq's Weapons of Mass Destruction. The Assessment of the British Government, and Saddam Hussein crimes and human rights abuses. A Government spokesman addressed the issue on 10 December 2002 and said that "[i]t is not clear that there are links between the Iraqi regime and al-Qaeda" see Hansard. House of Commons, 10 December 2002, columns 144-145. There has been no attempt in this hearing to make out a case for a link between Iraq and Al Qaeda; and neither counsel suggested that there is any such link, although Professor Aust did refer in general terms to Iraq's links with international terrorism.

38. There is evidence of Iraq's past links with international terrorism; and Professor Aust suggested that Iraq may now be supporting terrorism. He drew attention to the secrecy with which terrorists operate and to the dependence of governments upon secret intelligence to determine the nature of terrorist threats. That is undoubtedly true; but it is an axiom of the Rule of Law that a case must be made out. If, for reasons of secrecy or lack of information or whatever, a State does not make out the factual basis that would support a claim to use force in self-defence, no legal tribunal can admit that claim.

39. Professor Aust also suggested that Iraq could attack other States in the future but it is perfectly clear that Article 51 does not give States any right to pre-empt an attack. The right of self-defence necessarily exists only where an attack has already been made, or is so plainly imminent that there is no time to seek to avert the threat by any other means than by the use of force in self-defence.

40. Professor Aust conceded that any detailed argument on self-defence would be speculative, and therefore chose to rely upon his arguments concerning Security Council authorisation, rather than upon a right of self-defence. That seems to me a sensible decision, given the information available to us at the hearing.

41. I do, however, wish to add a few words on this point. There are official indications that the British Government does not consider that there is any imminent threat in this case. In the British Government dossier Iraq's Weapons of Mass Destruction. The Assessment of the British Government it was said (at p. 27) that while sanctions remain effective Iraq could not produce a nuclear weapon, and that if sanctions were removed it would take Iraq at least five years to produce sufficient fissile material for a weapon indigenously. If fissile components and other essential components were obtained from foreign sources, that timescale would be reduced to between one and two years. In any event, there is no nuclear threat that is 'imminent' in the sense required by the law on self defence.

42. The position on chemical and biological weapons is somewhat different. It is known that Iraq has had considerable stocks of chemical weapons and stocks of biological agents, and the means for their delivery. There is clear evidence of the use of chemical weapons by Iraqi forces against Iraqi citizens in Halabja in 1988, and against Iran in the Iran-Iraq war. The British Government estimates that Iraqi forces are able to deploy chemical and biological weapons within 45 minutes of a decision to do so. The British Government also believes that Iraq has retained, in breach of Security Council Resolution 687, up to 20 al-Hussein missiles, whose range would allow their use against targets in, for example, Israel and Cyprus. These matters are discussed in *Iraq's Weapons of Mass Destruction. The Assessment of the British Government,* pages 14-15, 17-19, 28.

43. There can be no doubt that Iraq's record of compliance with humanitarian law is appalling, and that it has acted with great brutality. One may accept, too, that it is imperative that something be done, and done quickly, to ensure that this pattern of behaviour does not repeat itself. But this does not necessarily mean that any individual State is entitled to take the law into its own hands. The right of self-defence

cannot justify the use of armed force to prevent a State acquiring, retaining or enhancing its capacity to attack other States in the future. 'Pre-emptive self-defence' is an oxymoron, unknown to international law and incoherent as a concept. If the threat is so grave and imminent that there is, in the familiar words of the Caroline case, "a necessity of self-defence, instant, overwhelming, leaving no choice of means and no moment for deliberation", proportionate force may be used to defend against that threat. If it is not so imminent, there is no such right. If the time allows, States must do what they committed themselves to do when they ratified the UN Charter, and take the matter to the Security Council.

44.   It may be observed that on the one occasion when a State did try to argue that it had a right akin to 'pre-emptive self-defence', when Israel attacked the Osirak reactor in 1981, the raid was unanimously and strongly condemned by the Security Council, in Resolution 487, as a "clear violation" of the Charter.

45.   In the present case, it is impossible to avoid the conclusion that the opportunity, and therefore the obligation, exists to allow the Security Council to determine what is the appropriate response to the threat posed by Iraq. The circumstances that exist at present do not, in my view, support any claim to act in self-defence.

A third exception? Humanitarian Intervention

46.   As counsel noted at the hearing, some people have argued in recent years that there is a further exception to the prohibition on the unilateral use of force set out in Article 2(4) of the Charter, comparable to the right of self-defence in as much as it would justify unilateral action by States, without the need for Security Council authorisation. This further exception is known as the right of humanitarian intervention, and was most notably articulated in relation to the NATO intervention in the former Yugoslavia. It is said that armed force may be used as an exceptional measure in extreme circumstances, in support of purposes already laid down by the UN Security Council, but without the Council's express authorisation for the use of force, when that use of force is the only means to avert an immediate and overwhelming humanitarian catastrophe.

47.   By no means all States took the view that even in the extreme circumstances of the Former Yugoslavia an individual State or group of States had the legal right to take it upon itself to override the explicit prohibition on the use of force in the UN Charter and to use force in another State. The so-called right of humanitarian intervention remains controversial, and is by no means a settled part of international law. Its uncertain status is, however, no obstacle to deciding upon the rights and duties of States in this hearing.

48. It has, admittedly, been widely alleged that the Government of Iraq has in the past subjected its own population to extreme abuse and cruel repression, including the use against its own civilian population of chemical weapons. That might at first sight be thought to provide a possible basis for a right of humanitarian intervention.

49. Indeed, the maintenance by the United States and the United Kingdom (and, initially, France) of the so-called 'no-fly zones' were a direct response to this. Iraq was said to be forcibly repressing its Kurdish population in the north of Iraq, and its population of Marsh Arabs living in the south. In order to protect those two groups, the United States and United Kingdom declared two zones, one in the north and one in the south, in which they stipulated that Iraq may not fly aircraft or helicopters. The zones have been, and still are, regularly patrolled by American and British aircraft, which have on many occasions fired upon Iraqi facilities that were considered to be threatening the American and British aircraft. (The international legality of these two no-fly zones is not itself an issue in this hearing. The legality of any use of military force of the kind now contemplated against Iraq does not depend upon the legality or illegality of the no-fly zones.)

50. Nonetheless, well-known as the accusations of past abuses of its people by the Iraqi government might be, and despicable and widespread as the abuses with which Iraq is charged undoubtedly are, they afford no basis upon which a claim of humanitarian intervention might be built. There is no suggestion that Iraq is currently engaged in massive killing of its own citizens on a scale comparable to that which was said to justify the NATO intervention in Kosovo, and in the Balkans more generally, as 'the only means to avert an immediate and overwhelming humanitarian catastrophe.' In the Balkans there had been almost daily accounts of the systematic rounding up and killing of large numbers of civilians during the forcible imposition of policies of ethnic cleansing. There is no such evidence in relation to Iraq at this moment. There is no suggestion that there is at the present moment any massive and systematic use of force against the Iraqi people. The situation in Iraq does not, as a matter of fact, constitute the kind of circumstance in which a right of humanitarian intervention could arise, even if that right were recognized in international law.

51. It may be said that Iraq has engaged in such policies in the past, and that it may engage in such policies in the future. Whether or not that is true, it does not advance the argument. The right of humanitarian intervention has only ever been asserted in the face of actual, current slaughter by a State of its citizens, demanding an immediate response. Any extension of that alleged right to allow the punishing of States for

past misdeeds, or to disable States from the commissioning of misdeeds in the future, quite clearly falls outside the scope of that right. Nor did Professor Aust seek to make out any case that the right of humanitarian intervention could justify military action against Iraq of the kind that we are now considering.

52. Having dealt with the scope of the right of defence, and the possible right of humanitarian intervention, and shown that neither would justify unilateral military action against Iraq at this time, I turn to the arguments advanced by Professor Aust in support of the legality of unilateral action. Those arguments focus upon the manner in which the Security Council has been dealing with the situation in Iraq over the past twelve years.

The scope of existing Security Council authorisation

The key resolution Resolution 1441

53. The argument that the Security Council has already provided sufficient authorisation for military action by the United States and the United Kingdom against Iraq is based upon the terms of a number of Security Council resolutions, and in particular upon Resolution 1441, adopted by the Security Council on 8 November 2002. The wording of that Resolution 1441 was negotiated intensively, over many days. Its analysis demands the same close and detailed attention.

54. The Resolution begins by recalling a series of earlier Security Council resolutions passed between 1990 and 1999. Those earlier resolutions form part of the context within which Resolution 1441 must be understood; and it is therefore necessary to pause to examine those earlier resolutions before proceeding with the analysis of Resolution 1441 itself.

The earlier resolutions

Resolutions 660 and 661

55. The earlier resolutions specifically identified begin with Resolution 661, adopted on 6 August 1991. That resolution was adopted under Chapter VII of the Charter. It reaffirmed the condemnation of the Iraqi invasion of Kuwait in resolution 660, which the Council had adopted on 2 August 1990, and imposed binding obligations upon States to apply economic sanctions against Iraq.

Resolution 678.

56. The series of resolutions includes resolution 678, by which Member States co-operating with the Government of Kuwait were authorized, in the well-known words of that resolution, "to use all necessary force to uphold and implement resolution 660 and all subsequent relevant resolutions and to restore international peace and security in the area."

Resolution 687.

57. The November 2002 resolution also specifically identifies resolution 687, the so-called "armistice" or "cease-fire" resolution adopted at the end of the 1991 'Operation Desert Storm' in Iraq. Resolution 687 is a measure of central importance. It imposed an extensive series of obligations upon Iraq and other States.

58. It is necessary to consider those obligations in some detail for two reasons. First, because they demonstrate the comprehensive, inter-linked and long-term nature of the cease-fire terms imposed by the Security Council, and make clear that resolution 687 was neither ephemeral nor of merely incidental significance. As the Security Council itself put it, in the preamble to resolution 1441, resolution 687 imposed obligations on Iraq as a necessary step for achievement of the Council's stated objective of restoring international peace and security in the area. Secondly, it is resolution 687 that imposed the legal obligations on Iraq to disarm.

59. The specific obligations imposed by the cease-fire resolution include the following (and I summarize the obligations for brevity's sake)-

" respect by Iraq and Kuwait of the international boundary between them;

" unconditional acceptance by Iraq of "the destruction, removal, or rendering harmless, under international supervision, of all chemical and biological weapons... and all research, development, support and manufacturing activities, [and] all ballistic missiles with a range greater than 150 kilometres, and related major parts, and repair and production facilities";

" an unconditional undertaking by Iraq not to use, develop, construct or acquire chemical or biological weapons or ballistic missiles with a range exceeding 150 kilometres;

" unconditional agreement by Iraq not to acquire or develop nuclear missiles or nuclear-weapons-useable material;

" payment by Iraq of compensation of all direct loss and damage, including environmental damage and the depletion of natural resources, resulting from its invasion and occupation of Kuwait;

" payment by Iraq of the foreign debt that it had purported to repudiate;

" the maintenance of sanctions against Iraq of sanctions in the terms decided upon by the Security Council;

" cooperation by Iraq with the Red Cross in securing the repatriation of Kuwaiti and third country nationals; and

" the requirement that Iraq inform the Security Council that it will not commit or support an act of international terrorism.

60. The 1991 cease-fire resolution also provided for the establishment of a UN Special Commission, UNSCOM, to go into Iraq in order to monitor Iraq's compliance with its disarmament obligations.

61. It is particularly important to note that the obligations relating to the destruction of Iraq's chemical and biological weapons capacity, and its renunciation of nuclear weapons, were imposed by the Security Council and not by the United States, or any other State, acting unilaterally. It is also important to note that the obligations are without any doubt binding as a matter of law upon Iraq. Their binding nature follows from Article 25 of the UN Charter, which binds all UN Member States "to accept and carry out the decisions of the Security Council."

The terms of Resolution 144.

62. These resolutions formed the background to Resolution 1441, adopted by the Security Council on 8 November 2002. Resolution 1441 began by noting that Iraq had not fulfilled its obligations under the cease-fire resolution 687 and other UN resolutions. It specifically deplored Iraq's failure to provide accurate, full, final and complete disclosure of its weapons of mass destruction - a term that embraces chemical, biological and nuclear weapons - and related facilities. It also expressly deplored Iraq's repeated obstruction of the activities of the UNSCOM inspection team and the international inspectors sent, again under Security Council direction, by the International Atomic Energy Agency, the IAEA. (UNSCOM was in fact succeeded in 1999 by a new Commission, the UN Monitoring, Verification and Inspection Commission, UNMOVIC, under the terms of Security Council resolution 1284.)

63. Next, there follow the five key operative provisions of Resolution 1441.

64. First, the Security Council "Decides that Iraq has been and remains in material breach of its obligations under relevant resolutions, including resolution 687 (1991), in particular through Iraq's failure to cooperate with United Nations inspectors and the IAEA."

65. Second, the Security Council set up an enhanced inspection regime in Iraq with the aim of bringing to full and verified completion Iraq's disarmament obligations.

66. Third, the Security Council ordered Iraq to provide to the Council and to the UN weapons inspectors "a currently accurate, full, and complete declaration of all aspects of its programmes to develop chemical, biological and nuclear weapons, ballistic missiles and other delivery systems," by 8 December 2002. The weapons inspectors were also given the right to a list of the names of all personnel currently and formerly

associated with Iraq's chemical, biological, nuclear and ballistic missile programmes.

67. Fourth, the Security Council decided that "false statements or omissions" in declarations made by Iraq and failures to cooperate in the implementation of resolution 1441 "shall constitute a further material breach of Iraq's obligations and will be reported to the Council for assessment in accordance with [the procedure set out in resolution 1441]."

68. Fifth, the Security Council ordered Iraq to provide the UN weapons inspectors with "immediate, unimpeded, unconditional, and unrestricted access" to any and all sites and facilities that they might wish to inspect, including Presidential palaces.

The procedure regarding material breaches

69. Among those provisions, the most important in the present context is the fourth the decision that "false statements or omissions" in declarations made by Iraq and failures to cooperate in the implementation of resolution 1441 "shall constitute a further material breach of Iraq's obligations and will be reported to the Council for assessment in accordance with [the procedure set out in Resolution 1441]." That is the language used in operative paragraph 4 of Resolution 1441.

70. That procedure is set out in two paragraphs, which are specifically referred to in operative paragraph 4. The first, paragraph 11, "Directs the Executive Chairman of UNMOVIC and the Director-General of the IAEA to report immediately to the Council any interference by Iraq with inspection activities, as well as any failure by Iraq to comply with its disarmament obligations, including its obligations regarding inspections under this resolution."

71. In the second, paragraph 12, the Security Council "Decides to convene immediately upon receipt of a report in accordance with paragraphs 4 or 11 above, in order to consider the situation and the need for full compliance with all of the relevant Council resolutions in order to secure international peace and security."

72. Those two paragraphs are followed by another paragraph, which, in contrast to paragraphs 11 and 12, is not referred to as part of the "procedure" to which instances of material breach are subject. It is paragraph 13, in which the Security Council "Recalls, in that context, that the Council has repeatedly warned Iraq that it will face serious consequences as a result of its continued violations of its obligations."

73. These provisions are clearly drafted. The scheme that they establish is simple. According to paragraph 4, any "false statements or omissions" made by Iraq, or failures by Iraq to cooperate in the implementation of

resolution 1441, is deemed to be a "material breach" of Iraq's legal obligations under the resolution and under the UN Charter. It is saying, in effect, that the obligations in Resolution 1441 are particularly important, not peripheral matters where less than full compliance by Iraq might be tolerated by the Security Council.

74. Lawyers are familiar with the drawing of a distinction between 'serious' or 'material' breaches of obligations on the one hand and less serious breaches on the other hand. The distinction is relevant to the consequences of the breach, material breaches generally leading to a wider range of possible remedies or sanctions against the violator. This is, of course, a reflection of the common-sense distinction between more and less serious violations of obligations.

75. The next question is, what is to happen when there is a material breach? The answer is given plainly by paragraph 4. Iraq's conduct "will be reported to the Council for assessment." That provision applies to any false statements or declarations made by Iraq, and to any failure by Iraq to cooperate in the implementation of any of the provisions of Resolution 1441.

76. That obligation is reinforced by paragraph 11, which stipulates that "any interference by Iraq with inspection activities, as well as any failure by Iraq to comply with its disarmament obligations, including its obligations regarding inspections under [Resolution 1441]" must be reported immediately to the Security Council.

77. The Resolution does not expressly say so, but the British Government has taken the view that a report to the Security Council may be made either by the UN weapons inspectors or by a State Member of the Security Council: see Hansard, House of Lords, 25 November 2002, column 559. This point was not discussed at the hearing.

78. Paragraph 12 of Resolution 1441 then records the Security Council's decision that immediately upon receiving any such report it (the Security Council) will "convene immediately... in order to consider the situation and the need for full compliance with all of the relevant Council resolutions in order to secure international peace and security."

79. That is the entire procedure stipulated in Resolution 1441 for dealing with 'material breaches' by Iraq.

80. Resolution 1441 was adopted unanimously. No Member of the Security Council dissented from its terms. The States Members of the Security Council at the time that the resolution was adopted explained their votes see UN Document S/PV.4644, 8 November 2002. On two points, there was complete agreement.

81.   First, there is no 'automatic trigger' in the Resolution. There is no provision that imposes upon Iraq a duty, failure to comply with which would automatically lead to the use of force against Iraq.

82.   Second, the Resolution establishes a two-stage process. The first stage is the imposition by the Security Council of specific obligations upon Iraq by Resolution 1441. The second stage would be, in the event of a material breach by Iraq of its obligations being reported to the Security Council, the immediate consideration by the Council of "the situation and the need for full compliance with all of the relevant Council resolutions in order to secure international peace and security." There is no doubt that if the Security Council decided to authorize the use of force against Iraq, that would be lawful.

83.   On one point, however, there was not complete agreement on the proper interpretation of the Resolution. What happens if the Security Council is unable to reach an agreed decision on steps to be taken in response to a material breach by Iraq? May an individual State or States proceed to use armed force against Iraq without any further authorization from the Security Council? This is the question that is at the centre of this hearing.

84.   The representative of Mexico took the view that the answer is, no. He said "the use of force is valid only as a last resort, with prior explicit authorization required from the Security Council." The representative of Ireland said that "it is for the Council to decide on any ensuing action." The representative of Syria said that "[t]he resolution should not be interpreted, through certain paragraphs, as authorizing any State to use force. It reaffirms the central role of the Security Council in addressing all phases of the Iraqi issue." The representative of China said that "[t]he text no longer includes automaticity for authorizing the use of force," and that on a report of non-compliance by Iraq with its obligations, "the Security Council [will] consider the situation and take a position". The statements are set out in UN Document S/PV.4644, 8 November 2002.

85.   The United States representative took what might be thought to be a somewhat different view. He said, "[i]f the Security Council fails to act decisively in the event of further Iraqi violations, this resolution does not constrain any Member State from acting to defend itself against the threat posed by Iraq or to enforce relevant United Nations resolutions and protect world peace and security."

86.   That statement, read literally, is certainly true. The Resolution does not expressly set out any constraints upon responses by anyone to material breaches by Iraq. The United States statement, however, implies that there is a right for any State, acting without Security Council authorization, to use armed force "to defend itself against the threat

posed by Iraq or to enforce relevant United Nations resolutions and protect world peace and security." It is the implication of the latter part of that phrase that is controversial.

87. It is not controversial that States have a right to act in self-defence in accordance with Article 51 of the Charter. But, as was explained above, it was not argued in the hearing that this right would in present circumstances warrant armed action against Iraq. The suggestion by the United States that individual States have the right to use armed force to enforce UN resolutions and protect world peace and security is, however, highly controversial.

88. Representatives of other States explained their positions in less precise and unequivocal terms. The representative of the United Kingdom, for instance, said that "there is no 'automaticity' in this resolution. If there is a further Iraqi breach of its disarmament obligations, the matter will return to the Council for discussion as required in paragraph 12. We would expect the Security Council then to meet its responsibilities." [see UN Document S/PV.4644, 8 November 2002]

89. The British Government has subsequently expanded upon its interpretation of the Resolution. A Government spokeswoman said "United Nations Security Council Resolution 1441 does not stipulate that there has to be a second Security Council resolution to authorise military action. Such a stipulation was never tabled as part of UNSCR 1441, which has enjoyed the unanimous support of the Security Council. My right honourable friend has made plain that the preference of the British Government in the event of a material breach is that there should be a second resolution. But we are not about rewriting UNSCR 1441. It says what it says, and it does not say that such a second resolution would be necessary." [Hansard, House of Lords, 25 November 2002, column 559.]

90. In the absence of a clear and unanimous interpretation of this provision, how is its meaning to be determined? Is there, or is there not, a need for a second resolution authorising the use of force?

91. The question becomes one of presumption. Professor Grief argued that the starting point under the Charter is the prohibition on the threat or use of force, and that exceptions to that prohibition had to be made out clearly and interpreted strictly and with due regard for the Purposes and Principle of the United Nations. It cannot be assumed that Resolution 1441 authorised the unilateral use of armed force simply because the resolution did not expressly forbid the use of armed force.

92. Professor Aust, on the other hand, argued that this position is wrong. He says that no State apart from Mexico in the Security Council expressly

contradicted the United States and United Kingdom statements indicating their view that Resolution 1441 would in the last resort entitle them to use force against Iraq in response to continuing material breaches of its international obligations, even if the Security Council was unable to reach an agreed decision authorising the use of force. The Resolution must therefore be interpreted in that context of that known intention of the United States and United Kingdom, the proposers of the resolution.

93. The Resolution was, Professor Aust says, drafted with painstaking care and attention to every word, and it is an essential and intended element of the resolution that it does not require any 'second resolution' authorising the use of force. This approach was adopted in the light of the fact that the Security Council had already expressly authorised the use of force against Iraq in 1990, in Resolution 678. That authorisation was "to use all necessary force to uphold and implement resolution 660 and all subsequent relevant resolutions and to restore international peace and security in the area." The subsequent resolutions plainly include the cease-fire resolution, Resolution 687, and the disarmament obligations that it set out. Accordingly, the authorisation already exists to use "all necessary means" (which phrase is accepted as including the use of armed force) in order to enforce Iraq's disarmament obligations. Moreover, the restoration of international peace and security in the area would also warrant the use of force. Resolution 1441 does not remove or limit that authorisation, but rather confirms and builds upon it, he says.

94. I should begin my analysis with the actual wording of Resolution 1441. It is self-evident that nothing in the language of its provisions expressly authorizes States unilaterally to take military action against Iraq.

95. The statement in paragraph 13 of the Resolution that "the Council has repeatedly warned Iraq that it will face serious consequences as a result of its continued violations of its obligations" is a simple statement of what the Security Council has done in the past. It cannot in my opinion possibly be interpreted as an express or implied authorization to States unilaterally to take military action against Iraq in the future. Certainly, paragraph 13 amounts to an implied threat of 'serious consequences' if Iraq breaches its obligations in the future. But nothing in paragraph 13 suggests that the consequences would be decided upon and taken by anyone other than the body that has, under the procedure established in the immediately preceding paragraphs 11 and 12, been given responsibility for deciding how to respond to material breaches that is, by the Security Council itself.

96. Equally, the simple fact that Resolution 1441 does not expressly forbid the use of armed force plainly cannot itself amount to an implied authorisation to use force. That argument has no merit whatever. Most Security Council resolutions do not expressly forbid the use of force no one would argue that they therefore all authorise it.

97. Nor, in my view, do the circumstances of the adoption of Resolution 1441 alter the position. It may well be that the proposers of the resolution knew what they wished the effect of the resolution to be. But as the quotations that I have given from the explanations of votes of Security Council members indicate, the public positions of other States do not entirely support that view.

98. It is tempting to say that for all the skill and patience with which Resolution 1441 was drafted, the result is a resolution that, far from pinning down with precision the unanimous understanding of the Members of the Council, but rather left enough room for different interpretations to make it possible for all Members to accept the text. That may be unfair. A more cautious, and perhaps fairer and more accurate, conclusion would be that there was indeed unanimity on the matters set out in the resolution, including the need for a two-stage process and the reference of material breaches to the Security Council. But there the resolution stops. The resolution does not specify what could or should happen if the Council then fails to agree upon a response.

99. What is to be done where there is agreement upon a single text, understood to mean different things, or not providing answers to crucial questions concerning its meaning? In my view this is a question of truly fundamental importance, that can admit of only one answer.

100. We must all be entitled to assume that legal instruments mean what they say. Often, there will be room for interpretation. It is well established that the proper approach to interpretation is to read the instrument in good faith in accordance with the ordinary meaning to be given to its terms in their context and in the light of the instrument's object and purpose see Article 31 of the Vienna Convention on the Law of Treaties.

101. In my view, therefore, it is completely clear from the wording of Resolution 1441 that the Security Council did not in that resolution itself give any authorization to any State or States to use military force against Iraq. The natural interpretation of these provisions is that it is left to the Security Council to decide how to respond to any material breaches notified to it. I do not see that any State, asked to support Resolution 1441, would be bound to accept that the Resolution itself authorised the use of armed force against Iraq by individual States even

if the Security Council did not decide to authorise such force when it met to consider a material breach by Iraq reported to the Council. Some members of the Council have, as was noted above, clearly taken a different view.

102. It may be added that the limitations on the use of force, in the UN Charter and in customary international law, are so fundamental to the international legal system that it seems to me arguable that there would in any event be a presumption to be overcome against implied authorisations of the use of force. Professor Grief submitted that this was indeed the case. But the wording of Resolution 1441 is sufficiently clear for it to be unnecessary to rely upon any such presumption.

103. That conclusion is enough to settle this point; but I feel obliged to add a further observation. If one can no longer read texts - agreements, laws, letters or whatever - and take them at their face value on the basis of their ordinary meaning, diplomacy and the Rule of Law become quite literally impossible. Not only the parties to agreements, but the rest of the world has an interest in knowing that when States publicly make agreements, the agreements mean what they say. Interpretations of resolutions that are reminiscent of the Looking-Glass world are corrosive of the Rule of Law and incompatible with the conduct in good faith of international relations.

104. I turn to Professor Aust's argument that the authorisation already given by the Security Council, in Resolution 678, has survived and would serve as a sound legal basis for the use of armed force in order to enforce Iraq's disarmament obligations.

105. This argument has considerable force. The UN Charter does not merely constrain the unilateral use of force. It imposes positive obligations, to take effective collective measures to maintain international peace and security. That is, indeed, given first place in the list of Purposes of the UN in Article 1 of the Charter. If the collective procedures contemplated when the Charter was drafted fifty years ago are inadequate for these purposes, the UN must find some other way of achieving them. Authorising Member States to take action on behalf of the UN is one way of doing this. Resolution 678 was such an authorisation; and it should be interpreted in such a way as to make the UN effective rather than ineffective.

106. For the argument to succeed, however, it would have to be shown that Security Council resolutions, including Resolution 678, are not - or are not necessarily - ephemeral instruments. This is indeed so. There are resolutions that impose obligations regarding mandatory sanctions, or that include determinations of the status of territory, which are plainly intended to have a lasting effect, and do so. There are, however, other

resolutions that are equally clearly temporary, being expressly or impliedly superseded by subsequent resolutions.

107. Into which category does Resolution 678 fall? Its authorisation to use force "to uphold and implement resolution 660 and all subsequent relevant resolutions and to restore international peace and security in the area" might suggest that it was intended to have a long, perhaps indefinite, life. On the other hand, Professor Grief drew attention to strong indications that this was not the intention.

108. First, Resolution 678 specifically authorised, not States in general but "Member States co-operating with the Government of Kuwait" to use force. There were such States in 1990. They co-operated in Operation Desert Storm. While many States 'co-operate' with Kuwait now, and Professor Aust submitted that, in effect, the coalition still exists, I find that proposition difficult to accept. The common understanding is that Operation Desert Storm is over; Kuwait is liberated; any new threat to Kuwait would be met by a new coalition, rather than by calling a continuing coalition into action.

109. Second, one of the Resolutions that followed 678 expressly affirmed that resolution 678 continued "to have full force and effect." That provision appeared in operative paragraph 1 of Security Council Resolution 686, adopted on 2 March 1991. Resolution 687 - the cease-fire resolution - , in contrast, affirmed in its operative paragraph 1 previous resolutions, including Resolution 678, "except as expressly changed below to achieve the goals of this resolution, including a formal cease-fire." There is no express revocation of Resolution 678. But does that mean that the authorisation to use force survived?

110. Perhaps the strongest evidence to this effect is to be found in the Preamble to Resolution 1441. That specifically recalls, in paragraph 4, that Resolution 678 authorised the use of all necessary means "to restore international peace and security in the area." The following paragraph then further recalls that the cease-fire resolution 687 "imposed obligations on Iraq as a necessary step for achievement of its stated objective of restoring international peace and security in the area." It might therefore be said that the clear implication is that the 678 authorisation to use force to restore peace and security included an authorisation to use force to enforce compliance by Iraq with the cease-fire terms.

111. This is a powerful argument. Its force is, however, diminished by three factors. First, the provision appears in the Preamble, and not in the operative provisions of the Resolution. This must inevitably affect its legal force.

112. Second, the Preamble to Resolution 1441 also states that "the resolutions of the Council constitute the governing standards of Iraqi compliance." That suggests that the Council, and not the coalition, determines whether there is a breach by Iraq. It is true that Resolution 1441, in operative paragraph 4, deems any false statement or omission by Iraq, or failure to co-operate, to be "a further material breach." Evidently, the Council regards Iraq as being already in material breach; and arguably Resolution 1441 automatically attaches the label of "material breach" to further acts of Iraqi non-compliance (although on the latter point I note that the British Foreign Secretary stated that "aside from the particular definition in paragraph 4, a material breach has to be something serious" [Hansard, House of Commons, 25 November 2002, column 52], which indicates the need for an appraisal of any breach in order that its materiality be established). Nonetheless, in a document that so boldly asserts that the Security Council has assumed its (legal and political) responsibility for the Iraq crisis, and has so clearly stamped the demands on Iraq with the authority of the Council, it is a remarkable proposition that there should be an implied authorisation to unnamed "Member States co-operating with the Government of Kuwait" - or States who were, twelve years ago, co-operating with the Government of Kuwait - to decide whether or not to go to war with Iraq in order "to restore international peace and security in the region."

113. The point was not argued in the hearing, but there is an important question of legal principle, as to the extent of the legal power of the Security Council to delegate decisions concerning the discharge of its responsibilities for the maintenance of international peace and security.

114. The third weakness in this argument is that it sits awkwardly with the history of the Council's dealings with Iraq in the period between Resolution 678 and Resolution 1441.

115. There are in Resolution 687 itself indications that the Council did not see the authorisation to use force as continuing beyond the period of the coalition occupation of Iraq. It must remembered that at the time that Resolution 687 was adopted, coalition forces were still in Iraq. Their presence there demanded a legal justification, as paragraph 4 of Resolution 686 recognised. Resolution 678 provided that justification. But Resolution 687 stated, in operative paragraph 6, that the coalition could bring its military presence in Iraq to an end once the UN had deployed an observer unit. There was, therefore, a logical need for Resolution 687 to provide a continuing but temporary authority for the remaining days of the forcible occupation of Kuwait by the coalition; and one reading of Resolution 687 is that its reference to Resolution 678 was intended to do no more than that.

116. Perhaps the clearest indication that the Council considered that the authorisation granted to the coalition would be shortly be spent is to be found in operative paragraph 4 of Resolution 687, in which the Council "Decides to guarantee the inviolability of the... international boundary [sc., between Iraq and Kuwait] and to take as appropriate all necessary measures to that end in accordance with the Charter." It is plainly asserted that it is the Council, and not States co-operating with Kuwait, that will take such action; but if any coalition power could survive the cease-fire resolution it is surely the power to use force to guarantee the inviolability of the boundary.

117. One might point, too, to the comprehensiveness of the cease-fire resolution, on which Professor Aust remarked. It has all the marks of a comprehensive settlement of the matter. There is no sense of 'unfinished business', or of the Council dealing with only a part of the problem while the rest of the problem remained in the hands of the coalition. Compliance with the resolution did, of course, remain an urgent and serious concern but the natural reading of the resolution is that compliance was thenceforth the concern of the Council, not of the individual States that had been acting in coalition with Kuwait.

118. It is hard to avoid the implication that by the time of Resolution 687, adopted on 3 April 1991, the Security Council had decided that the force that it had authorised had been used and that the situation was in the Council's hands and not those of the Member States co-operating with Iraq. Indeed, the final operative paragraph of Resolution 687 says just that. In it, the Council "Decides to remain seized of the matter and to take such further steps as may be required for the implementation of the present resolution and to secure peace and security in the region." It is quite plainly the Council, and not the coalition States, that is to decide upon and take whatever further steps might be necessary. The same approach was taken in, for example, Resolution 1154, in March 1998.

119. Professor Aust referred to a practice during the 1990s of the Security Council being informed of Iraqi violations, to which the Security Council responded by issuing a Presidential Statement warning Iraq of the serious consequences of non-compliance with its obligations. Continued non-compliance resulted in the bombing of selected targets by British and American aircraft. He suggested that this practice evidenced a belief that the coalition forces retained the right to use force to enforce Iraq's international obligations. If it could be shown that there was a consistent practice that pointed unequivocally to a settled belief on the part of the Security Council that such powers of unilateral action persisted, it would be a very significant matter. But no detailed evidence was put before the hearing on this point; and it is in any event very

difficult to see how any such belief in the Security Council could have existed, given the difficulties in negotiating Resolution 1441 and the statements made by Security Council members, already quoted, explaining their view of that resolution.

120. In my view, these indications establish that the authorisation to use armed force that was given in Resolution 678 does not survive today. Even less can it be argued that the authorisation expanded so as to authorise the use of force by individual States to compel Iraq to comply with the disarmament obligations in the cease-fire resolution 687. It may be true that acceptance of the 687 disarmament terms was a condition of the cessation of hostilities and the adoption of Resolution 687; but it does not follow that the coalition States retained an indefinite right to take the initiative back from the Security Council even while the Council remains seised of the matter and to use force against Iraq as they see fit. The matter was taken back under the control of the Security Council in Resolution 687; and in my view it remains there today.

121. My conclusion, therefore, is that under present circumstances it would be contrary to international law for the United Kingdom to engage in military action against Iraq, or assist any other State in taking such action, unless it was expressly authorised to do so by the United Nations Security Council.

122. It follows from this that the United Kingdom would incur responsibility not only if United Kingdom forces themselves engaged in an unauthorised armed attack upon Iraq, but even if the United Kingdom merely provided material assistance to the United States. As Article 16 of the International Law Commission's Articles on State Responsibility, adopted in 2001, makes clear, States are responsible not only for the wrongs that they themselves do, but also for helping other States to do wrong. Since an unauthorised attack by the United States would be unlawful for the reasons given above, if the United Kingdom were in any way materially to facilitate such an attack it would be internationally responsible for the assistance that it gave.

123. I have not reached this conclusion without much thought and reflection; and there is one final point that I wish to make. The Security Council has a clear responsibility for the maintenance of international peace and security, and it is the Council's duty, legal and political, to respond appropriately to any further material breach by Iraq of its obligations. Resolution 1441 recognises that; and it indicates that the Council will immediately convene to discuss any further material breaches. If the Security Council decides to use force against Iraq, there will be no doubt concerning its legality. The Council is plainly entitled to decide to use or authorise the use of force, and all Member States are bound to

accept that decision. Similarly, all States would be bound to accept any formal decision of the Council not to use force against Iraq.

124. It is, however, possible that events may unfold in such a way that a very unsatisfactory situation arises, in which the Security Council clearly regards Iraq as being engaged in further material breaches of its obligations, and regards those breaches as threatening international peace and security. But it may be that, because of the use of a veto by a Permanent Member or because of wider opposition, the Council is unable to adopt any agreed decision on how to deal with the problem.

125. I am conscious that the view taken here would rule out the possibility of any State taking military action in such circumstances, and could therefore result in very serious breaches of international law passing 'unpunished', or (since the purpose of international law is not to punish but rather to induce compliance) more accurately, without a decisive and forcible response. That may be so; but the question is, if the structure of a legally-binding instrument such as the UN Charter is found to be seriously defective, who should put it right? In this hearing I was asked to put myself in the role of an international tribunal. I have no hesitation in saying that, however serious the defects in the Charter might be, and however urgent the need to remedy them, it is not the proper role of a tribunal to revise the Charter. Any revision is, and must be, the responsibility of the States Parties to the Charter; and until they do revise it, it is the responsibility of any legal tribunal to hold them bound by the terms of the Charter that they have solemnly accepted.

126. I would accordingly give Professor Grief the declaration that he seeks, and declare that under present circumstances it would be contrary to international law for the United Kingdom to engage in military action against Iraq, or assist any other State in taking such action, unless it was expressly authorised to do so by the United Nations Security Council.

Part IV:
LEAD-UP TO HOSTILITIES
AN OPINION GIVEN TO THE CAMPAIGN FOR NUCLEAR DISARMAMENT (CND): RABINDER SINGH QC AND CHARLOTTE KILROY, 23 JANUARY 2003
****

10. In the Matter of the Potential Use of Armed Force by the UK against Iraq

---
FURTHER OPINION
---

1. Further to our previous Opinion dated 15 November 2002 on whether the United Kingdom (**UK**) can rely on United Nations Security Council Resolution 1441 (**Resolution 1441**) to use force against Iraq, we are asked to advise the Campaign for Nuclear Disarmament (**CND**) on whether the UK can rely on the authorisation to use force contained in UN Security Council Resolution 678 (**Resolution 678**), which was adopted on 29 November 1990, to take military action against Iraq.

Summary of advice

2. For the reasons set out below, our opinion is that the UK cannot rely on the authorisation to use force in Resolution 678 to take military action against Iraq.

Background

3. On 2 August 1990 Iraq invaded Kuwait. In response, on the same day, the United Nations Security Council adopted Resolution 660 which, at paragraph 2, called upon Iraq to "*withdraw immediately and unconditionally all its forces to the positions in which they were located on 1 August 1990*". When Iraq failed to comply with Resolution 660, the Security Council on 6 August 1990 adopted Resolution 661, which imposed sanctions on Iraq in order to secure its compliance with Resolution 660. Nine further resolutions followed, including Resolution 674, adopted on 29 October 1990, paragraph 10 of which stated that the Security Council

"*Requires that Iraq comply with the provisions of the present resolution and its previous resolutions, failing which the Council will need to take further measures under the Charter.*"

Resolutions 678, 686 and 687

4.   On 29 November 1990 the Security Council adopted Resolution 678. It stated that the Security Council:

"..Noting that, despite all efforts by the United Nations, Iraq refuses to comply with its obligation to implement resolution 660 (1990) and **the above-mentioned subsequent relevant resolutions**, *in flagrant contempt of the Security Council...*

Acting under Chapter VII of the Charter,

    1.   Demands that Iraq comply fully with resolution 660 (1990) and all subsequent relevant resolutions, and decides, while maintaining all its decisions, to allow Iraq one final opportunity, as a pause of goodwill, to do so;

    *2.   **Authorises member States co-operating with the Government of Kuwait, unless Iraq on or before 15 January 1991 fully implements, as set forth in paragraph 1 above the above-mentioned resolutions, to use all necessary means to uphold and implement resolution 660 (1990) and all subsequent relevant resolutions and to restore international peace and security in the area...**"* (emphasis added)

5.   Following the suspension of hostilities, the Security Council adopted Resolution 686 on 2 March 1991. Resolution 686 stated that the Security Council;

"...Noting the suspension of offensive combat operations by the forces of Kuwait and the Member States cooperating with Kuwait pursuant to resolution 678 (1990).

Bearing in mind the need to be assured of Iraq's peaceful intentions, and the objective expressed in resolution 678 (1990) of restoring international peace and security in the region.

Underlining the importance of Iraq taking the necessary measures which would permit a definitive end to the hostilities....

Acting under Chapter VII of the Charter ..

    2.   Demands that Iraq implement its acceptance of all twelve resolutions noted above and in particular that Iraq:

        (a)   Rescind immediately its actions purporting to annex Kuwait;..

    3.   Also demands that Iraq:

        (a)   Cease hostile or provocative actions by its forces against all Member States, including missile attacks and flights of combat aircraft;...

> *4.*   *Recognises that during the period required for Iraq to comply with paragraphs 2 and 3 above, the provisions of paragraph 2 of resolution 678 (1990) remain valid;"...* (emphasis added)
>
> *8.*   *Also decides, in order to secure the rapid establishment of a definitive end to the hostilities, **to remain actively seized** of the matter."*

6.   On 3 April 1991 the Security Council adopted Resolution 687. That Resolution, by paragraphs 8 to 13, established the conditions for a formal cease-fire and the requirement on Iraq to accept the destruction of all chemical and biological weapons, and to agree not to acquire or develop nuclear weapons or nuclear-weapon usable material, to submit declarations on its possession of any such weapons or materials and to submit to a regime of inspections. The Resolution stated as follows:

"...Bearing in mind its objective of restoring international peace and security in the area as set out in its recent resolutions,

Conscious of the need to take the following measures acting under Chapter VII of the Charter,

> *1.*   *Affirms all thirteen resolutions noted above, except as expressly changed below to achieve the goals of the present resolution, including a formal cease-fire....*
>
> *4.*   *Decides to guarantee the inviolability of the above-mentioned international boundary and to take, as appropriate, all necessary measures to that end in accordance with the Charter of the United Nations;*
>
> *5.*   *Requests the Secretary-General, after consulting with Iraq and Kuwait, to submit within three days to the Council for its approval a plan for the immediate deployment of a United Nations observer unit to monitor the Khawr' Abd Allah and a demilitarised zone, which is hereby established....*
>
> *6.*   *Notes that as soon as the Secretary-General notifies the Council of the completion of the deployment of the United Nations observer unit, the conditions will be established for the Member States cooperating with Kuwait in accordance with resolution 678 (1990) to bring their military presence in Iraq to an end consistent with resolution 686 (1991)....*
>
> *33.*   ***Declares that, upon official notification by Iraq to the Secretary-General and to the Security Council of its acceptance of the above provisions, a formal cease-fire is effective between Iraq and Kuwait and the Member States cooperating with Kuwait in accordance with resolution 678 (1990).***

34. *Decides to remain seized of the matter and to take such further steps as may be required for the implementation of the present resolution and to secure peace and security in the region.*" (emphasis added)

Issues

7. It has been argued by the United Kingdom and the United States in the past that a material breach of the terms of the formal cease-fire contained in Resolution 687 would reactivate the authorization to use force contained in Resolution 678. In particular the UK and the US have argued that breach of the requirements of paragraphs 8 to 13 of Resolution 687, relating to the destruction of chemical and biological weapons and to the non-development of nuclear capability, entitle Member States to use force against Iraq under Resolution 678 without a further UN Security Council Resolution.

8. In this Opinion therefore we will address the following question:

> Whether the authorization to use force contained in Resolution 678 may be reactivated on Iraq's breach of Resolution 687 so as to entitle the UK to take military action against Iraq without a further UN Security Council resolution.

9. In our previous opinion we addressed the issue of whether the use of force by a Member State in the absence of express authorization from the Security Council was as a matter of principle compatible with the UN Charter and with customary international law, and concluded that it was not (at paragraph 48). In our view those observations apply with equal force here.

10. Furthermore Peacerights[1] has received an opinion dated 10 September 2002[2] which addressed the extent to which the UK can rely on the existing body of UN Security Council resolutions as authorising the use of force without a Security Council Resolution. That opinion concluded at paragraph 70 that none of the existing Security Council Resolutions authorised the use of force.

11. We will concentrate therefore in this Opinion on the specific question of whether the authorisation to use force in Resolution 678 can be reactivated upon a breach of the provisions of Resolution 687 so as to permit the use of force without a further UN Security Council Resolution expressly authorizing such force.

Analysis

12. Resolution 678 authorised Member States acting in co-operation with Kuwait to use all necessary means to uphold and implement resolution

660 (1990) and all subsequent resolutions (which, in the context of the resolution read as a whole and having regard to the words we have emphasised above, was clearly a reference to the subsequent relevant resolutions listed in the Preamble to the Resolution 678) and to restore international peace and security in the area. Since Resolution 660 and the resolutions subsequent to it were devoted to ending the invasion of Kuwait and restoring her territorial integrity and independence, and since that invasion is now at an end, the argument that force is still authorised by Resolution 678 has focused on the authorisation to use all necessary means to '*restore international peace and security in the area*'.

13. The argument appears to be constructed as follows:

(1) Resolution 687 does not explicitly revoke the authorisation to use force contained in Resolution 678, but rather affirms it at paragraph 1.

(2) The cease-fire contained in resolution 687 was therefore only a suspension of the authorisation to use force.

(3) Resolution 687 had as its objective the restoration of international peace and security in the area in conformity with Resolution 678.

(4) The provisions of Resolution 687 relating to disarmament of Iraq's nuclear, chemical and biological weapon capability (paragraphs 8 to 13) were designed to restore international peace and security in the area.

(5) Resolution 687 required Iraq to accept the provisions relating to disarmament of its nuclear, chemical and biological weapon capability as a condition precedent to the effecting of the formal cease-fire.

(6) Iraq's failure to comply with those provisions is therefore a threat to international peace and security, and a breach of the terms of the cease-fire.

(7) The suspension of the authorisation to use force represented by the cease-fire is therefore lifted and Resolution 678 reactivated in order to ensure Iraq's compliance with the terms of Resolution 687.

14. In our view, however, it is clear from the terms of Resolution 687, and from the context in which it was adopted that the formal cease-fire, once effected, terminated the authorization to use force in Resolution 678, and that any steps to be taken for the implementation of Resolution 687 and to secure peace and security in the region were now once more a matter for the Security Council and not for the Member States.

15. Our reasons for this conclusion are set out below.

Resolution 686

16. Resolution 686 provides the clearest possible indication that Resolution 687 was not intended to continue the authorization to use force in Resolution 678. Resolution 686 was adopted in acknowledgement of the suspension of hostilities which had by that point occurred. It required Iraq to abide by the terms of a provisional cease-fire with the ultimate aim of achieving '*a definitive end to the hostilities*' (see Preamble paragraph 7, Operative paragraph 8). Paragraph 4, however, explicitly recognised that *during the period required for Iraq to comply with the terms of the provisional cease-fire*, the authorization to use force in Resolution 678 would remain valid. Paragraph 4 provided this explicit recognition despite the fact that paragraph 1 had affirmed that Resolution 678 continued to have full force and effect.

17. No such explicit language is used in Resolution 687. On the contrary, Resolution 687 clearly provides for the Member States cooperating with Kuwait to bring their military presence to an end following the deployment of the United Nations observer unit (paragraph 6), and for a formal cease-fire to be effective upon official notification by Iraq of '*its acceptance*' of the provisions of Resolution 687. It also provides that Resolution 678 was affirmed "*except as expressly changed ...to achieve the goals of the present resolution, including a formal cease-fire*". If the Security Council had sought to keep the authorization to use force contained in Resolution 678 alive pending Iraq's **compliance** with the provisions of Resolution 687, in our view Resolution 686 demonstrates that it could and would have done so (see Jules Lobel and Michael Ratner, *Bypassing the Security Council: Ambiguous Authorisations to Use Force, Cease-Fires and the Iraqi Inspection Regime*, AJIL [1999] 124 at 148-9; "Judgment" of Professor Vaughan Lowe, 21 December 2002, Today Programme, Radio 4 website

, at paragraph 109; Opinion of Professor Colin Warbrick of 30 September 2002, at at page 11.).

Resolution 678

18. Resolution 678 authorised not Member States in general but "*Member States co-operating with the Government of Kuwait*". In our view therefore, it is clear that although the authorization was not just to restore the sovereignty and territorial integrity of Kuwait, but also to restore international peace and security in the area, once the coalition authorized to achieve those goals was no longer in existence, a cease-fire having been implemented, the authorization could not outlive it (see Professor Lowe above at paragraph 108, and Professor Warbrick above at page 12). This point is reinforced by the fact that the specific goals

for which the UK and the US are attempting to revive the authorization, namely paragraphs 8 to 13 of 687, were formulated after the adoption of Resolution 678, and after the coalition had achieved its main goal, the liberation of Kuwait. Resolution 687 is clearly not one of the "subsequent" resolutions to which Resolution 678 referred because that was confined to the resolutions which had been passed *up to that time.* The goals of Resolution 687 for the most part were not directly related to the conflict which Resolution 678 had been designed to solve, but were intended to prevent future and potentially more devastating conflicts (see the Preamble, operative paragraph 14 and below).

The language of Resolution 687

19. In our view it is clear from the language of Resolution 687 that, the coalition having achieved its main goal, the liberation of Kuwait, and the restoration of international peace and security in the area at that time at least, the Security Council imposed a cease-fire and then assumed its proper responsibility for the long-term restoration of international peace and security in the area. It expressly remained seized of the matter.

20. Paragraph 4 of Resolution 687 expressly reserves to the Security Council and not Member States the right to use force to guarantee the inviolability of the boundary between Iraq and Kuwait. As Professor Lowe points out in his "judgment" (above, at paragraph 116) this is a clear indication that the Security Council considered that the authorization granted to the coalition would not survive the cease-fire, as if any authorization to the coalition under Resolution 678 were to remain active it would be the power to protect Kuwait from further incursions into its territory by Iraq (see also Lobel and Ratner, above, at 149).

21. Paragraph 34 of Resolution 687 meanwhile expressly states that the Security Council decides to remain seized of the matter and to take such further steps as may be required for the implementation of the present resolution and to secure peace and security in the region. As both Professor Lowe (above, at paragraph 118) and Lobel and Ratner (above, at 150) point out, this paragraph makes it clear that it is the Security Council that will decide upon, and take, whatever steps are necessary to implement the terms of the resolution and to secure peace and security in the area, and not Member States.

22. Moreover it is simply not correct to assert that the implementation of the obligations to which Iraq agreed under paragraphs 8 to 13 was a condition of the formal cease-fire. As pointed out above the condition of the cease-fire was Iraq's notification of its acceptance of the provisions of Resolution 687 (paragraph 33), and a condition of the withdrawal of the military presence of the coalition from Iraq was the deployment of the United Nations observer unit (paragraph 6). Once those steps had

been taken, the cease-fire was formally in place, the role of the coalition was brought to an end and any decisions on the further steps to be taken to ensure compliance with the terms of the Resolution 687 were to be taken by the Security Council under paragraph 34.

23. The long-term nature of the obligations in paragraphs 8 to 13 in our view supports the view that their implementation was not a condition of the cease-fire, and was to be monitored by the Security Council and not the coalition of Member States. As paragraph 14 of Resolution 687 states, the Security Council notes that '*the actions to be taken by Iraq in paragraphs 8 to 13 represent steps towards the goal of establishing in the Middle East a zone free from weapons of mass destruction and all missiles for their delivery and the objective of a global ban on chemical weapons*'.

Conclusion

24. In our view therefore, the language of Resolution 687 and the context in which it was adopted make it clear that the authorization to Member States to use force against Iraq under Resolution 678 did not outlive the formal cease-fire agreement which was effected pursuant to paragraph 33 of Resolution 687. In our view, the argument that the authorization to use force was simply suspended by Resolution 687 and may be reactivated in the event of a breach of paragraphs 8 to 13 thereof is, on proper analysis, incorrect.

25. Even if, we are wrong about this, however, and the authorization may be reactivated it would not be open to a Member State, even a member of the Security Council, unilaterally to decide to do so. Given the fundamental nature of the prohibition on the use of force contained at Article 2(4) of the Charter and the requirement for the Security Council to retain a measure of control over the operations it authorises, in our view it is not open to a Member State to make a unilateral decision to revive an authorisation which was granted 12 years earlier and which has been the subject of a subsequent cease-fire agreement imposed by the Security Council. [3]

26. As Professor Thomas Franck stated at proceedings of the American Society of International Law in 1998:

"*The Security Council has authorised a combined military operation; has terminated a combined military operation; has established the terms under which various UN agency actions will occur to supervise the cease-fire, to establish the standards with which Iraq must comply; has established the means by which it may be determined whether those standards have been met (and this has been done by a flock of reports by the inspection system); and has engaged in negotiations to secure compliance. After all these actions, to now state that the United Nations has not in fact occupied the field, that there remains under Article 51 or*

188

*under Resolution 678, which authorised the use of force, which
authorisation was terminated in Resolution 687, a collateral total
freedom on the part of any UN member to use military force against
Iraq at any point that any member considers there to have been a
violation of the conditions set forth in Resolution 687, is to make a
complete mockery of the entire system.*" (ASIL Proceedings, 1998,
'*Legal Authority for the Possible Use of Force Against Iraq*, at 139.)

(See also the Opinion of Rabinder Singh QC and Alison Macdonald,
above, at paragraphs 71-76).

27.   The Security Council in passing Resolution 1441 on 8 November 2002
      determined that Iraq was in material breach of its obligations under
      Resolution 687 (at paragraph 1). For the reasons we have set out above,
      we do not consider that Resolution 678 can be reactivated, or that it is
      compatible with the UN Charter for Member States to rely on anything
      other than an express authorization to use force. Even if we are wrong
      on these points, however, in our view this declaration in Resolution
      1441 would not be sufficient to reactivate the authorization in
      Resolution 678 given that the negotiations leading up to the adoption of
      Resolution 1441, as set out in our earlier Opinion, provide clear
      evidence that the Security Council did not consider its declaration to
      amount in any way to an authorization to any Member State to use force
      without a further UN Security Council Resolution.[4]

28.   In our view therefore any military action taken by the UK against Iraq
      on the basis of the authorization to use force contained in Resolution
      678 would not be justified under international law.

Rabinder Singh QC
Charlotte Kilroy
23 January 2003

**IN THE MATTER OF THE POTENTIAL USE
OF ARMED FORCE BY THE UK AGAINST IRAQ**

FURTHER OPINION

Rabinder Singh QC
Charlotte Kilroy
Matrix Chambers

**Public Interest Lawyers
on Behalf of the
Campaign for Nuclear Disarmament**

189

FOOTNOTES

[1]A recently formed non-governmental organisation concerned with issues of international law and international human rights law particularly in the context of weapons of mass destruction and the peaceful resolution of conflict.

[2]Opinion of 10 September 2002, Rabinder Singh QC and Alison Macdonald

[3]We have seen a memorandum on the Legality of Using Force Against Iraq by Professor Greenwood QC dated 24 October 2002, which states, at paragraph 19: *"..it is open to the Security Council to determine that Iraq continues to be in breach of the ceasefire conditions in resolution 687 and that that breach involves a threat to international peace and security which peaceful means have failed to resolve. The effect of such a determination would be that the authorization of military action in Resolution 678 would again be rendered active. That would not necessarily require a Security Council resolution. It could be done by means of a Presidential Statement (which would require a consensus in the Council)."* Even on this argument therefore the reactivation of Resolution 678 is a matter for the Security Council to consider whether by adopting a new Resolution, or by means of a Presidential Statement. What is crucial is that it is not open to Member States, even members of the Security Council, to take unilateral action: they have to act through decisions of the Security Council.

[4]The argument has also been made that a violation of the cease-fire agreement of itself justifies those States who were involved in the hostilities that preceded the cease-fire in using military action, whether or not the authorisation to use force in Resolution 678 remains alive. The United Nations Charter makes it clear that the use of force may only be used where it is authorised by the Security Council, or under the right of self-defence contained in Article 51. Where it is clear that the authorisation to use force has been terminated by the Security Council by a formal cease-fire agreement, in our view Member States may not rely on a breach of that cease-fire alone as a justification for military action without further authorisation from the Security Council (see Christopher Greenwood QC at paragraph 28 of his Memorandum, above).

11. Further Opinion of Rabinder Singh QC and Charlotte Kilroy, made Public 3 March 2003
****

IN THE MATTER OF THE POTENTIAL USE OF ARMED FORCE BY THE UK AGAINST IRAQ AND THE DRAFT US/UK RESOLUTION PUBLISHED ON 24 FEBRUARY 2003

OPINION

1. Further to our previous advice (**OP1441**) on whether the United Kingdom (**UK**) can rely on United Nations Security Council Resolution 1441 (**Resolution 1441**) to use force against Iraq[1].we are asked to advise the Campaign for Nuclear Disarmament on whether the draft resolution released by the United States and the United Kingdom on 24 February 2003 (the "**Draft Resolution**") would, if adopted by the United Nations Security Council, authorise the US and the UK to take military action against Iraq.

Summary of advice

2. For the reasons set out below, our opinion is that:

    (1) The Draft Resolution would not authorise the US and the UK to use force against Iraq if it were adopted.

    (2) In the present circumstances as known to us, if there is no further Resolution clearly authorising force, the US and the UK would be acting in violation of international law if they were to attack Iraq.

The text of the Draft Resolution

3. The Draft Resolution comprises a long preamble and two short operative paragraphs. The preamble 'recalls' all the Security Council's previous relevant resolutions, and continues:

    "Recalling that in its Resolution 687 (1991) the Council declared that a ceasefire would be based on acceptance by Iraq of the provisions of that resolution, including the obligations on Iraq contained therein,

    "Recalling that its Resolution 1441 (2002), while acknowledging that Iraq has been and remains in material breach of its obligations, afforded Iraq a final opportunity to comply with its disarmament obligations under relevant resolutions,

"Recalling that in its Resolution 1441 (2002) the Council decided that false statements or omissions in the declaration submitted by Iraq pursuant to that resolution and failure by Iraq at any time to comply with, and to cooperate fully in the implementation of that resolution would constitute a further material breach,

"Noting, in that context, that in its Resolution 1441 (2002), the Council recalled that it has repeatedly warned Iraq that it will face serious consequences as a result of its continued violations of its obligations,

"Noting that Iraq has submitted a declaration pursuant to its Resolution 1441 (2002) containing false statements and omissions and has failed to comply with, and cooperate fully in the implementation of that resolution,

"Reaffirming the commitment of all member states to the sovereignty and territorial integrity of Iraq, Kuwait and the neighbouring states,

Mindful of its primary responsibility under the charter of the United Nations for the maintenance of international peace and security,

"Recognising the threat of Iraq's non compliance with Council resolutions and proliferation of weapons of mass destruction and long range missiles poses to international peace and security,

"Determined to secure full compliance with its decisions and to restore international peace and security in the area, ..."

4. The operative part of the Draft Resolution states that the Security Council:

"Acting under Chapter VII of the charter of the United Nations,

(1) Decides that Iraq has failed to take the final opportunity afforded to it in Resolution 1441 (2002),

(2) Decides to remain seized of the matter."

5. In an article in the *Guardian* dated 25 February 2003 Julian Borger reported that the Draft Resolution was far milder than the US originally had in mind. The article reported that prior to the report of Hans Blix on 14 February 2003 the US had considered going further, '*demanding the security council approve the use of "all necessary means" to enforce its*

will.' A British official was reported as saying, *"The Americans' original language was quite tough on requiring the words 'material breach' and so on. We said you simply have to refer back to resolution 1441 otherwise you're simply not going to get the nine votes."* (Emphasis added)

6. Newspaper reports suggest that it is anticipated that the Draft Resolution will be put to the vote at the Security Council in the week beginning 10 March 2003, and that war will begin shortly afterwards.

Issues

7. In our earlier opinion OP1441 we concluded that Resolution 1441 did not authorise the US and the UK to use force against Iraq in the event that it breached the terms of Resolution 1441. We concluded that a further Security Council Resolution clearly authorising force would be needed.

8. The Draft Resolution appears to be the US and the UK 's proposal for meeting this requirement. It seems clear that, if it is adopted by the Security Council, the US and the UK will seek to rely on the Draft Resolution either on its own or in conjunction with Resolution 1441 as authorising them to attack Iraq.

9. The crucial question therefore is whether the Draft Resolution would in fact authorise the use of force against Iraq.

Legal Background

10. The United Nations Charter provides the framework for the use of force in international law.

11. Article 1 states:

> "The Purposes of the United Nations are:
>
> (1)   *To maintain international peace and security, and to that end: to take effective collective measures for the prevention and removal of threats to the peace, and for the suppression of acts of aggression or other breaches of the peace, and to bring about by peaceful means, and in conformity with the principles of justice and international law, adjustment or settlement of international disputes or situations which might lead to a breach of the peace."*

12. Article 2(4) states:

> *"All Members shall refrain in their international relations from the threat or use of force against the territorial integrity or political independence of any state, or in any other manner inconsistent with the Purposes of the United Nations."*

13. Chapter VII of the Charter (Articles 3951) confers on the Security Council the duty of determining the existence of any threat to the peace,

breach of the peace, or act of aggression, and of deciding what action should be taken to maintain or restore international peace and security.

14. Article 39 states

"The Security Council shall determine the existence of any threat to the peace, breach of the peace, or act of aggression and shall make recommendations, or decide what measures shall be taken in accordance with Articles 41 and 42, to maintain or restore international peace and security."

15. Article 41 states

"The Security Council may decide what measures not involving the use of armed force are to be employed to give effect to its decisions, and it may call upon the Members of the United Nations to apply such measures. These may include complete or partial interruption of economic relations and of rail, sea, air, postal, telegraphic, radio, and other means of communication, and the severance of diplomatic relations."

16. Article 42 states

"Should the Security Council consider that measures provided for in Article 41 would be inadequate or have proved to be inadequate, it may take such action by air, sea, or land forces as may be necessary to maintain or restore international peace and security. Such action may include demonstrations, blockade, and other operations by air, sea, or land forces of Members of the United Nations."

Advice

What is the effect of a breach by Iraq of Resolution 1441?

17. Much of the Draft Resolution refers back to Resolution 1441. It is important therefore to examine the meaning of that Resolution.

18. In OP1441 we considered whether Resolution 1441 authorised the use of force in the event that Iraq failed to comply with its terms. We concluded that it did not for three principal reasons.

19. First, Resolution 1441 does not expressly authorise Member States to use force. The resolutions adopted by the Security Council over the years, including Resolution 678, show that that the language used to authorise force is bold and consistent. Member states are '*authorised*' to '*use all necessary means*' or '*take all necessary measures*' in pursuit of a specified goal.[2] These words are manifestly absent from Resolution 1441.

20. Secondly, as a matter of principle international law precludes Member States from relying on any implied authorisation to use force. The

prohibition on the use of force contained in Article 2(4) of the UN Charter is one of the most fundamental principles in the Charter. Member States may only derogate from that prohibition in self-defence or following an authorisation from the Security Council to use force made under Chapter VII of the Charter.

21. The fundamental nature of the prohibition against the use of force means that if a resolution is ambiguous on the question of whether force is authorised, then it should be assumed that force is not authorised. Furthermore the power given to the Security Council alone under Chapter VII to decide to use force to restore peace is intended to ensure that any decisions on the use of force are reached collectively. Article 1 of the Charter which sets out the Purposes of the UN makes it clear that collective measures are all that is envisaged by the Charter. Use of force without clear collective authorisation would therefore be in conflict with the fundamental principles of the Charter and in violation of international law.

22. Thirdly, even if implied authorisation to use force were permissible under international law, Resolution 1441 does not contain such an implied authorisation. The wording and scheme of Resolution 1441 and the discussions leading up to its adoption make it abundantly clear that any decision on the actions to be taken in the event of breach of Resolution 1441 by Iraq will be taken by the Security Council. Paragraphs 4 and 11 provide that, in the event of false statements or omissions in Iraq's weapons declaration or non-compliance with its disarmament obligations, either UNMOVIC or the IAEA will make a report to the Security Council. Paragraph 12 of Resolution 1441 provides as follows:

> 12.[The Security Council] Decides to convene immediately upon receipt of a report in accordance with paragraphs 4 or 11 above, in order to consider the situation and the need for full compliance with all of the relevant Council resolutions in order to secure international peace and security".

23. This contemplates that the Security Council, not Member States acting unilaterally, will decide on any further action to be taken against Iraq in the event of any non-compliance by Iraq with its obligations under Resolution 1441. In other words Resolution 1441 does not set out what will happen if it is breached, but leaves it to the Security Council to decide.

24. We also made it clear in OP1441 that in our view the use of the word 'serious consequences' in paragraph 13 of Resolution 1441 does not amount to an authorisation to Member States to use force. Paragraph 13 of Resolution 1441 states that the Security Council *"Recalls, in that context, that the Council has repeatedly warned Iraq that it will face*

serious consequences as a result of its continued violations of its obligations." The words '*in that context*', clearly indicate that any serious consequences which Iraq will face are to be decided upon in the context of the discussion by the Security Council envisaged by paragraph 12 of Resolution 1441. In any event, this paragraph does not itself warn of serious consequences but is a reference to warnings made on previous occasions which this part of the Resolution "recalls". The new Draft Resolution simply "notes" in the preamble that that is what Resolution 1441 said and does not itself authorise "serious consequences".

25.   In summary the effect of Resolution 1441 in international law is as follows. If Hans Blix (for UNMOVIC) or Mohamed El Baradei (for IAEA) conclude that Iraq is not complying with the terms of Resolution 1441 they will make a report to the Security Council. The Security Council will then consider the situation and the need to secure full compliance with its resolutions and will decide, in accordance with Chapter VII of the UN Charter, what action to take. Iraq is reminded that the consequences of breach will be serious, but it remains a matter for the Security Council to determine what the precise consequences will be and when they will take effect.

26.   The question arises, therefore, of what the Security Council will have determined if it adopts the Draft Resolution.

Does the Draft Resolution authorise force?

27.   It is clear that the Draft Resolution does not expressly authorise force any more than Resolution 1441 does. There is no paragraph which authorises Member States to use "*all necessary means*" or "*take all necessary measures*". Indeed the newspaper report referred to above indicates that this wording was contemplated by the US but not pursued on the grounds that it would not receive the full support of the Security Council.

28.   In our view, if wording exists which clearly authorises force, and this wording has not been pursued in favour of alternative wording which does not, then this is the clearest indication that, if adopted, this Draft Resolution would do something less than authorise force. To conclude otherwise not only flies in the face of common sense but severely undermines the fundamental principles of the Charter for the reasons set out above (see also OP1441). Those principles require that decisions on the use of force be taken by the Security Council, not Member States, and that the authorisation of force be enunciated in the clearest of terms so that it is beyond doubt that the Security Council has in fact authorised the use of force. They also enable the Security Council to retain control and supervision over such use of force as it does authorise, for example with clear timescales set out in its resolutions. In contrast, unilateral use of force by one or more Member States carries

the serious risk that there will be a "free for all", threatening rather than maintaining international peace and security.

29. Even assuming this argument is wrong, however, in our view the Draft Resolution cannot be construed as authorising force either alone or in combination with Resolution 1441.

30. The bulk of the Draft Resolution is the Preamble. Preambles do not have operative effect, and cannot therefore be relied upon as authorising action of any kind. Where the words of the operative part of the Resolution are ambiguous, however, the Preamble may be used as a tool of interpretation.

31. The Preamble to the Draft Resolution sets out the history of Iraq's international obligations and failure to comply with those obligations and at Preamble paragraph 9 '*recognises*' the threat to international peace and security posed by Iraq's non-compliance with Security Council resolutions.

32. Operative paragraph 1 in the Draft Resolution then states that the Security Council acting under Chapter VII of the UN Charter "*Decides that Iraq has failed to take the final opportunity afforded to it by Resolution 1441.*" This is a decision as to a *question of past fact*, not an authorisation as to *future action by other Member States*.

33. All that paragraph 1 does is refer back to the "final opportunity" afforded in Resolution 1441. As set out above, however, Resolution 1441 does not authorise force in the event that Iraq fails to take the final opportunity afforded to it, but expressly envisages that a further decision will be taken by the Security Council as to what steps should be taken under Chapter VII.

34. In our view the most that paragraph 1 of the Draft Resolution can be said to determine, when read in conjunction with the Preamble, is that Iraq poses a threat to the peace. Paragraph 1 of the Draft Resolution might therefore be said to be a determination under Article 39 of the Charter, which determination is a prerequisite to any decision to use measures short of force under Article 41 or force under Article 42 of the Charter. What paragraph 1 clearly does not do, however, is go on to decide what measures shall be taken in accordance with Articles 41 and 42 in order to restore international peace and security.

35. This interpretation is reinforced by the consideration that it would have been very easy for the Draft Resolution to include an operative paragraph setting out what it was that it authorised in the form of *future action by Member States*. That paragraph would state what measures the Security Council should take in the light of its decision under paragraph 1. The Security Council might decide to take measures under either Article 41 (for example, further sanctions or an enhanced weapons inspection regime) or under Article 42 (blockades or military action).

36. In our view the fact that the words 'final opportunity' are used cannot mean that force automatically follows. The Security Council might, for example, decide to take measures under Article 41 before it takes measures under Article 42. Under Article 42, it might decide to mount a blockade before it takes military action. A determination that there has been a breach of the peace under Article 39 does not automatically entail military action. That is why Article 39 expressly provides that the Security Council should make recommendations or decide what measures to take.

37. It is not open to the US and the UK to simply assume that the Security Council has authorised measures under Article 42. Those measures are for the Security Council to decide upon. Even if the Security Council were to decide to authorise measures under Article 42 it might, for example, wish to limit the measures to action by land in order to minimise civilian casualties, bearing in mind its obligation to take into account human rights and humanitarian considerations under Article 1 of the Charter.

38. Nor in our view does the reference to 'serious consequences' in Resolution 1441 mean that, once Iraq has been declared by the Security Council to have failed to take the final opportunity afforded to it, those 'serious consequences', whatever they are, will automatically ensue. As set out above, the context in which the 'serious consequences' were referred to in paragraph 13 of Resolution 1441 makes it clear that the Security Council was to decide upon what those serious consequences would be and when they would ensue. Indeed, as explained above, any other interpretation of that paragraph would be in conflict with Articles 39, 41 and 42 of the UN Charter.

Conclusion

39. In our view, the Draft Resolution, if adopted, would not provide the US and the UK with an authorisation to use force against Iraq , either alone or in conjunction with Resolution 1441. Nor does Resolution 1441 authorise force in the event that it is breached by Iraq.

40. Any attack by US and the UK on Iraq in reliance on the Draft Resolution either alone or in conjunction with Resolution 1441 would be in breach of international law.

RABINDER SINGH QC CHARLOTTE KILROY
Matrix Chambers
Griffin Building, Gray's Inn
3 March 2003

FOOTNOTES

[1.] Dated 15 November 2002

[2.] See inter alia S/Res/940 (Haiti), S/ Res/1264 (East Timor), S/Res/1080 (The Great Lakes).

12. Attorney General's Parliamentary Written Answer on the legality of Hostilities against Iraq

17 March 2003

1. In resolution 678 the Security Council authorised force against Iraq, to eject it from Kuwait and to restore peace and security in the area.

2. In resolution 687, which set out the ceasefire conditions after Operation Desert Storm, the Security Council imposed continuing obligations on Iraq to eliminate its weapons of mass destruction in order to restore international peace and security in the area.

    Resolution 687 suspended but did not terminate the authority to use force under resolution 678.

3. A material breach of resolution 687 revives the authority to use force under resolution 678.

4. In resolution 1441 the Security Council determined that Iraq has been and remains in material breach of resolution 687, because it has not fully complied with its obligations to disarm under that resolution.

5. The Security Council in resolution 1441 gave Iraq "a final opportunity to comply with its disarmament obligations" and warned Iraq of the "serious consequences" if it did not.

6. The Security Council also decided in resolution 1441 that, if Iraq failed at any time to comply with and cooperate fully in the implementation of resolution 1441, that would constitute a further material breach.

7. It is plain that Iraq has failed so to comply and therefore Iraq was at the time of resolution 1441 and continues to be in material breach.

8. Thus, the authority to use force under resolution 678 has revived and so continues today.

9. Resolution 1441 would in terms have provided that a further decision of the Security Council to sanction force was required if that had been intended.

Thus, all that resolution 1441 requires is reporting to and discussion by the Security Council of Iraq's failures, but not an express further decision to authorise force.

I have lodged a copy of this answer, together with resolutions 678, 687 and 1441 in the Library of both Houses.

13. Response to the Attorney General's Statement by Rabinder Singh QC and Charlotte Kilroy 18 March 2003, published in the Solicitor's Journal

By the time you read this article the UK government will most probably have embarked with the US on an attack against Iraq which has not been authorised by a fresh resolution of the United Nations Security Council. If they do so, in our view they will be acting in contravention of international law.

On 17 March 2003 the Attorney General issued a written statement to the House of Lords in which he set out what he called 'the legal basis' for war. On the same day the UK and the US announced at the United Nations that they would not put their so called 'second resolution' to the vote, and that they 'reserved their right' to take their own steps to secure the disarmament of Iraq.

In our view the argument set out in the Attorney General's statement is wrong. The UK and the US have no right to take military action to secure the disarmament of Iraq, and in our view a war against Iraq in present circumstances without clear authorisation from the Security Council would be contrary to international law.

The prohibition on the use of force by one state against another, set out in Article 2(4) of the UN Charter, is one of the most fundamental principles of international law. It is not only a treaty obligation but part of customary international law. It is recognised as having the status of 'ius cogens', in other words a peremptory norm of international law from which states may not derogate.

The UN Charter recognises two exceptions to this fundamental prohibition on the use of force. The first is the right of self-defence in the face of an armed attack, preserved by Article 51. As Iraq has not attacked the UK and there is no evidence that an attack is imminent, the UK and the US may not rely on this exception. The other exception is authorisation by the Security Council under Article 42.

The Attorney General's view appears to be that Resolution 1441, combined with Resolution 687, 'revives' the authorisation to Member States acting in cooperation with the government of Kuwait which the Security Council gave at the beginning of the Gulf War in Resolution 678. This argument implicitly accepts that Resolution 1441 alone does not authorise force.

Resolution 1441 cannot be said to authorise force for three clear reasons. Firstly, nowhere in Resolution 1441 is there any language indicating that the Security Council has authorised Member States to use force. The clear and consistent formula used by the UN Security Council when authorising force is that 'Member States' are 'authorised' 'to use all necessary means' or 'take all necessary measures' in pursuit of a specified goal. None of this language appears in Resolution 1441. Secondly, Resolution 1441 provides at paragraphs 4 and 11 that if the inspectors of UNMOVIC or IAEA find that Iraq has made false statements or omissions in its declaration under Resolution 1441, and that it is not cooperating with the in*spectors in revealing and destroying weapons or materials, then they will make a report to the Security Council. Paragraph 12 of Resolution 1441 provides that on receipt of such a report the Security Council* will convene to consider the situation and the need for compliance. In other words the Security Council has specifically stated that it will monitor compliance itself. Thirdly, on the passage of Resolution 1441, all the Permanent Members including the ambassadors of the US and the UK made clear statements to the Security Council that the resolution contained no `automaticity' and `no hidden triggers'. It was only on this understanding that the Resolution was adopted at all. The first draft of Resolution 1441 had been rejected by France, Russia and China precisely because it stated that "breach [of Resolution 1441] authorises Member States to use all necessary means to restore international peace and security in the area."

In an apparent attempt to circumvent these arguments the Attorney General asserts in his statement that Resolution 687, which imposed a formal ceasefire after the end of the Gulf War, suspended and did not terminate the authorisation to use of force. He states that a material breach of Resolution 687 `revives' the authorisation for the use of force contained in Resolution 678.

This argument is flawed for several reasons. There is no language anywhere in Resolution 687 which indicates that the authorisation to use force in Resolution 678 was merely suspended by the ceasefire, pending compliance with the disarmament obligations contained in paragraphs 8-13 of that Resolution. On the contrary, paragraph 33 of Resolution 687 provided that once Iraq had notified the Security Council of its acceptance of the provisions in 687 the formal ceasefire would be effective. Iraq did notify its acceptance to the Security Council and the formal ceasefire became effective. Paragraph 34 then provided that the Security Council `decides to remain seized of the matter and to take such further steps as may be required for the implementation of the present resolution and to secure peace and security in the region.' In other words, once the formal ceasefire was in place the Security Council took over the task of implementing the disarmament provisions of Resolution 687.

The wording of Resolution 686, the provisional ceasefire resolution adopted before the adoption of Resolution 687, makes it clear that if the Security Council had wanted to keep the authorisation to use force alive, it would have used clear language to do so. Paragraph 4 of Resolution 686 stated that 'during the period required for Iraq to comply with' the terms of that resolution, the authorisation to use force contained in Resolution 678 would remain valid. This indicates that the Security Council considered it necessary explicitly to state that the authorisation to use force would remain alive during a provisional ceasefire. The fact that the Security Council did not make the same explicit statement in Resolution 687 is the clearest indication that it did not intend merely to suspend the authorisation for the use of force.

Resolution 678 was adopted for a specific purpose, the liberation of Kuwait. This is reflected in the fact that the authorisation was to 'Member States cooperating with the government of Kuwait.' The phrase 'restore international peace and security in the area' has to be read in the context of the invasion of Kuwait by Iraq. It cannot credibly be argued that a Member State can revive that authorisation twelve years after the ceasefire was put in place and the coalition disbanded.

The Attorney General concludes his statement with the observation that Resolution 1441 would have provided that a further decision of the Security Council to sanction force was required if that had been intended. He states that all that resolution 1441 requires is reporting to and discussion by the Security Council of Iraq's failures, but not an express further decision to authorise force. In our view, this is wrong. The UN Charter requires that force only be used in self-defence or with authorisation from the Security Council. It is not necessary for this to be repeated in Resolution 1441 for it to apply to the US and the UK. The prohibition on the use of force is so basic a principle that the onus is on those seeking to show that they have authorisation to use force to demonstrate that it has in fact been authorised.

Even if we are wrong and Resolution 678 could be revived now, it would need a clear decision by the Security Council itself: unilateral decisions by members of the UN will not suffice. As we have illustrated above, Resolution 1441 cannot provide that clear decision, as the Security Council members who adopted it clearly agreed that it contained no 'automaticity'.

Part V:
AFTERMATH
14. OPINION OF OF RABINDER SINGH QC & CHARLOTTE KILROY ON THE LEGALITY OF THE USE OF FORCE AGAINST IRAQ, 6 JUNE 2003

In the Matter of the Legality of the Use of Force against Iraq
and the Alleged Existence of
Weapons of Mass Destruction

OPINION

1.　Further to our previous advices on whether the United Kingdom (**UK**) could rely either on United Nations Security Council Resolution 1441 (**Resolution 1441**) (**OP1441**), or on Resolutions 678 and 687 (**OP678**) to use force against Iraq, we are asked to advise the Campaign for Nuclear Disarmament and Peacerights on the implications of the absence to date of discovery of weapons of mass destruction in Iraq since its invasion on 20 March 2003.

Summary of advice

2.　In summary our view is that the allegations made by former members of the Cabinet in the recent past, that the evidence of the existence of weapons of mass destruction was exaggerated by the UK and the US prior to the invasion of Iraq in March 2003, call into question the factual foundation for the Attorney-General's view that the invasion was lawful in international law. In our view there is therefore a strong case for establishing a judicial inquiry to examine that legal question.

The Attorney-General's Statement of 17 March 2003

3.　In OP1441 and OP678 we concluded as follows:

(1)　Security Council Resolution 1441 did not authorise the use of force by member states of the UN.

(2)　The UK would be in breach of international law if it were to use force against Iraq in reliance on Resolution 1441 without a further Security Council Resolution.

(3)　The UK could not rely on the authorisation to use force in Resolution 678 to take military action against Iraq.

4.   However, the Attorney-General, the Rt. Hon. Lord Goldsmith QC, set out a different view in his statement of 17 March 2003. He stated that *"authority to use force exists from the combined effect of resolutions 678, 687 and 1441."* It is instructive that even he did not state that Resolution 1441 itself authorised the use of force. It is important to set out the steps of his argument:

1.   In resolution 678 the Security Council authorised force against Iraq, to eject it from Kuwait and to restore peace and security in the area.

2.   In resolution 687, which set out the ceasefire conditions after Operation Desert Storm, **the Security Council imposed continuing obligations on Iraq to eliminate its weapons of mass destruction in order to restore international peace and security in the area.** Resolution 687 suspended but did not terminate the authority to use force under resolution 678.

3.   A material breach of resolution 687 revives the authority to use force under resolution 678.

4.   **In resolution 1441 the Security Council determined that Iraq has been and remains in material breach of resolution 687, because it has not fully complied with its obligations to disarm under that resolution.**

5.   **The Security Council in resolution 1441 gave Iraq "a final opportunity to comply with its disarmament obligations"** and warned Iraq of the "serious consequences" if it did not.

6.   The Security Council also decided in resolution 1441 that, if Iraq failed at any time to comply with and cooperate fully in the implementation of resolution 1441, that would constitute a further material breach.

7.   **It is plain that Iraq has failed so to comply and therefore Iraq was at the time of resolution 1441 and continues to be in material breach.**

8.   **Thus, the authority to use force under resolution 678 has revived and so continues today. (emphasis added)**

5.   The Attorney-General's statement of 17 March 2003 (**"the Statement"**) was not his detailed legal opinion, but a short summary setting out a legal conclusion. The statement does not set out the factual basis for his argument, nor does it fully explain his legal reasoning or provide an assessment of the strength of the argument he has put forward or of counter-arguments (as was well-publicised at the time, many professors of international law and others in this country took the view that the

resolutions relied on by him did not authorise the invasion of Iraq in March 2003). It is fair to assume therefore that this Statement was based on a formal legal opinion which has not been published.

6.   The Statement does, however, give a strong indication of the factual evidence on which the Attorney-General was relying. He states at paragraphs 7: "*It is plain that Iraq has failed so to comply and therefore Iraq was at the time of resolution 1441 and continues to be in material breach.*"

7.   In his leaked Confidential Note to the Prime Minister of 26 March 2003, there is a further hint of what the Attorney-General had advised in his formal legal opinion on the legality of an invasion of Iraq. He states at paragraph 6:

> "Finally and in any event, it must be borne in mind that the lawfulness of any occupation after the conflict has ended is still governed by the legal basis for the use of force. **As you know, any military action pursuant to the authorisation in resolution 678 (1990) must be limited to what is necessary to achieve the objectives of that resolution, namely Iraqi disarmament, and must be a proportionate response to that objective. The Government has concluded that the removal of the current Iraqi regime from power is necessary to secure disarmament,** but the longer the occupation of Iraq continues, and the more tasks undertaken by an interim administration depart from the main objective, the more difficult it will be to justify the lawfulness of the occupation. So in the absence of a further Security Council resolution, in addition to the issues raised in paragraph 2 above, it is likely to be difficult to justify the legality of the continued occupation of Iraq once the disarmament requirements of the relevant Security Council resolutions have been completed." (emphasis added)

8.   This paragraph makes two points very clear:

(1)   the Attorney-General had advised that military action was only lawful to the extent that it was necessary to achieve disarmament;

(2)   the Attorney-General had been told that the removal of the current Iraqi regime from power was necessary to secure disarmament. In other words, it was the Attorney General's view (and we think that view was correct) that "regime change" could not be an end in itself; it could only be achieved by force as a necessary means to achieve the end of disarmament.

Allegations of misuse of intelligence

9. In September 2002 the UK Government published a dossier entitled: *"Iraq's Weapons of Mass Destruction: the Assessment of the British Government."* (**"The September Dossier"**)

10. In his foreword to the September Dossier, the Prime Minister, the Rt. Hon. Tony Blair MP, stated as follows:

> *The document published today is based, in large part, on the work of the Joint*
>
> *Intelligence Committee (JIC). The JIC is at the heart of the British intelligence*
>
> *machinery. ....*
>
> *Its work, like the material it analyses, is largely secret. It is unprecedented for the Government to publish this kind of document. But in light of the debate about Iraq and Weapons of Mass Destruction (WMD), I wanted to share with the British public the reasons why I believe this issue to be a current and serious threat to the UK national interest.*
>
> *In recent months, I have been increasingly alarmed by the evidence from inside Iraq that despite sanctions, despite the damage done to his capability in the past, despite the UN Security Council Resolutions expressly outlawing it, and despite his denials, Saddam Hussein is continuing to develop WMD, and with them the ability to inflict real damage upon the region, and the stability of the world...*
>
> *What I believe the assessed intelligence has established beyond doubt is that Saddam has continued to produce chemical and biological weapons, that he continues in his efforts to develop nuclear weapons, and that he has been able to extend the range of his ballistic missile programme. ...*
>
> *The picture presented to me by the JIC in recent months has become more not less worrying. It is clear that, despite sanctions, the policy of containment has not worked sufficiently well to prevent Saddam from developing these weapons.*
>
> *I am in no doubt that the threat is serious and current, that he has made progress on WMD, and that he has to be stopped.*
>
> *Saddam has used chemical weapons, not only against an enemy state, but against his own people. Intelligence reports make clear that he sees the building up of his WMD capability, and the belief overseas that he would use these weapons, as vital to his strategic interests, and in particular his goal of regional*

domination. And the document discloses that his military planning allows for some of the WMD to be ready within 45 minutes of an order to use them."

11. In his introduction to the debate held in the House of Commons on 18 March 2003, the Prime Minister Tony Blair made the following statement:

> *"...what is the claim of Saddam today? Why, exactly the same as before: that he has no weapons of mass destruction. Indeed, we are asked to believe that after seven years of obstruction and non-compliance, finally resulting in the inspectors' leaving in 1998-seven years in which he hid his programme and built it up, even when the inspectors were there in Iraq-when they had left, he voluntarily decided to do what he had consistently refused to do under coercion.*
>
> *When the inspectors left in 1998, they left unaccounted for 10,000 litres of anthrax; a far-reaching VX nerve agent programme; up to 6,500 chemical munitions; at least 80 tonnes of mustard gas, and possibly more than 10 times that amount; unquantifiable amounts of sarin, botulinum toxin and a host of other biological poisons; and an entire Scud missile programme. **We are asked now seriously to accept that in the last few years-contrary to all history, contrary to all intelligence-Saddam decided unilaterally to destroy those weapons. I say that such a claim is palpably absurd.***
>
> *... this much is accepted by all members of the UN Security Council: the 8 December declaration is false...Iraq continues to deny that it has any weapons of mass destruction, **although no serious intelligence service anywhere in the world believes it.***

12. On 1 June 2003 the Rt. Hon. Clare Short MP, the former Secretary of State for International Development who resigned from the Cabinet on 12 May 2003 told the *Sunday Telegraph* that the Prime Minister Tony Blair had "duped" the public over the threat posed by Saddam Hussein in order to ensure that Britain invaded Iraq.

13. Clare Short stated in her interview:

> *"I have concluded that the PM had decided to go to war in August sometime and he duped us all along. He had decided for reasons that he alone knows to go to war over Iraq and to create this sense of urgency and drive it: the way the intelligence was spun was part of that drive.*
>
> *There was political spin put on the intelligence information to create a sense of urgency. It was a political decision that came*

from the Prime Minister. We were misled: I think we were deceived in the way it was done ...

The suggestion that there was a risk of chemical and biological weapons being weaponised and threatening us in a short time was spin ... That didn't come from the security services."

14. In an article published in the *International Herald Tribune* on 4 June 2003, the Rt. Hon. Robin Cook MP, the former Leader of the House of Commons who resigned from the Cabinet on 17 March 2003, stated as follows:

"When the cabinet of Prime Minister Tony Blair's government discussed the dossier on Saddam's weapons of mass destruction, I argued that I found the document curiously derivative. It set out what we knew about Saddam's chemical and biological arsenal at the time of the Gulf War. It rehearsed our inability to discover what had happened to those weapons. It then leaped to the conclusion that Saddam must still possess all those weapons. There was no hard intelligence of a current weapons program that would represent a new and compelling threat to our interests. .

Nor did the dossier at any stage admit the basic scientific fact that biological and chemical agents have a finite shelf life. Nerve agents of good quality have a shelf life of about five years and anthrax in liquid solution of about three years. Saddam's stocks were not of good quality. The Pentagon itself concluded that Iraqi chemical munitions were of such poor standard that they were produced on a "make-and-use" regimen under which they were usable for only a few weeks. Even if Saddam had destroyed none of his arsenal from 1991 it would long ago have become useless. .

It is inconceivable that no one in the Pentagon told Rumsfeld these home truths, or at the very least tried to tell him. So why did he build a case for war on a false claim of Saddam's capability? .

Enter stage right - far right - his deputy, Paul Wolfowitz, a man of such ferociously reactionary opinion that he has at least the advantage to his department of making Rumsfeld appear reasonable. He has now disclosed: "For bureaucratic reasons we settled on weapons of mass destruction because it was the one issue everyone could agree on."

15. In an article dated 6 June 2003, the *Guardian* newspaper carried the following report by Simon Jeffery:

"The United Nations' chief weapons inspector, Hans Blix, has hit out at the quality of intelligence given to him by the United States and Britain on Iraq's alleged chemical and biological weapons programmes.

As the prime minister, Tony Blair, continued to be dogged by claims he had exaggerated the threat posed by Saddam Hussein, Mr Blix said today he was disappointed with the tip-offs provided for his inspection teams.

"Only in three of those cases did we find anything at all, and in none of these cases was there any weapons of mass destruction, and that shook me a bit, I must say," he told BBC News 24.

"I thought, my God, if this is the best intelligence they have and we find nothing, what about the rest?"

The BBC also reported last night that British intelligence services were asked at least six times to rewrite the controversial dossier on Iraq's weapons of mass destruction.

A source, described as "close to British intelligence", said Mr Blair was at one stage personally involved in the decision to get the document redrafted.

The new claim appears to back up the allegation, originally made by the BBC's defence correspondent Andrew Gilligan on Radio 4's Today programme, that intelligence services were told by Downing Street to "sex up" the dossier to boost support for the war.

The final version claimed Iraq could launch chemical or biological weapons within 45 minutes of Saddam giving the order.

In a valedictory appearance in front of the UN security council yesterday, Mr Blix, who retires this month, criticised Britain for "jumping to conclusions" that Iraq posed a serious threat to world security.

He said Saddam's regime might have hidden weapons of mass destruction in Iraq, or destroyed them ahead of the US-British invasion, but stressed that neither evidence of the "continuation or resumption of programmes of weapons of mass destruction or significant quantities of proscribed items" had been unearthed by his inspectors.

"As I have noted before, this does not necessarily mean that such items could not exist," he said. "They might -- there remain long lists of items unaccounted for - but it is not

justified to jump to the conclusion that something exists just because it is unaccounted for."

16. In another article in the *Guardian* dated 6 June 2003, Nicholas Watt, John Hooper and Richard Norton-Taylor also reported on Hans Blix's remarks made to the UN Security Council on 5 June 2003:

> *"As a UN official, Mr Blix did not name Britain and the US. But there was no doubt who he had in mind when he said there was no evidence that Saddam had continued with his banned weapons programme after the 1991 Gulf war. This contradicted Mr Blair's warning last year that Iraq's banned weapons programme was "active, detailed and growing".*
>
> *A former UN inspector, Bernd Birkicht, 39, said he believed the CIA had made up intelligence on weapons of mass destruction to provide a legal basis for the war. He told the Guardian how supposedly top-secret, high-quality intelligence had led the inspectors on an absurd wild goose chase.*
>
> *"We received information about a site, giving the exact geographical coordinates, and when we got there we found nothing. Nothing on the ground. Nothing under the ground. Just desert."*
>
> *He said the so-called decontamination trucks which figured in satellite photographs presented to the security council were fire engines."*

17. Richard Norton-Taylor in an article published in the *Guardian* on 4 June 2003, made the following comments on the September dossier:

> *" The dossier contains four references to the claim that Iraq could deploy chemical and biological weapons within 45 minutes of an order to do so. A senior British official told the BBC this was one of several claims added against the wishes of intelligence agencies. Adam Ingram, the armed forces minister, admitted the claim was made by an uncorroborated, single, source.*
>
> *The dossier said Iraq was seeking uranium from Africa - a reference to Niger. Colin Powell, US secretary of state, omitted it from his speech to the UN security council on February 5. "It turned out to be untrue; that happens a lot in the intelligence business," he said this week.*
>
> *The dossier said aluminium tubes Iraq tried to buy could be for nuclear weapons. The US energy and state departments dismissed the claim. That very month, the US defence*

intelligence agency concluded: "There is no reliable information on whether Iraq is producing and stockpiling chemical weapons."

18. On 3 June 2003, the BBC reported that a full-scale Congressional inquiry had been ordered in the United States on the use and possible abuse of intelligence information on weapons of mass destruction in Iraq. The inquiry - being conducted by the Senate Armed Services and Intelligence Committees - is expected to compare comments made by the US administration in the run-up to war with what it was given in terms of intelligence briefing and to decide whether or not there was a deliberate attempt to exaggerate intelligence material. In the UK there are to be inquiries by the Foreign Affairs Select Committee and the Parliamentary Intelligence and Security Committee.

Issue

19. The issue which we will consider in this advice is to what extent the allegations made by former Cabinet ministers and intelligence officials that intelligence material has been exaggerated and misused affect the argument set out in the Attorney-General's Statement, on which the UK Government relied to justify the legality of the invasion of Iraq.

Advice

20. As highlighted above the Attorney-General's argument that the invasion of Iraq was lawful depended on the assumption that this invasion was necessary to achieve the disarmament of Iraq. It was only on the basis of this assumption that the Attorney-General could argue that the authority to use force contained in Resolution 678, which had been adopted by the UN Security Council in 1990, and which authorised the use of force in order to ensure the withdrawal of Iraq from Kuwait and to restore peace and security to the area, had been revived. This was because the Attorney-General's argument depended on the following premises:

(1) The cease-fire contained in Resolution 687 was only a suspension of the authorisation to use force contained in Resolution 678.

(2) Resolution 687 had as its objective the restoration of international peace and security in the area in conformity with Resolution 678.

(3) In Resolution 1441 the Security Council determined that Iraq was in breach of the provisions of Resolution 687 relating to disarmament of Iraq's nuclear, chemical and biological weapon capability (paragraphs 8 to 13), which provisions were designed to restore international peace and security in the area in accordance with Resolution 678.

(4)   Iraq failed to take to final opportunity afforded to it by Resolution 1441 to comply with its disarmament obligations under Resolution 687.

21.   Any reliance on Resolution 678 to authorise the use of force was therefore restricted to what was necessary to enforce the disarmament provisions of Resolution 687 (and Resolution 1441) with the objective of restoring international peace and security to the area. It follows that the quality, reliability and strength of the evidence which was made available to the Government, in particular to the Attorney-General, are essential for an assessment of whether in fact there was any lawful basis for the invasion of Iraq even on the Attorney-General's legal view.

22.   Furthermore, the quality, reliability and strength of that evidence are essential for an assessment of whether the invasion had to take place when it did on 20 March 2003 because there was insufficient time to allow the UN inspectors, including Dr Blix, any more time, as they had requested. If, as the Government now suggest, it will take time before weapons of mass destruction are discovered in Iraq, this raises the question why it was not possible to allow Dr Blix more time and calls into question the proportionality of the invasion and use of force to effect regime change in March-April 2003. As we have noted above, the Attorney-General himself was acutely aware of the need for any use of force to comply with the legal principle of proportionality.

23.   In our view the allegations made in the media over the past week call into question the factual foundation of the Attorney-General's legal advice to the Government. If those allegations are well-founded they mean that it was far from plain that Iraq had not complied with its disarmament obligations, and far from certain that invasion and/or regime change was necessary in order to secure disarmament.

Conclusion

24.   Without any disrespect to the two Parliamentary inquiries which are to take place, we consider that there is a strong case for establishing a judicial inquiry to examine what are essentially legal questions about:

(1)   the basis in international law for the Government's participation in the invasion of Iraq and the use of force to effect regime change there; and

(2)   the quality, reliability and strength of the evidence which was relied on to lay the factual foundation for any such basis in law.

25.   It is quintessentially the task of independent judges to decide questions of law and to assess evidence. We conclude that there is a strong case for those two questions to be the subject of a judicial inquiry.

Rabinder Singh QC
Charlotte Kilroy
6 June 2003

AN OPINION GIVEN TO THE CAMPAIGN FOR NUCLEAR DISARMAMENT (CND) : RABINDER SINGH QC AND CHARLOTTE KILROY, 23 JULY 2003

****

15. In the Matter of the Legality of the Occupation of Iraq by UK Armed Forces

OPINION

1.   We are asked to advise the Campaign for Nuclear Disarmament (CND) and Peacerights on the legality of the occupation of Iraq by the armed forces of the United Kingdom (UK) and the United States (US). In particular we are asked to consider the effect that UN Security Council Resolution 1483 adopted on 22 May 2003 (**"Resolution 1483"**) has on the lawfulness of the occupation.

Summary of Opinion

2.   For the reasons set out below, our opinion is that:

(1)   while the invasion and subsequent occupation of Iraq by the US and the UK were unlawful at international law, Resolution 1483 has, since its adoption, rendered the continuing occupation of Iraq by the US and the UK lawful;

(2)   the conduct of that occupation is subject to the limits placed on it by international law;

(3)   in particular, the legality of what the occupying powers are authorised to do and their responsibilities and obligations remain limited by the Hague Regulations and Geneva Convention IV; and

(4)   on a proper interpretation of Resolution 1483 the *primary* responsibility for nation-building, judicial reform and economic reconstruction rests with the UN Special Representative appointed in accordance with paragraph 8 of that Resolution and *not* with the occupying powers.

Factual background

3.   On 20 March 2003 the US and the UK commenced military action against Iraq. By 9 April 2003 US forces had reached Baghdad, toppling Saddam Hussein's regime. The major figureheads of the regime went into hiding and the Iraqi administration crumbled. On 1 May 2003 George W. Bush, the President of the United States, announced what he described as the end of combat operations in Iraq.

4.   Since at least that date the US and the UK have been in control of most of Iraq; UK forces are primarily in the south-east, where they control the city of Basra.

Resolution 1483

5.   On 22 May 2003 the UN adopted Resolution 1483 relating to Iraq. The relevant parts of Resolution 1483 for the purposes of this opinion are set out below:

Stressing the right of the Iraqi people freely to determine their own political future and control their own natural resources, *welcoming* the commitment of all parties concerned to support the creation of an environment in which they may do so as soon as possible, and *expressing* resolve that the day when Iraqis govern themselves must come quickly,

Encouraging efforts by the people of Iraq to form a representative government based on the rule of law that affords equal rights and justice to all Iraqi citizens without regard to ethnicity, religion, or gender, and, in this connection, *recalls* resolution 1325 (2000) of 31 October 2000,

...*Resolved* that the United Nations should play a vital role in humanitarian relief, the reconstruction of Iraq, and the restoration and establishment of national and local institutions for representative governance,

...*Stressing* the need for respect for the archaeological, historical, cultural, and religious heritage of Iraq, and for the continued protection of archaeological, historical, cultural, and religious sites, museums, libraries, and monuments,

Noting the letter of 8 May 2003 from the Permanent Representatives of the United States of America and the United Kingdom of Great Britain and Northern Ireland to the President of the Security Council (S/2003/538) and recognizing the specific authorities, responsibilities, and obligations under applicable international law of these states as occupying powers under unified command (the "Authority"),

....*Determining* that the situation in Iraq, although improved, continues to constitute a threat to international peace and security,

***Acting* under Chapter VII of the Charter of the United Nations,**

...4. *Calls upon* the Authority, consistent with the Charter of the United Nations and other relevant international law, to promote the welfare of the Iraqi people through the effective administration of the territory, including in particular working towards the restoration of conditions of security and stability and the creation of conditions in which the Iraqi people can freely determine their own political future;

5. *Calls upon* all concerned to comply fully with their obligations under international law including in particular the Geneva Conventions of 1949 and the Hague Regulations of 1907;

....8. *Requests* the Secretary-General to appoint a Special Representative for Iraq whose independent responsibilities shall involve reporting regularly to the Council on his activities under this resolution, coordinating activities of the United Nations in post-conflict processes in Iraq, coordinating among United Nations and international agencies engaged in humanitarian assistance and reconstruction activities in Iraq, and, in coordination with the Authority, assisting the people of Iraq through:

(a) coordinating humanitarian and reconstruction assistance by United Nations agencies and between United Nations agencies and non-governmental organizations;

(b) promoting the safe, orderly, and voluntary return of refugees and displaced persons;

(c) working intensively with the Authority, the people of Iraq, and others concerned to advance efforts to restore and establish national and local institutions for representative governance, including by working together to facilitate a process leading to an internationally recognized, representative government of Iraq;

(d) facilitating the reconstruction of key infrastructure, in cooperation with other international organizations;

(e) promoting economic reconstruction and the conditions for sustainable development, including through coordination with national and regional organizations, as appropriate, civil society, donors, and the international financial institutions;

(f) encouraging international efforts to contribute to basic civilian administration functions;

(g) promoting the protection of human rights;

(h) encouraging international efforts to rebuild the capacity of the Iraqi civilian police force; and

(i) encouraging international efforts to promote legal and judicial reform;

9. *Supports* the formation, by the people of Iraq with the help of the Authority and working with the Special Representative, of an Iraqi interim administration as a transitional administration run by Iraqis, until an internationally recognized, representative government is established by the people of Iraq and assumes the responsibilities of the Authority;

..12. *Notes* the establishment of a Development Fund for Iraq to be held by the Central Bank of Iraq and to be audited by independent public accountants approved by the International Advisory and Monitoring Board of the Development Fund for Iraq and looks forward to the early meeting of that International Advisory and Monitoring Board, whose members shall include duly qualified representatives of the Secretary-General, of the Managing Director of the International Monetary Fund, of the Director-General of the Arab Fund for Social and Economic Development, and of the President of the World Bank;

13. *Notes further* that the funds in the Development Fund for Iraq shall be disbursed at the direction of the Authority, in consultation with the Iraqi interim administration, for the purposes set out in paragraph 14 below;

14. *Underlines* that the Development Fund for Iraq shall be used in a transparent manner to meet the humanitarian needs of the Iraqi people, for the economic reconstruction and repair of Iraq's infrastructure, for the continued disarmament of Iraq, and for the costs of Iraqi civilian administration, and for other purposes benefiting the people of Iraq;

...20. *Decides* that all export sales of petroleum, petroleum products, and natural gas from Iraq following the date of the adoption of this resolution shall be made consistent with prevailing international market best practices, to be audited by independent public accountants reporting to the International Advisory and Monitoring Board referred to in paragraph 12 above in order to ensure transparency, and *decides further* that, except as provided in paragraph 21 below, all proceeds from such sales shall be deposited into the Development Fund for Iraq until such time as an internationally recognized, representative government of Iraq is properly constituted;

..21. *Decides further* that 5 per cent of the proceeds referred to in paragraph 20 above shall be deposited into the Compensation Fund established in accordance with resolution 687 (1991) and subsequent relevant resolutions and that, unless an internationally recognized, representative government of Iraq and the Governing Council of the United Nations Compensation Commission, in the exercise of its authority over methods of ensuring that payments are made into the Compensation Fund, decide otherwise, this requirement shall be binding on a properly constituted, internationally recognized, representative government of Iraq and any successor thereto;

22. *Noting* the relevance of the establishment of an internationally recognized, representative government of Iraq and the desirability of prompt completion of the restructuring of Iraq's debt as referred to in paragraph 15 above, further *decides* that, until December 31, 2007,

unless the Council decides otherwise, petroleum, petroleum products, and natural gas originating in Iraq shall be immune, until title passes to the initial purchaser from legal proceedings against them and not be subject to any form of attachment, garnishment, or execution, and that all States shall take any steps that may be necessary under their respective domestic legal systems to assure this protection, and that proceeds and obligations arising from sales thereof, as well as the Development Fund for Iraq, shall enjoy privileges and immunities equivalent to those enjoyed by the United Nations except that the above-mentioned privileges and immunities will not apply with respect to any legal proceeding in which recourse to such proceeds or obligations is necessary to satisfy liability for damages assessed in connection with an ecological accident, including an oil spill, that occurs after the date of adoption of this resolution;

...25. *Decides* to review the implementation of this resolution within twelve months of adoption and to consider further steps that might be necessary;

26. *Calls upon* Member States and international and regional organizations to contribute to the implementation of this resolution;

27. *Decides* to remain seized of this matter.

6.   The letter of 8 May 2003 to which the Preamble refers stated as follows:

"The United States of America, the United Kingdom of Great Britain and Northern Ireland and Coalition partners continue to act together to ensure the complete disarmament of Iraq of weapons of mass destruction and means of delivery in accordance with United Nations Security Council resolutions. The States participating in the Coalition will strictly abide by their obligations under international law, including those relating to the essential humanitarian needs of the people of Iraq. We will act to ensure that Iraq's oil is protected and used for the benefit of the Iraqi people.

In order to meet these objectives and obligations in the post-conflict period in Iraq, the United States, the United Kingdom and Coalition partners, acting under existing command and control arrangements through the Commander of Coalition Forces, have created the Coalition Provisional Authority, which includes the Office of Reconstruction and Humanitarian Assistance, to exercise powers of government temporarily, and, as necessary, especially to provide security, to allow the delivery of humanitarian aid, and to eliminate weapons of mass destruction.

The United States, the United Kingdom and Coalition partners, working through the Coalition Provisional Authority, shall inter alia, provide for security in and for the provisional administration of Iraq, including by: deterring hostilities; maintaining the territorial integrity of Iraq and securing Iraq's borders; securing, and removing, disabling, rendering harmless, eliminating or destroying (a) all of Iraq's weapons of mass destruction, ballistic missiles, unmanned aerial vehicles and all other chemical, biological and nuclear delivery systems and (b) all elements of Iraq's programme to research, develop, design, manufacture, produce, support, assemble and employ such weapons and delivery systems and subsystems and components thereof, including but not limited to stocks of chemical and biological agents, nuclear-weapon-usable material, and other related materials, technology, equipment, facilities and intellectual property that have been used in or can materially contribute to these programmes; in consultation with relevant international organizations, facilitating the orderly and voluntary return of refugees and displaced persons; maintaining civil law and order, including through encouraging international efforts to rebuild the capacity of the Iraqi civilian police force; eliminating all terrorist infrastructure and resources within Iraq and working to ensure that terrorists and terrorist groups are denied safe haven; supporting and coordinating demining and related activities; promoting accountability for crimes and atrocities committed by the previous Iraqi regime; and assuming immediate control of Iraqi institutions responsible for military and security matters and providing, as appropriate, for the demilitarization, demobilization, control, command, reformation, disestablishment, or reorganization of those institutions so that they no longer pose a threat to the Iraqi people or international peace and security but will be capable of defending Iraq's sovereignty and territorial integrity.

The United States, the United Kingdom and Coalition partners recognize the urgent need to create an environment in which the Iraqi people may freely determine their own political future. To this end, the United States, the United Kingdom and Coalition partners are facilitating the efforts of the Iraqi people to take the first steps towards forming a representative government, based on the rule of law, that affords fundamental freedoms and equal protection and justice under law to the people of Iraq without regard to ethnicity, religion or gender. The United States, the United Kingdom and Coalition partners are facilitating the establishment of representative institutions of government, and providing for the responsible administration of the Iraqi financial sector, for humanitarian relief, for economic reconstruction, for the transparent operation and repair of Iraq's infrastructure and natural resources, and for the progressive transfer of administrative responsibilities to such representative institutions of government, as appropriate. Our goal is to transfer responsibility for administration to representative Iraqi authorities as early as possible. The United Nations has a vital role to play in providing humanitarian relief, in supporting the reconstruction of Iraq, and in helping in the formation of an Iraqi interim authority. The United States, the United Kingdom and Coalition partners are ready to work closely with representatives of the United Nations and its specialized agencies and look forward to the appointment of a special coordinator by the Secretary-General. We also welcome the support and contributions of Member States, international and regional organizations, and other entities, under appropriate coordination arrangements with the Coalition Provisional Authority."

Legal Background

7.   The international law on belligerent occupation is for the most part contained in the 1949 Geneva Convention Relative to the Protection of Civilian Persons in Time of War (**Geneva Convention IV**), in particular Articles 27-34 and 47-78, and the Annex to the 1907 Hague Convention IV Respecting the Laws and Customs of War on Land, Regulations Respecting the Laws and Customs of War on Land (**the Hague Regulations**), Articles 42-56.

8.   As Hans-Peter Gasser puts it in the Handbook of Humanitarian Law in Armed Conflicts[1] at 525:

"The first step towards an understanding of the international legal consequences of the occupation of foreign territory is to recognise the general ban on acquiring foreign territory by force, derived from the prohibition of the use of force in the UN Charter [see Declaration on Principles of International Law concerning Friendly Relations and Co-operation among States in accordance with the Charter of the United Nations, Resolution of the UN General Assembly No. 2625 (XXV) of 24 Oct. 1970.). The annexation of conquered territory is prohibited by international law. This necessarily means that if one state achieves power over parts of another state's territory by force or threat of force, the situation must be considered temporary by international law. The international law of belligerent occupation must therefore be understood as meaning that the occupying power is not sovereign, but exercises provisional and temporary control over foreign territory. The legal situation of the territory can be altered only through a peace treaty or debellatio. International law does not permit annexation of territory of another state. It follows from this that all measures taken by the occupying authorities should affect only the administration of the territory, avoiding far-reaching changes to the existing order. In this sense, the occupying power assumes 'responsibility for the occupied territory and its inhabitants.'"

The Hague Regulations

9.   Article 42 of the Hague Regulations states:

"Territory is considered occupied when it is actually placed under the authority of the hostile army. The occupation extends only to the territory where such authority has been established and can be exercised."

10.   Article 43 of the Hague Regulations states:

"The authority of the legitimate power having in fact passed into the hands of the occupant, the latter shall take all the measures in his power to restore, and ensure, as far as possible, public order and safety, while respecting, unless absolutely prevented, the laws in force in the country."

11.   Article 43 is at the heart of the rules set out in Geneva Convention IV and the Hague Regulations. It encapsulates the responsibilities imposed upon occupying powers and the limits to the action they may take.

12.   Article 46 of the Hague Regulations states:

"Family honour and rights, the lives of persons and private property, as well as religious convictions and practice, must be respected. Private property cannot be confiscated."

13.   Article 48 states:

"If, in the territory occupied, the occupant collects the taxes, dues and tolls imposed for the benefit of the State, he shall do so, as far as is possible, in accordance with the rules of assessment and incidence in force, and shall in consequence be bound to defray the expenses of the administration of the occupied territory to the same extent as the legitimate Government was so bound."

14.   Article 55 states:

"The occupying State shall be regarded only as administrator and usufructuary of public buildings, real estate, forests and agricultural estates belonging to the hostile state, and situated in the occupied country. It must safeguard the capital of these properties, and administer them in accordance with the rules of usufruct."

15.   Article 56 states:

"The property of municipalities, that of institutions dedicated to religion, charity and education, the arts and sciences, even when State property, shall be treated as private property.

All seizure of, destruction or wilful damage done to institutions of this character, historic monuments, works of art and science, is forbidden, and should be made the subject of legal proceedings."

220

Geneva Convention IV

16. Article 54 of Geneva Convention IV states:

"The Occupying Power may not alter the status of public officials or judges in the occupied territories, or in any way apply sanctions to or take any measures of coercion or discrimination against them, should they abstain from fulfilling their functions for reasons of conscience.

This prohibition does not prejudice the application of the second paragraph of Article 51. It does not affect the right of the Occupying Power to remove public officials from their posts."

17. Article 55 states:

"To the fullest extent of the means available to it, the Occupying Power has the duty of ensuring the food and medical supplies of the population; it should, in particular, bring in the necessary foodstuffs, medical stores and other articles if the resources of the occupied territory are inadequate....."

18. Article 56 states:

"To the fullest extent of the means available to it, the Occupying Power has the duty of ensuring and maintaining, with the co-operation of national and local authorities, the medical and hospital establishments and services, public health and hygiene in the occupied territory, with particular reference to the adoption and application of the prophylactic and preventive measures necessary to combat the spread of contagious diseases and epidemics. Medical personnel of all categories shall be allowed to carry out their duties... In adopting measures of health and hygiene and in their implementation, the Occupying Power shall take into account the moral and ethical susceptibilities of the population of the occupied territory."

19. Article 58 states:

"The Occupying Power shall permit ministers of religion to give spiritual assistance to the members of their religious communities..."

20. Article 59 states:

"If the whole or part of the population of an occupied territory is inadequately supplied, the Occupying Power shall agree to relief schemes on behalf of the said population, and shall facilitate them by all the means at its disposal.

Such schemes, which may be undertaken either by States or by impartial humanitarian organisations such as the International Committee of the Red Cross, shall consist, in particular, of the provision of consignments of foodstuffs, medical supplies and clothing...."

21. Article 63 states:

"*Subject to temporary and exceptional measures imposed for urgent reasons of security by the Occupying Power:*

(a)   *recognised National Red Cross (Red Crescent, Red Lion and Sun Societies shall be able to pursue their activities in accordance with Red Cross principles, as defined by the International Red Cross Conferences. Other relief societies shall be permitted to continue their humanitarian activities under similar conditions;*

(b)   *the Occupying Power may not require any changes in the personnel or structure of these societies which would prejudice the aforesaid activities....*"

22. Article 64 provides:

"*The penal laws of the occupied territory shall remain in force, with the exception that they may be repealed or suspended by the Occupying Power in cases where they constitute a threat to its security or an obstacle to the application of the present Convention. Subject to the latter consideration and to the necessity for ensuring the effective administration of justice, the tribunals of the occupied territory shall continue to function in respect of all offences covered by the said laws.*

The Occupying Power may, however, subject the population of the occupied territory to provisions which are essential to enable the Occupying Power to fulfil its obligations under the present Convention, to maintain the orderly government of the territory, and to ensure the security of the Occupying Power, of the members and property of the occupying forces or administration, and likewise of the establishments and lines of communication used by them."

Issues

23. We have in earlier Opinions[2] written before the start of military action against Iraq on 20 March 2003 set out our view that, in the absence of a UN Security Council Resolution clearly authorising the US and the UK to take military action against Iraq, such military action would be unlawful and in breach of international law. No such UN Security Council Resolution was ever adopted. In our view, therefore, the UK's military action against Iraq was taken in breach of international law. We are aware that many international lawyers around the world, academic and practitioner, share that view.

24. The UK Government was advised, however, that there was a legal basis for its military action against Iraq in the combined effect of Resolutions 678, 687 and 1441[3]. The Government was also advised by the Attorney

General, Lord Goldsmith QC, in an opinion dated 26 March 2003 (and published in *The New Statesman*) that *"the lawfulness of any occupation after the conflict has ended is still governed by the legal basis for the use of force . . . .any military action pursuant to the authorisation in resolution 678 (1990) must be limited to what is necessary to achieve the objectives of that resolution, namely Iraqi disarmament, and must be a proportionate response to that objective. The Government has concluded that the removal of the current Iraqi regime from power is necessary to secure disarmament, but the longer the occupation of Iraq continues, and the more tasks undertaken by an interim administration depart from the main objective, the more difficult it will be to justify the lawfulness of the occupation."*

25. This raises a number of issues which we will address in this opinion:

   (1)   Whether the occupation of Iraq by the US and the UK is lawful;

   (2)   whether Resolution 1483 renders the occupation of Iraq by the US and the UK lawful;

   (3)   the scope of the powers and responsibilities of the US and the UK under international law generally and under Resolution 1483 in particular.

Advice

Is the occupation of Iraq by the US and the UK lawful?

26. Article 42 defines the state of occupation as *"territory.. actually placed under the authority of the hostile army."* The occupation extends only to the territory where such authority has been established and can be exercised.

27. As stated above, in our view the military action taken by the US and the UK was in breach of international law. It follows therefore that the ensuing occupation of Iraq as the invasion unfolded was also unlawful. The fact, however, that the occupation was unlawful does not mean that the US and the UK were not bound by the provisions of the Hague Regulations and Geneva Convention IV, nor does the UK's compliance with these treaties mean that the occupation is lawful. The principles of international humanitarian law apply to unlawful occupying powers in the same way as they apply to lawful occupying powers.[4]

28. The question of whether the UK is <u>conducting</u> its occupation of Iraq in a lawful way is therefore distinct at international law from the question of whether the occupation itself was lawful, the latter question being inextricably linked to the justification for taking the military action which led to the occupation.

29. In relation to the former question, as the Attorney-General pointed out in his opinion of 26 March 2003, the powers and actions of the occupying powers are limited by the Hague Regulations and Geneva Convention IV. In particular Article 43 of the Hague Regulations limits the ability of the occupier to make permanent changes to the constitution of the occupied territory. As Professor Christopher Greenwood QC stated in *The Administration of Occupied Territory* in International Law and the Administration of Occupied Territories (Clarendon, 1992),

> "*.the fact that a belligerent occupant does not acquire sovereignty and has a duty under Article 43 of the Hague Regulations to respect the laws in force in the occupied territory makes any change introduced by the occupant in the constitution or institutions of the occupied territory of doubtful legality.....an attempt by an occupying power to effect permanent changes in the constitution of occupied territory may, in itself, involve a violation of the Hague Regulations. Article 43, it has been suggested, "protects the separate existence of the State, its institutions and its laws."[5] An occupant is entitled to suspend the operation of certain constitutional guarantees and the functioning of the political organs of the constitution (at least at the level of central government) for the duration of the occupation. Permanent changes in the constitution of the occupied territory, on the other hand, are probably lawful only if they are necessary to enable the full implementation of the Hague Regulations and the Fourth Geneva Convention or other rules of international law."[6]*

30. Equally Article 43 of the Hague Regulations combined with Article 64 of Geneva Convention IV shows "*that international law does not recognise a general legislative competence in the belligerent occupant. Changes in the law of the territory will be contrary to international law unless they are required for the legitimate needs of the occupation.*"[7]

31. The desire of the US and the UK to oversee, if not themselves make, far-reaching changes to the structures of government of Iraq and in particular to institute a representative democracy would therefore almost certainly have been in breach of Article 43 of the Hague Regulations. Under the Hague Regulations and the Geneva Convention, the occupying powers have a duty to "take all the measures in his power to restore, and to ensure, as far as possible, public order and safety." They may not, however, by virtue of Article 43 of the Hague Regulations and Article 64 of Geneva Convention IV replace the administration and

judicial organisation of the occupied territory with their own administration. If there is a power vacuum because, for example authorities, public officials and judges have left the occupied territory, or are unwilling to perform their duties then, as a matter of urgency, the occupying powers may set up their own civilian administration. *"According to the principle of subsidiarity, they may intervene and take their own decisions only to the extent that this is absolutely necessary in the interests of the population of the occupied territory. National administrative bodies or courts which are still functioning may not be altered."* [8]

32.   The Hague Regulations and Geneva Convention IV also contain important limitations on the occupying power's ability to control the economy. The basic principle is that the occupying power must not exercise its authority in order to further its own interests or to meet the needs of its own population. Antonio Cassese states:[9] *"In no case can it exploit the inhabitants, the resources or other assets of the territory under its control for the benefit of its own territory or population.... In my view it follows from the provisions of the Hague Regulations referred to above [Articles 46, 52, 53, 55 and 56] that the occupant can interfere in the economic activity of the territory under its control (by requisitioning private property, seizing public movables, or using state-owned immovables) only for the following purposes: (a) to meet its own military or security needs (i.e. the exigencies posed by the conduct of its military operations in the occupied territory); (b) to defray the expenses involved in the belligerent occupation; (c) to protect the interests and the well-being of the inhabitants."*

33.   Perhaps the most important restriction on the occupying powers derives from the assumption that the occupation will be temporary. Article 6 of Geneva Convention IV expressly provides, for instance, that save for certain core provisions the Convention will cease to apply one year after the close of military operations, although this is a provision which has been much criticised. [10]

34.   As a result of these restrictions, the US and the UK sought authorisation for their administration of Iraq from the UN Security Council in the form of Resolution 1483. In this advice we will address two questions which arise from Resolution 1483: first whether it legitimises the US and the UK's occupation of Iraq; second, to what extent it extends the US and the UK's powers and responsibilities as occupying powers under international law.

Does Resolution 1483 render the US and the UK occupation of Iraq lawful?

35.   As is clear from the extracts from Resolution 1483 set out above, nowhere in that Resolution does the Security Council state that the

military action against Iraq was lawful or justified. Although the third recital of the Preamble reaffirms the importance of the disarmament of Iraqi weapons of mass destruction and of eventual confirmation of the disarmament of Iraq, and the 13th recital recognises that the UK and the US are occupying powers, both fall short of endorsing the military action.[11] As explained above, the US and the UK's status as occupying powers and the powers and responsibilities which go with that status, are not dependent on the lawfulness of the military action which led to the occupation.

36. In any event, in our view it would be difficult to see how such retrospective endorsement would be compatible with the UN Charter, unless the Security Council were to conclude that the US and the UK had acted properly under Article 51, the self-defence provision of the Charter, which permits force to be used by Member States in self-defence as long as the matter is promptly referred to the Security Council. Either the US and the UK were authorised to take military action by the Security Council under Chapter VII of the UN Charter or they were not. If they were not then that action was unlawful, and in our view *no ex post facto* resolution can authorise that action. Furthermore, although the Security Council has a quasi-judicial function insofar as it is called upon to judge whether there has been a violation of international law in order to enforce the provisions of the Charter, in our view the scope of that function is limited to what is necessary in order for it to enforce the law. As Bruno Simma's Commentary on the Charter of the UN[12] states:

> *"..the tendency of the S[ecurity] C[ouncil] to assume quasi-judicial authority, though certainly conducive to the maintenance of peace, is difficult to reconcile with the legal order of the UN Charter which, as has been shown above, limits Chapter VII powers, in principle, to preliminary measures while excluding the imposition of specific terms of settlement by the SC. Moreover, the final determination of rights and obligations of States (and of individuals) partly establishes a compulsory jurisdiction, whereas the Charter has opted for a system of voluntary submission of States to third-party settlement. Therefore in cases of doubt a legal determination by the SC should be interpreted as possessing only preliminary and not final character, thus allowing for challenges when the conflict is over and when a reconsideration of the legal question does not add to the threat to the peace any more...In any event, quasi-judicial determinations should remain exceptional and should be confined to cases where they are indispensable for the exercise*

> *of the police function of the SC. In consequence, their effects*
> *should be limited to the particular situation. In addition, they*
> *should conform to the general standards for judicial findings,*
> *and thus meet the respective procedural requirements and*
> *respect the substantive law in place."*

37. In our view, therefore, for the reasons set out above the lawfulness of the military action against Iraq by the US and the UK is still very much an open question.

38. The question remains, however, to what extent Resolution 1483 legitimises the continuing occupation of Iraq by the US and the UK. As stated above, the 13th recital of the Preamble recognises that the US and the UK are occupying powers and recognises the specific authorities, responsibilities and obligations under applicable international law which follow from this status. Although this is far from a condemnation of the US and the UK's presence in Iraq,[13] equally it does not in our view amount to an endorsement of their presence because the relevant obligations apply to those powers whose occupation is unlawful as well as those whose occupation is lawful.

39. Operative paragraph 4, however, calls upon the Authority (the US and the UK) to promote the welfare of the Iraqi people through the effective administration of the territory including working towards the restoration of conditions of security and stability and the creation of conditions in which the Iraqi people can freely determine their own political future. Operative paragraph 8 meanwhile sets out responsibilities for the UN Special Representative in coordination with the Authority, thereby anticipating the involvement of the Authority in the carrying out of those responsibilities, and operative paragraph 9 supports the formation by the people of Iraq with the help of the Authority and working with the Special Representative, of an interim administration as a transitional administration run by Iraqis until a recognised representative government is established by the people of Iraq and assumes the responsibilities of the Authority.

40. The Security Council has called upon the US and the UK to remain as administrator and to promote the welfare of the Iraqi people in the ways described in operative paragraph 4; has envisaged by operative paragraph 8 that the US and the UK will be involved in carrying out specific functions over and above those provided for in the Hague Regulations and Geneva Convention IV; and by operative paragraph 9 has anticipated that the US and the UK will remain until an internationally recognised representative government is established by the people of Iraq which assumes the responsibilities of the Authority. By those means, in our view, Resolution 1483 renders lawful the

continuing occupation of Iraq by the US and the UK, in order to carry
out the responsibilities described in the Resolution. Operative paragraph
4 in particular, as a measure under Chapter VII which "calls upon" the
US and the UK to take a particular action, is binding on the US and the
UK. [14] Article 48 of the UN Charter provides that *"the action required
to carry out the decisions of the Security Council for the maintenance of
international peace and security shall be taken by all the Members of
the United Nations or by some of them, as the Security Council may
determine"*.

41. In our view therefore, although we remain of the view that the military
action taken against Iraq by the US and the UK was taken in breach of
international law, and although the Security Council in Resolution 1483
does not make any finding that this military action was lawful, by
calling upon the US and the UK to carry out the role of administering
Iraq in order to promote the welfare of the Iraqi people, and by
expressly contemplating that the US and the UK will remain in Iraq
until their responsibilities are assumed by an Iraqi representative
government, the Security Council has authorised the continuing
occupation of Iraq by the US and the UK for the purposes set out in
Resolution 1483.

What is the scope of the UK's responsibilities and authority under
international law and Resolution 1483?

42. Resolution 1483 expressly calls at operative paragraph 5 upon 'all
concerned to comply fully with their obligations under international law
including in particular the Geneva Conventions of 1949 and the Hague
Regulations of 1907' and in the 13th recital of the Preamble recognises
the specific authorities, responsibilities and obligations which the US
and the UK have as occupying powers under international law. There is
no question therefore that the UK must continue to comply with the
Hague Regulations and Geneva Convention IV, not to mention Geneva
Convention III which concerns prisoners of war.

43. As indicated above, however, Resolution 1483 also appears to anticipate
a role for the US and the UK which goes beyond that permitted of an
occupying power under the Hague Regulations and Geneva Convention
IV (see below). It is significant that operative paragraph 4 which confers
a direct responsibility on the UK and the US does not in fact endow
them with more power to change the *status quo* than permitted by the
Hague Regulations or Geneva Convention IV, but expressly states that
they should act consistently with relevant international law and calls
upon them to promote the welfare of the Iraqi people in particular by
inter alia creating the conditions in which the Iraqi people can freely
determine their own political future. Although the words 'creation of

conditions' is open to interpretation, in the context of the paragraph as a whole, which requires compliance with relevant international law and specifies the restoration of conditions of security and stability as a means of promoting the welfare of the Iraqi people (entirely in keeping with Article 43 of the Hague Regulations which requires the occupier to restore public order and safety), in our view, this would limit the US and the UK to the powers set out in the Hague Regulations and Geneva Convention IV. It is only operative paragraphs 8 and 9 which appear to expand the role of the UK and the US as occupying powers.

44. Operative paragraph 8 is addressed to the Secretary-General of the UN and requests him to appoint a special representative with the responsibilities set out in that paragraph and paragraph 9. These responsibilities are in fact less far-reaching than those set out in UN Security Council Resolution 1244, which provided for the establishment of an international civil presence in Kosovo, which had widespread administrative powers, and UN Security Council Resolution 1272, which provided for the establishment of an international transitional administration in East Timor whose overall responsibility included all legislative and executive authority and the administration of justice. As indicated above, because paragraphs 8 and 9 require the Special Representative to work in co-ordination with the Authority in carrying out these responsibilities it appears that they are therefore implicitly also conferred on the US and the UK (see below).

45. Operative paragraph 8 (c) provides that the Special Representative should work intensively with the Authority and the people of Iraq to advance efforts to restore and establish national and local institutions for representative governance, and work together to facilitate a process leading to an internationally recognised, representative government of Iraq; 8 (e) provides that he should in co-ordination with the Authority promote economic reconstruction and conditions for sustainable development; 8 (i) provides that he should in co-ordination with the Authority encourage international efforts to promote legal and judicial reform; and operative paragraph 9 supports the establishment with the help of the Authority and the Special Representative of a transitional administration run by Iraqis.

46. It is immediately clear from the above that Resolution 1483 gives the Special Representative and the Authority a considerable amount of influence over the process of creating a new government and constitution in Iraq, over the creation of a temporary civil administration, over economic reconstruction and over legal and judicial reform. In our view this influence is far greater than would be lawful for an occupying power under the Hague Regulations and Geneva

Convention IV, and in particular exceeds the remit set out in Article 43 of the Hague Regulations. Although as indicated above, there are circumstances where an occupying power might be entitled to create a new temporary civil administration compatibly with the Hague Regulations, economic reconstruction, judicial reform and permanent changes to the system of government are flatly contradictory to the basic principle underlying the Hague Regulations, namely that the occupation is '*a temporary state of affairs and any change in the status of the territory has to wait until the conclusion of a treaty of peace or the complete subjugation of the State which had formerly exercised sovereignty in the territory*'.[15]

47.   As Christopher Greenwood states:[16]

> "*Existing administrative and legislative structures and the political process may be suspended for the duration of the occupation but an occupant will exceed its powers if it attempts, for example, to create a new State, to change a monarchy into a republic or a federal into a unitary government. An occupant may, therefore, suspend or bypass the existing administrative structure where there is a legitimate necessity of the kind discussed in the preceding paragraph but any attempt at effecting permanent reform or change in that structure will be unlawful.*"

48.   There is no doubt that nation-building has increasingly become part of the practice of the Security Council.[17] As Frederic Megret and Florian Hoffmann put it:[18]

> "*Whereas old-style mandates and trusteeships under the League of Nations were administered by states with the League merely exercising supervisory power, the United Nations is henceforth engaged in an unprecedented experience of massive direct rule with broader competence over a territory than ever before bestowed upon an international body.*
>
> *That this 'international civil presence' to use the prevalent euphemism, is meant to be temporary, does not change the fact that it is effective, often exclusive and, in most cases, likely to last a number of years. Concretely this means that in a context of renewed commitment to 'nation-building' the United Nations is asked to build state structures from scratch in a process that has variously been described as post-conflict 'reconstruction', 'management' or, perhaps even more adequately, 'international social engineering'.*"

49. It is generally accepted,[19] that although these functions are newly exercised by the Security Council, they do fall within the wide and non-exhaustive range of measures envisaged by Article 41 of the UN Charter.[20] Furthermore the United Nations does not naturally fit the definition of an occupying power and it is a matter of debate whether the Geneva Conventions of 1949 and the Hague Regulations apply to it.[21]

50. The responsibilities endowed upon the Special Representative by operative paragraphs 8 and 9 are therefore in keeping with the role increasingly taken by the United Nations. The important question therefore arises, whether the Security Council has by Resolution 1483 shared or delegated those responsibilities to a Member State which is also an occupying power.

51. The powers of the Security Council under Chapter VII of the UN Charter are broad. There is a view that when acting under Chapter VII with the arguable exception of *ius cogens* (i.e. peremptory norms of international law which permit of no derogation) the Security Council is not bound to respect international law apart from the Charter itself,[22] although it must be guided by the purposes and principles of the UN Charter set out in Articles 1 and 2 and by the principle of proportionality.[23] This view is, however, rejected by Judge Mohammed Bedjaoui in the New World Order and the Security Council, Testing the Legality of Its Acts[24] at 34-5. The Security Council has nonetheless a very wide margin of appreciation in making determinations under Article 39 that there is a threat to the peace or breach of the peace, limited by the purposes and principles of the UN Charter and the obligation to act in good faith.[25] The Security Council also has a wide discretion to select measures under Articles 41 and 42, though it would also be bound by the purposes and principles of the UN Charter.[26] Schweigman states:[27]

> "As seen above this inter alia implies a duty to act in good faith, meaning that one should determine "whether the responsive measure selected by the Security Council was commensurate with the threat to the peace it had identified. In this context Brownlie observes that the concepts of "purpose and necessity" are relevant to the Council's choice of measures under Articles 41 and 42 particularly because it "cannot be ex hypothesi necessary to select a method of implementation which is incompatible with general international law." And Shaw also takes note of the "extensive" discretion afforded the Security Council under the Charter scheme "as regards actions taken consequent upon the determination in order to maintain or restore international peace and security". At the same time he maintains that:

> *the more subsidiary such measures are and the further away from the initial action taken in the exercise of the primary responsibility to restore international peace and security, the stronger grows the case for the application of international legal principles.*"

52. As explained above, in our view, the military action taken by the US and the UK against Iraq was taken in breach of international law. The Security Council adopted Resolution 1483 without making a determination one way or the other about the lawfulness of the US and UK action against Iraq and ensuing occupation. Can the Security Council be said to be acting in accordance with the purposes and principles of the UN Charter by calling upon an unlawful aggressor to administer the territory of the country it has unlawfully invaded? To the extent that the Security Council is doing no more than calling upon the US and the UK to comply with the obligations which those states have in any event under the Hague Regulations and Geneva Convention IV, in our view this does not exceed the limits of the Security Council's powers. As highlighted above the Security Council has a broad discretion in deciding whether there is a threat to the peace, breach of the peace or act of aggression under Article 39, and a broad discretion in deciding what actions to take in order to eliminate it under Articles 41 and 42. In our view the Security Council cannot be said to be obliged to call upon the US and the UK to withdraw from Iraq, nor can it be said to be acting in bad faith or otherwise in contravention of the purposes and principles of the UN Charter for deciding that it was in the interests of peace and security for the US and the UK to remain in Iraq as administering powers in accordance with international law.

53. The position is, in our view, more complex in relation to any argument that Resolution 1483 implicitly authorises the US and the UK to play a role in the nation-building and economic reconstruction of Iraq. Neither are rights or powers which the US and the UK can claim at international law for the reasons set out above. These are powers reserved exclusively to the Security Council under Article 41 of the Charter. Furthermore Resolution 1483 expressly confirms the UK and the US's status as occupying powers and calls upon them (operative paragraph 5) to act in accordance with their obligations under Geneva Convention IV and the Hague Regulations.

54. Danesh Sarooshi argues that, since the Security Council is exercising powers delegated to it by Member States under Article 24 of the UN Charter, powers which it must exercise in compliance with the Purposes and Principles of the United Nations, it cannot delegate certain of its functions under Chapter VII to a Member State, and must retain

effective authority and control over those functions which it does delegate (Danesh Sarooshi, The United Nations and the Development of Collective Security, (Oxford, 1999), at pp154-5). Sarooshi also argues that the limitations on delegation mean that the terms of a resolution which delegates Chapter VII powers are to be interpreted narrowly (The United Nations and the Development of Collective Security, above, at p 44). The argument that Chapter VII resolutions should be narrowly interpreted is echoed in the Charter of the United Nations, A Commentary:[28]

> *"..Chapter VII resolutions should, in general, be interpreted narrowly. If their wording is ambiguous, this most often reflects a compromise and therefore indicates that no agreement has been reached on a certain measure. Such agreement of nine members and the absence of objection by the permanent members, however, constitute the sole authority upon which this measure rests. In their absence, the basis of such a far-reaching encroachment upon the rights of a member State as caused by enforcement action is doubtful. For SC resolutions under Chapter VII, it seems therefore warranted to have recourse to the old rule of interpretation according to which limitations of sovereignty may not be lightly assumed."*

55.   The US and the UK's joint letter of 8 May 2003, which envisages the UN's Special Representative playing a minor role, notwithstanding, there is no point in Resolution 1483 where the Security Council expressly delegates its powers under Article 41 to the Authority. It follows, in our view, that operative paragraphs 8 and 9, when they refer to '*in coordination with the Authority*" or "*with the help of the authority*" or "*working intensively with the Authority*" should be construed narrowly. When construed narrowly, with the UK and the US's obligations under international law, which have been carefully emphasised in the earlier parts of the Resolution, in mind, it becomes clear that the responsibilities for nation-building set out in those paragraphs rest primarily with the Special Representative and the people of Iraq, with the US and the UK as the occupying powers playing merely a facilitating and not a decisive role.

56.   If therefore the UK seeks to play more than a facilitating role in the carrying out of the functions described at operative paragraphs 8 and 9, it would be acting in breach of its obligations under international law, and exceeding its mandate under Resolution 1483.

Conclusion

57. In our view while the invasion and subsequent occupation of Iraq by the US and the UK was unlawful at international law, Resolution 1483 has rendered the continuing occupation of Iraq by the US and the UK lawful, subject to the limits on the conduct of that occupation contained in international law. In our view, the responsibilities and obligations of the US and the UK remain limited by the Hague Regulations and Geneva Convention IV, and on a proper construction of Resolution 1483 the primary responsibility for nation-building, judicial reform and economic reconstruction rests with the Special Representative appointed in accordance with operative paragraph 8. While Resolution 1483 envisages that the US and the UK will be involved in those processes, in our view such involvement must remain administrative and logistical in order for it to comply with the US and the UK's obligations under international law, which are reaffirmed by Resolution 1483.

Rabinder Singh QC
Charlotte Kilroy
Matrix Chambers
Gray's Inn
London WC1R 5LN
23 July 2003

IN THE MATTER OF THE LEGALITY OF THE OCCUPATION OF IRAQ BY UK ARMED FORCES

OPINION

Charlotte Kilroy
Matrix Chambers
Public Interest Lawyers

FOOTNOTES

[1] Edited by Dieter Fleck, OUP, 1995, 1999

[2] Opinion dated 15 November 2002 on whether the United Kingdom (**UK**) could rely on United Nations Security Council Resolution 1441 (**Resolution 1441**) (**OP1441**); Opinion dated 23 January 2003 on whether the UK could rely on Resolutions 678 and 687 (**OP678**) to use force against Iraq

[3] See the Statement of the Attorney General given to the House of Lords on 17 March 2003.

[4] See Adam Roberts, *What is a Military Occupation?*, 55 British Yearbook of International Law, 249 at 294, and Christopher Greenwood, *The Administration of Occupied Territory in International Law*, in International Law and the Administration of Occupied Territories, Clarendon, 1992 at 243.

[5] Geneva Convention IV, Commentary, Pictet, Geneva, 1958 at 273

234

[6]Page 245

[7]Greenwood, op cit at 247

[8]Gasser, Op cit at p. 256.

[9]See also Christopher Greenwood op cit at p 256: *"Where there is no functioning administrative structure or that structure is not capable of providing an adequate government in the unusual circumstances of belligerent occupation, the occupant is entitled to create such new administrative bodies as are necessary. Where, however the occupant finds a functioning administrative structure already in place, there is a presumption that that structure will be retained even if some or all of the officials are removed from their posts. Departures from the existing structure will be justified only where they are necessary to enable the occupant to meet the needs of its armed forces or to discharge its governmental duties under the Hague Regulations and the Fourth Geneva Convention."*

[10]*Powers and Duties of an Occupant in Relation to Land and Natural Resources*, in International Law and the Administration of Occupied Territories, Clarendon, 1992 at 422-423

[11]See for example Gasser, op cit at p 251-2

[12]See *ASIL Insights* Security Council Resolution 1483 on the Rebuilding of Iraq by , May 2003, http://www.asil.org/insights/insigh107.htm

[13]Second Edition, 2002 at p 708

[14]See by contrast UN Security Council Resolutions 384 and 389 in which the Security Council called upon Indonesia to immediately withdraw its forces from East Timor

[15]See Bruno Simma, op cit at p 739

[16]Christopher Greenwood, op cit at 244-5

[17]Op cit at p 257

[18]The UN as Human Rights Violator? Some Reflections on the United Nations Changing Human Rights Responsibilities, Human Rights Quarterly, 25, 2003 314, at 327- 330

[19]Ibid at 329

[20]See Bruno Simma ed, op cit at 743-4; The United Nations Transitional Administrations in Kosovo and East Timor: A First Analysis, Carsten Stahn, Max Planck UNYB (2001) 105 at 139

[21]The Security Council may decide what measures not involving the use of armed force are to be employed to give effect to its decisions, and it may call upon the Members of the United Nations to apply such measures. These may include complete or partial interruption of economic relations and of rail, sea, air, postal, telegraphic, radio, and other means of communication, and the severance of diplomatic relations

[22]See Frederic Megret and Florian Hoffman op cit at 330-333

[23]Bruno Simma ed at 711

[24]See Simma at 711; and The Authority of the Security Council under Chapter VII of the UN Charter, Legal Limits and the Role of the ICJ, David Schweigman, Kluwer, 2001 at 165-182

[25]1994, Kluwer

[26]Schwiegman ibid at 185-189

[27]Schweigman ibid at page 189-192

[28]Ibid at page 190- 91

[29]Op cit at 713

APPENDIX: NOTICE TO HER MAJESTY'S GOVERNMENT REGARDING WAR CRIMES

16. LETTER TO PRIME MINISTER TONY BLAIR FROM PUBLIC INTEREST LAWYERS, 22 JANUARY 2003

The Right Honourable Tony Blair,
10 Downing Street, London SW1A 2AA

Fax: 0207 925 0918

22 January 2003

Your ref:

Our ref: PS/SA/

Dear Prime Minister

The legality of the use of force against Iraq

We enclose a copy of a letter sent today to your Cabinet colleagues, the Secretaries of State for Defence and Foreign and Commonwealth Affairs.

We are sure that your lawyers will advise you as to its contents and implications. It deals with the consequences for you, and other leaders of the UK Government, if the UK decides to become involved in the further use of force in Iraq, and if that use of force violates rules of international humanitarian law (IHL). Specifically, we make clear that if the UK acts so as to bring any breaches of IHL within the definition of "war crimes" we, and others, will take steps to ensure that you, and other leaders of the UK Government are held accountable within International Criminal Law.

We wish to address an additional and important point. It concerns your personal responsibility for the crime of aggression and a crime against peace. It is our clients' position that in present circumstances it appears likely that a decision by the UK Government to use further force against Iraq without a specific Security Council authorisation (which is as we write absent) will be a crime of aggression and, therefore, accordingly, a crime against peace. On the question of an authorisation from the Security Council we note that you told the House of Commons Liaison Committee on 21 January 2003 that the UK would be willing to use force against Iraq without a Security Council authorisation and specifically if one of the Permanent Members vetoed a resolution authorising force. Thus, as far as aggression is concerned, we wish to draw your attention to a specific passage of our attached letter to the Secretary of State for Defence in which we write:

"We wish to raise with you at the outset of this letter our clients' concerns that the UK Government (and its leaders) are about to use force in circumstances where a "crime of aggression" is being committed and, thus, a "crime against peace." Our reasoning on this is as follows:

1. You will be aware that the crime of aggression is included under Article 5 of the ICC Statute as one of the crimes along with genocide, crimes against humanity and war crimes, over which the ICC has jurisdiction. The ICC may not yet exercise jurisdiction over this crime, however, and will not be able to do so until an agreed definition of the crime is adopted in accordance with Articles 121 and 123 of the ICC Statute. There is nonetheless a broad consensus that the crime of aggression is a crime under international law.

2. Crimes against peace were punishable under Principle 6 of the Nuremberg Principles. Principle 6 defines crimes against peace as

   i) Planning, preparation, initiation or waging of a war of aggression or a war in violation of international treaties, agreements or assurances;

   ii) Participation in a common plan or conspiracy for the accomplishment of any of the acts mentioned under (i).

3. The International Military Tribunal at Nuremberg described aggression as the 'supreme international crime.'

4. The outlawing of aggressive war is reflected in Articles 1 and 2 of the United Nations Charter, and in particular in the prohibition on the use of force at Article 2(4). Article 1 (1) of the United Nations Charter states that the Purposes of the United Nations are (amongst other things)

   "To maintain international peace and security, and to that end: to take effective collective measures for the prevention and removal of threats to the peace, and for the suppression of acts of aggression or other breaches of the peace, and to bring about by peaceful means, and in conformity with the principles of justice and international law, adjustment or settlement of international disputes or situations which might lead to a breach of the peace."

   Article 2 states

   "..(3) All Members shall settle their international disputes by peaceful means in such a manner that international peace and security, and justice, are not endangered.

   (4) All Members shall refrain in their international relations from

the threat or use of force against the territorial integrity or political independence of any state, or in any other manner inconsistent with the Purposes of the United Nations."

5. On 9 September 2002 the Assembly of States Parties to the ICC Statute adopted a resolution proposed by the Preparatory Commission for the International Criminal Court in which it stated that it was desirous of continuing and completing the work on the crime of aggression and to that end established a special Working Group on the crime of aggression. The discussion paper which was attached to the Preparatory Commission's Draft Resolution suggested the following basic definition of the crime:

"For the purpose of the present Statute, a person commits a "crime of aggression" when, being in a position effectively to exercise control over or to direct the political or military action of a State, that person intentionally and knowingly orders or participates actively in the planning, preparation, initiation or execution of an act of aggression which, by its character, gravity and scale, constitutes a flagrant violation of the Charter of the United Nations."

6. Paragraph 2 of the discussion paper suggested that act of aggression be defined as an act referred to in United Nations General Assembly resolution 3314 (XXIX) ("Resolution 3314") of 14 December 1974. Article 1 of Resolution 3314 states:

"Aggression is the use of armed force by a State against the sovereignty, territorial integrity or political independence of another State, or in any other manner inconsistent with the Charter of the United Nations, as set out in this Definition."

Article 3 provides as follows:

"Any of the following acts, regardless of a declaration of war, shall, subject to and in accordance with the provisions of article 2, qualify as an act of aggression:

(a) The invasion or attack by the armed forces of a State of the territory of another State, or any military occupation, however temporary, resulting from such invasion or attack, or any annexation by the use of force of the territory of another State or part thereof;

(b) Bombardment by the armed forces of a State against the territory of another State or the use of any weapons by a State against the territory of another State;

(c) The blockade of the ports or coasts of a State by the armed forces of another State;

(d) An attack by the armed forces of a State on the land, sea or air forces, or marine and air fleets of another State;

(e) The use of armed forces of one State which are within the territory of another State with the agreement of the receiving State, in contravention of the conditions provided for in the agreement or any extension of their presence in such territory beyond the termination of the agreement;

(f) The action of a State in allowing its territory, which it has placed at the disposal of another State, to be used by that other State for perpetrating an act of aggression against a third State;

(g) The sending by or on behalf of a State of armed bands, groups, irregulars or mercenaries, which carry out acts of armed force against another State of such gravity as to amount to the acts listed above, or its substantial involvement therein.

7.   It is the widely held view of legal experts in the field that in the absence of the inherent right arising to take action in self-defence under Article 51 of the UN Charter, any military action taken by the United Kingdom against Iraq without a United Nations Security Council Resolution expressly authorising such force would be in clear violation of the UN Charter and international law."[1]

Thus the purpose of this letter is to put you on notice of two consequences of an illegal use of force against Iraq by the UK. First, as it is you who exercises the prerogative power to wage war it is you who will ultimately be held responsible for the crime of aggression and "crime against peace" we refer to above; second you and other leaders of the UK Government will be held accountable to the ICC in the Hague as we make clear in the attached letter to the Defence Secretary.

Please acknowledge receipt of this letter.

Yours faithfully

Public Interest Lawyers

[1].See Opinion of Professor Colin Warbrick, 30 October 2002, at www.matrixlaw.co.uk, and Opinion of Professor Vaughan Lowe of 19 December 2002 at http://www.bbc.co.uk/radio4/today/reports/international/iraq_hearing.shtml; ; Opinion of Rabinder Singh QC and Alison Macdonald, 10 September 2002; Opinion of Rabinder Singh QC and Charlotte Kilroy, 15 November 2002

17. LETTER FROM PUBLIC INTEREST LAWYERS TO DEFENCE SECRETARY GEOFF HOON, 22 JANUARY 2003

The Right Honourable Geoffrey Hoon MP

The Secretary of State for Defence, Ministry Of Defence

Whitehall, London SW1A 2HB

2 January 2003

Your ref:

Our ref: PS/SA/

Dear Sir,

PROPOSED USE OF FORCE AGAINST IRAQ – ISSUES OF INTERNATIONAL HUMANITARIAN LAW AND "WAR CRIMES"

We are acting for Mark Thomas, The Campaign for Nuclear Disarmament (CND) and other non-governmental organisations (NGOs).[1] We are asked to write to you to put you on notice as to the consequences of any decisions by the UK Government to use further force against Iraq[2] involving methods of attack or weapon systems that breach rules of international humanitarian law (IHL).[3] Specifically we make clear that if the UK acts so as to bring any breaches of IHL within the definition of "war crimes" we, and other, will take steps to ensure that you, and other leaders of the UK Government, are held accountable within international criminal law.

Summary

The purpose of this letter is to put the UK Government on notice as to the position if requirements of IHL are breached in the forthcoming war. From the outset of the use of force various NGOs working in the field will be collecting evidence as to whether the use of force against Iraq adheres to the fundamental requirements of the international humanitarian law, in particular to the principles of distinction, military necessity and proportionality. In analysing this evidence, our clients will seek to determine whether the force used provides evidence of crimes against humanity and war crimes in violation of international criminal law, specifically, Articles 7 and 8 of the International Criminal Court Statute (the ICC Statute) and sections 50 and 51 and schedule 8 of the International Criminal Court Act 2001. In due course, either before the end of the use of force or shortly after its end, NGOs' written and oral evidence will be presented to a tribunal. The tribunal will be organised by the Permanent People's Tribunal (PPT) based in Italy. Its panel will consist of eminent international lawyers and others experienced in this field. The panel will hear evidence from various NGOs and others as to whether requirements of IHL have been breached. If the panel finds that there have been breaches it will prepare a report giving its judgement. That judgement, and the supporting evidence of NGOs and others, will then be presented to the Prosecutor of the International Criminal Court (ICC). The Prosecutor will be urged to initiate investigations on his own initiative, on the basis of this report and evidence as he is empowered to do under Article 15 of the ICC Statute. Thereafter, those who have initiated this process including various NGOs will work with the Prosecutor as he analyses the seriousness of the information received and makes a decision as to whether or not there is a reasonable basis to proceed with an investigation (Articles 15 (2) and (3) of the ICC Statute). If there is, in the opinion of the tribunal, and the various NGOs a reasonable basis to proceed with an investigation we shall urge that this investigation proceed against yourself and other senior members of the UK Government responsible, at the highest level, for decisions as to how force is used against Iraq and its civilian population. It is our position that pursuant to Article 25 of the ICC Statute, you and other senior members of the UK Government will be responsible for any breaches of Articles 7 and 8 of the ICC Statute (defining "crimes against humanity" and "war crimes") notwithstanding the culpability of senior members of the armed forces. Thus we urge that you proceed in any forthcoming war with Iraq on the basis that if there are breaches by the UK Government of IHL you will at least be investigated by the Prosecutor and could likely face prosecution. Accordingly you should ensure that the use of force against Iraq complies with IHL and the principles of distinction, necessity, proportionality and humanity.

"Crime of Agression" and "Crimes against Peace"

We wish to raise with you at the outset of this letter our clients' concerns that the UK Government (and its leaders) are about to use force in circumstances where a "crime of aggression" is being committed and, thus, a "crime against peace." Our reasoning on this is as follows:

1.   You will be aware that the crime of aggression is included under Article 5 of the ICC Statute as one of the crimes along with genocide, crimes against humanity and war crimes, over which the ICC has jurisdiction. The ICC may not yet exercise jurisdiction over this crime, however, and will not be able to do so until an agreed definition of the crime is adopted in accordance with Articles 121 and 123 of the ICC Statute. There is nonetheless a broad consensus that the crime of aggression is a crime under international law.

2. Crimes against peace were punishable under Principle 6 of the Nuremberg Principles. Principle 6 defines crimes against peace as:

i) Planning, preparation, initiation or waging of a war of aggression or a war in violation of international treaties, agreements or assurances;

ii) Participation in a common plan or conspiracy for the accomplishment of any of the acts mentioned under (i).

3. The International Military Tribunal at Nuremberg described aggression as the 'supreme international crime.'

4. The outlawing of aggressive war is reflected in Articles 1 and 2 of the United Nations Charter, and in particular in the prohibition on the use of force at Article 2(4). Article 1 (1) of the United Nations Charter states that the Purposes of the United Nations are (amongst other things)

"To maintain international peace and security, and to that end: to take effective collective measures for the prevention and removal of threats to the peace, and for the suppression of acts of aggression or other breaches of the peace, and to bring about by peaceful means, and in conformity with the principles of justice and international law, adjustment or settlement of international disputes or situations which might lead to a breach of the peace."

Article 2 states

"..(3) All Members shall settle their international disputes by peaceful means in such a manner that international peace and security, and justice, are not endangered.

(4) All Members shall refrain in their international relations from the threat or use of force against the territorial integrity or political independence of any state, or in any other manner inconsistent with the Purposes of the United Nations."

5. On 9 September 2002 the Assembly of States Parties to the ICC Statute adopted a resolution [4] proposed by the Preparatory Commission for the International Criminal Court in which it stated that it was desirous of continuing and completing the work on the crime of aggression and to that end established a special Working Group on the crime of aggression. The discussion paper which was attached to the Preparatory Commission's Draft Resolution suggested the following basic definition of the crime:

"For the purpose of the present Statute, a person commits a "crime of aggression" when, being in a position effectively to exercise control over or to direct the political or military action of a State, that person intentionally and knowingly orders or participates actively in the planning, preparation, initiation or execution of an act of aggression which, by its character, gravity and scale, constitutes a flagrant violation of the Charter of the United Nations."

6.   Paragraph 2 of the discussion paper suggested that act of aggression be defined as an act referred to in United Nations General Assembly resolution 3314 (XXIX) ("Resolution 3314") of 14 December 1974. Article 1 of Resolution 3314 states:

"Aggression is the use of armed force by a State against the sovereignty, territorial integrity or political independence of another State, or in any other manner inconsistent with the Charter of the United Nations, as set out in this Definition."

Article 3 provides as follows:

"Any of the following acts, regardless of a declaration of war, shall, subject to and in accordance with the provisions of article 2, qualify as an act of aggression:

(a) The invasion or attack by the armed forces of a State of the territory of another State, or any military occupation, however temporary, resulting from such invasion or attack, or any annexation by the use of force of the territory of another State or part thereof,

(b) Bombardment by the armed forces of a State against the territory of another State or the use of any weapons by a State against the territory of another State;

(c) The blockade of the ports or coasts of a State by the armed forces of another State;

(d) An attack by the armed forces of a State on the land, sea or air forces, or marine and air fleets of another State;

(e) The use of armed forces of one State which are within the territory of another State with the agreement of the receiving State, in contravention of the conditions provided for in the agreement or any extension of their presence in such territory beyond the termination of the agreement;

(f) The action of a State in allowing its territory, which it has placed at the disposal of another State, to be used by that other State for perpetrating an act of aggression against a third State;

(g) The sending by or on behalf of a State of armed bands, groups, irregulars or mercenaries, which carry out acts of armed force against another State of such gravity as to amount to the acts listed above, or its substantial involvement therein.

It is the widely held view of legal experts in the field that in the absence of the inherent right arising to take action in self-defence under Article 51 of the UN Charter, any military action taken by the United Kingdom against Iraq without a United Nations Security Council Resolution expressly authorising such force would be in clear violation of the UN Charter and international law[5].

Background to our clients' concerns

Our clients' concerns are that, based on evidence of the use of armed force in the Gulf War in 1991, in Kosovo and in Afghanistan the US and the UK have clearly breached fundamental requirements of IHL in the past. Thus there is every reason to believe that these requirements will be breached again in any forthcoming war in Iraq. You are better placed than ourselves or the various NGOs that we represent to know the detail of the impacts of the use of force in the Gulf, Kosovo and, more recently, Afghanistan. You will, of course, appreciate that these three recent examples all pre-date July 2002 when the ICC came into being and that its jurisdiction over these matters requires now a fundamentally different approach by the UK. However, our clients' concerns include the following:

ILLEGITIMATE MEANS AND METHODS OF ATTACK

* The unannounced bombing of Amiraya Civilian Air Raid Shelter in Baghdad killing between 600 and 1000 civilians on February 13 1991 when it was known by coalition forces that the facility had been previously used as a civil-defence shelter;

* The deliberate killing of thousands of civilians especially Palestinians, killed as they tried to escape from Kuwait City after February 26 1991;

* What appears to have been the deliberate massacre, without quarter, of tens of thousands of Iraqi soldiers and civilians on the road to Basra on February 26 and 27, 1991;

* The bombing of cities which served as major military communications and supply centres, for example Basra, Ramadi, Diwaniya and Mosul;

* The fact that 93% of the bombs used were free-falling bombs and that most appeared to have been dropped from higher than 30,000 feet;

* The fact that only 7,000 tons were guided bombs leaving 82,000 tons of bombs used that were non-precision guided;

* The use by the US of massive amounts of fire bombs;

* The use by the US of fuel air explosives;

* The use by the US of BLU-82s (otherwise known as "daisy cutters");

* The use of cluster bombs and anti-personnel bombs;

- The use of the weapon system CBU-75 carrying 1800 bomblets called Sadeyes (each bomblet contains 600 razor sharp steel fragments lethal up to 40 feet).

- The declaration of Basra as a "free fire zone";

- The use of carpet bombing techniques;

- The targeting of chemical plants;

- The use of at least 320 tons of depleted uranium ammunition in air and tank rounds and sniper bullets.[6]

ATTACKS ON OBJECTS DEDICATED TO CIVILIAN PURPOSES

- The destruction of civilian targets such as the Iraqi Ministries of Justice and Municipal Affairs;

- The destruction of between 10 to 20,000 homes, apartments, and other dwellings;

- The destruction of commercial centres with shops, retail stores, offices, hotels, restaurants and other public accommodation destroyed;

- The destruction or damage of scores of schools, hospitals, mosques and churches;

- The targeting of isolated Bedouin tents in Western Iraq leaving 46 dead civilians, including infants and children;

- The bombing of the "baby-milk" factory in Abu Gharaib on January 22 1991

DESTRUCTION OF IRAQI INFRASTRUCTURE

- The deliberate disproportionate targeting and destruction of Iraq's infrastructure towards the end of the war leaving it in a pre-industrial condition. Among the facilities targeted and destroyed were:

- Electricity power generation, relay and transmission

- Water treatment, pumping and distribution systems and reservoirs

- Telephone and radio exchanges, relay stations, towers and transmission facilities

- Food processing, storage and distribution facilities and markets, infant milk formula and beverage plants, animal vaccination facilities and irrigation sites

- Railroad transportation facilities, bus depots, bridges, highway overpasses, highways, highway repair stations, trains, buses and other public transportation vehicles, commercial and private vehicles

- Oil wells and pumps, pipelines, refineries, oil storage tanks, gasoline filling stations and fuel delivery tanks, cars and trucks, and kerosene storage tanks

- Sewage treatment and disposal systems

- Factories engaged in civilian production, for example, textile and automobile assembly

- Historical markers and ancient sites

- As a result of the above the deaths of tens of thousands of civilians from dehydration, dysentery and diseases caused by impure water, inability to obtain effective medical assistance and debilitation from hunger, shock, cold and stress;

CIVILIAN LOSSES IN AFGHANISTAN

- Disproportionate and indiscriminate bombardment of Afghanistan resulting in at least 3,767 civilians being killed between October 7 and December 6, 2001, in particular:

- Repeated bombing of the farming village of 450 persons of Karam, killing at least 160 civilians on October 11;

- Falling of a cluster bomb on the military hospital and mosque in Herat, killing 100 on October 21;

- Carpet-bombing by B-52's of a frontline village near Khanabad, killing at least 150 civilians on November 18. •

CIVILIAN LOSSES DURING NATO AIR STRIKES IN KOSOVO

- At least 489 civilians killed in the ninety separate incidents in Operation Allied Force, almost half of which resulted from attacks during daylight hours, when civilians could have been expected to be on the roads and bridges or in public buildings which may have been targeted;

- The most dramatic losses of civilian life came from attacks on fleeing or travelling refugees including repeated attacks on refugees on the Djakovica-Decane road, near Korisa and Savine Vode;

- Bombing of Dubrava prison on 21 May 1998;

- Attacks on populated urban areas in Belgrade, Nis and Vranje

- Use of cluster bombs, resulting in deaths of some 90 to 150 civilians and Britain's refusal to discontinue their use even after NATO confirmation of responsibility for the attack on Nis airfield in southern Serbia on May 7, 1998 and subsequent prohibition of cluster bomb use imposed on the US forces by the White House.

- Failure to provide clear advance warning of the attacks on state Serb Radio and Television headquarters in Belgrade on April 23, 1998 resulting in civilian deaths

The information that leads us to these conclusion includes:

- Personal accounts from representatives of NGOs.

- The report of the Commission of Inquiry for the International War Crimes Tribunal ("War Crimes. A report on United States war crimes against Iraq to the Commission of Inquiry for the International War Crimes Tribunal" by Ramsey Clark and others, available at www.deoxy.org/wc/wc-index.htm)

- Needless Deaths in the Gulf War, Human Rights Watch, available www.hrw.org/reports/1991/ gulfwar/

- The Secret behind the Sanctions: how the US intentionally destroyed Iraq's water supply, Thomas Nagy, available at www.progressive.org/0801icsue/nagy0901.html

- Joint WHO/UNICEF team report: A visit to Iraq (New York: United Nations, 1991). A report to the Secretary General dated March 20 1991 by representatives of the UN Secretariat, UNICEF, UNDP, UNDRO, UNHCR, FAO and WHO.

- Amnesty International annual report 1991, pp122-124.

- Counting the Human Cost of the Gulf War, Medical Education Trust background paper, London, July 1991

- US Bombing: The myth of surgical bombing in the Gulf War, Paul Walker, evidence to the Commission of Inquiry for the International War Crimes Tribunal, May 11 1991, available at www.deoxy.org/wc/wc-myth.htm

- International Law and War Crimes, Michael Ratner, evidence to the Commission of Inquiry for the International War Crimes Tribunal, May 11 1991, available at www.deoxy.org/wc-ilaw.htm

- Highway to Hell, Michael Kelly, New Republic, April 1991: 12

- The Gulf War: Not so Clean, George Lopez, Bulletin of the Atomic Scientists, September 1991, vol 47, no.7, available at ww.thebulletin.org/issues/1991/ s91/s91lopez.html

- Iraqis Reduced to a "Rabble," General Asserts, R W Apple, JR, New York Times, March 1991, p1

- Report to the Secretary General on Humanitarian Needs in Kuwait and Iraq in the Immediate Post-Crisis Environment, Martti Ahtisaari, United Nations Report No. 5122366, March 20, 1991

- Testimony of Joyce Chediac, a Lebanese-American journalist, report presented to the Commission of Inquiry for the International War Crimes Tribunal, May 11, 1991 available at www.deoxy.org/wc/wc-death.htm

- Various reports from the Washington Post and the New York Times and agency reports from Reuters and Agence France Presse available at www.globalsecurity.org

- Collateral Damage: the health and environmental costs of war in Iraq, November 2002, available at www.medact.org
- Iraq: Consequences of a war, Professor Paul Rogers, Oxford Research Group, October 2002.
- War Plan Iraq, Milan Rai, ARROW Publications, 2002
- War on Iraq, Scott Ritter, Profile Books, 2002
- Targeting Iraq: Sanctions and Bombing in US Policy, Geoff Simons, Saqi Books, 2002
- Material from Defence publications particularly Defense News, Jane's Defence Weekly, Aviation Week and Space Technology.
- Depleted Uranium Weapons: Lessons from the 1991 Gulf War, Dan Fahey, Laka Foundation, May 1999
- A Dossier on Civilian Victims of United States' Aerial Bombing of Afghanistan: A Comprehensive Accounting, Professor Marc W. Herold, December 2001, available at www.ratical.org/ratville/CAH/civilDeaths.html
- Medical ethics and human rights violations: the Iraqi occupation of Kuwait and its aftermath, Troyan Brennan and Robert Kirschner, Annals of Internal Medicine, 117:78-82 (1992)
- Civilian Deaths in the NATO Air Campaign - The crisis in Kosovo, report by the Human Rights Watch, available at www.hrw.org/reports/2000/nato/Natbm200-01.htm

We should make clear that our clients' main concerns are the civilian casualties caused by indiscriminate and/or disproportionate attacks. Further our clients are extremely concerned about the consequent civilian casualties caused by attacks on the economic infrastructure of Iraq as happened in the 1991 Gulf War.

To add to our clients' concerns the following are noted:

Nuclear Weapons

We note that the US Nuclear Posture Review (NPR) submitted to Congress on 31 December 2001[7] makes clear that the United States continues to plan for massive retaliation or a pre-emptive counter force attack in response to an actual or imminent nuclear attack, and for use of nuclear weapons against an overwhelming conventional attack. Much concern has been expressed about the US's willingness to contemplate a "first strike" against non-nuclear weapons states and particularly those characterised as "rogue states." You have made clear to both the UK House of Commons Defence Committee and to the Jonathan Dimbleby programme on BBC TV that the UK also might under certain circumstances be willing to engage in a "first strike" use of nuclear weapons against a non-nuclear weapon state, namely Iraq. [8] This policy represents a fundamental breach of customary international law and particularly in the light of the International Court of Justice's Advisory Opinion on the Legality of the Threat or Use of Nuclear Weapons.[9] That opinion concludes at paragraph 105E:

"E. By seven votes to seven, by the president's casting vote,

It follows in the above-mentioned requirements that the threat or use of nuclear weapons would generally be contrary to the rules of international law applicable in armed conflict, and in particular the principles and rules of humanitarian law;

However, in view of the current state of international law, and of the elements of fact at its disposal, the Court cannot conclude definitively whether the threat or use of nuclear weapons would be lawful or unlawful in an extreme circumstance of self-defence, in which the very survival of a state would be at stake...."

It is clear that the threat to use chemical or biological weapons against UK deployed forces in the field is far short of a threat such that "the very survival" of the UK "is at stake." As such if the UK were to carry out the threat you have made to use nuclear weapons against Iraq in these circumstances it would be in clear breach of customary international law.

Other Weapons Systems

We know that in the Gulf War conflict from 1991, in Kosovo and in Afghanistan the following weapons systems have been used:

- Cluster bombs including the BL-755 and the US CBU-55B

- Fuel air explosives including the BLU-82B.

- The multiple launch rocket system

- Depleted uranium munitions including the British Challenger II and US M1A1, M1 and M60 tank rounds, aircraft rounds and 7.62mm calibre bullets.

Our client's concerns include that these weapons systems, and the UK's nuclear weapon system, all breach "intransgressible"[10] rules of IHL and in particular the rule on discrimination (Articles 48 and 51 (4) and (5) of the Protocol Additional to the Geneva Conventions of 12 August 1949, and relating to the protection of victims of international armed conflict (Protocol 1) adopted at Geneva, 8 June 1977 (hereafter referred to as AP1)).

Relevant provisions of International Humanitarian Law

The above noted incidents are all examples of where the use of force failed to comply with fundamental principles of IHL, in particular the conventional and customary rules of distinction, military necessity and

proportionality. You will be aware that failure to comply with these principles constitute grave breaches of the Geneva Conventions and will amount to violations of articles 7 and 8 of the ICC.

Art 35. Basic Rules

1. In any armed conflict, the right of the Parties to the conflict to choose methods or means or warfare is not unlimited.

2. It is prohibited to employ weapons, projectiles and materials and methods of warfare of a nature to cause superfluous injury or unnecessary suffering.

3. It is prohibited to employ methods or means of warfare which are intended or may be expected, to cause widespread, long-term and severe damage to the natural environment.

Art 48. Basic Rule

In order to ensure respect for and protection of the civilian population and civilian objects, the Parties to the conflict shall at all times distinguish between the civilian population and combatants and between civilian objects and military objectives and accordingly shall direct their operations against military objectives.

Art 49. Definition of attack and scope of application

1. "Attacks" means acts of violence against the adversary, whether inoffence or defence.

Art 51. Protection of the civilian population

1. The civilian population and individual civilians shall enjoy general protection against dangers arising from military operations. To give effect to this protection, the following rules, which are additional to other applicable rules of international law, shall be observed in all circumstances.

2. The civilian population as such, as well as individual civilians , shall not be the object of attack. Acts or threats of violence the primary purpose of which is to spread terror among the civilian population are prohibited.

3. Civilians shall enjoy the protection afforded by this section, unless and for such time as they take a direct part in hostilities.

4. Indiscriminate attacks are prohibited. Indiscriminate attacks are:

    (a)   those which are not directed at a specific military objective;

    (b)   those which employ a method or means of combat which cannot be directed at a specific military objective; or

    (c)   those which employ a method or means of combat the effects of which cannot be limited as required by this Protocol; and consequently, in each such case, are of a nature to strike military objectives and civilians or civilian objects without distinction.

5.   Among others, the following types of attacks are to be considered as indiscriminate:

(a)   an attack by bombardment by any methods or means which treats as a single military objective a number of clearly separated and distinct military objectives located in a city, town, village or other area containing a similar concentration of civilians or civilian objects;

and

an attack which may be expected to cause incidental loss of civilian life, injury to civilians, damage to civilian objects, or a combination thereof, which would be excessive in relation to the concrete and direct military advantage anticipated.

....

Art 52. General protection of civilian objects

1.   Civilian objects shall not be the object of attack or of reprisals. Civilian objects are all objects which are not military objectives as defined in paragraph 2.

2.   Attacks shall be limited strictly to military objectives. In so far as objects are concerned, military objectives are limited to those objects which by their nature, location, purpose or use make an effective contribution to military action and whose total or partial destruction, capture or neutralisation, in the circumstances ruling at the time, offers a definite military advantage.

3.   In case of doubt whether an object which is normally dedicated to civilian purposes, such as a place of worship, a house or other dwelling or a school, is being used to make an effective contribution, it shall be presumed not to be so used.

Art 54. Protection of objects indispensable to the survival of the civilian population

1.   ....

2.   It is prohibited to attack, destroy, remove or render useless objects indispensable to the survival of the civilian population, such as food-stuffs, agricultural areas for the production of food-stuffs, crops, livestock, drinking water installations and

supplies and irrigation works, for the specific purpose of denying them for their sustenance value to the civilian population or to the adverse Party, whatever the motive, whether in order to starve out civilians, to cause them to move away, or for any other motive. ....

Art 55. Protection of the natural environment

Care shall be taken in warfare to protect the natural environment against widespread, long-term and severe damage. This protection includes a prohibition of the use of methods or means of warfare which are intended or may be expected to cause such damage to the natural environment and thereby prejudice the health or survival of the population

....

Art 56. Protection of works and installations containing dangerous forces

1. Works or installations containing dangerous forces, namely dams, dykes and nuclear electrical generating stations, shall not be made the object of attack, even where these objects are military objectives, if such attack may cause the release of dangerous forces and consequent severe losses among the civilian population. Other military objectives located at or in the vicinity of these works or installations shall not be made the object of attack if such attack may cause the release of dangerous forces from the works or installations and consequent severe losses among the civilian population

....

Art 57. Precautions in attack

1. In the conduct of military operations, constant care shall be taken to spare the civilian population, civilians and civilian objects.

2. With respect to attacks, the following precautions shall be taken:

    (a) those who plan or decide upon an attack shall:

        (i) do everything feasible to verify that the objectives to be attacked are neither civilians nor civilian objects and are not subject to specific protection but are military objectives within the meaning of paragraph 2 of Article 52 and that it is not prohibited by the provisions of this Protocol to attack them;

        (ii) take all feasible precautions in the choice of

means and methods of attack with a view to avoiding, and in any event minimising, incidental loss of civilian life, injury to civilians and damage to civilian objects;

(iii) refrain from deciding to launch any attack which may be expected to cause incidental loss of civilian life, injury to civilians, damage to civilian objects, or a combination thereof, which would be excessive in relation to the concrete and direct military advantage anticipated;

(b) an attack shall be cancelled or suspended if it becomes apparent that the objective is not a military one or is subject to special protection or that the attack may be expected to cause incidental loss of civilian life, injury to civilians, damage to civilian objects, or a combination thereof, which would be excessive in relation to the concrete and direct military advantage anticipated;

(c) effective advance warning shall be given of attacks which may affect the civilian population, unless circumstances do not permit.

3. When a choice is possible between several military objectives for obtaining a similar military advantage, the objective to be selected shall be that the attack on which may be expected to cause the least danger to civilian lives and to civilian objects.

....

Art 59. Non-defended localities

1. It is prohibited for the Parties to the conflict to attack by any means whatsoever, non-defended localities.

....

Art 85. Repression of breaches of this Protocol

....

2. In addition to the grave breaches defined in Article 11, the following acts shall be regarded as grave breaches of this Protocol, when committed wilfully, in violation of the relevant provisions of this Protocol, and causing death or serious injury to body or health:

(a) making the civilian population or individual civilians the object of attack;

(b) launching an indiscriminate attack affecting the civilian population or civilian objects in the knowledge that such attack will cause excessive loss of life, injury to civilians or damage to civilian objects, as defined in Article 57, paragraph 2 (a)(i);

(c) launching an attack against works or installations containing dangerous forces in the knowledge that such attack will cause excessive loss of life, injury to civilians or damage to civilian objects, as defined in Article 57, paragraph 2 (a)(i);

(d) making non-defended localities and demilitarised zones the object of attack;

(e) making a person the object of attack in the knowledge that he is hors de combat;

(f) the perfidious use, in violation of Article 37, of the distinctive emblem of the red cross, red crescent or red lion and sun or of other protective signs recognised by the Conventions or this Protocol

. . . .

Specific Notice of Prohibition Under IHL of Certain Modes of Attack and Weapon Systems

Bearing in mind the above concerns our clients have emerging from the 1991 Gulf War and the use of force in Kosovo and Afghanistan, and in the light of the relevant provisions of ICC and IHL our clients wish to make clear that you are on notice that the following modes of attack or weapons systems are prohibited by IHL and if used will be the subject of evidence and a People's Tribunal report to the prosecutor of the Hague:

1. High level, indiscriminate, air-strikes on known centres of civilian population.

2. The use of carpet bombing techniques or other methods of attack that do not discriminate against civilians.

3. The use of fuel-air explosives, cluster bombs, multiple rocket launcher systems, depleted uranium, uranium, or uranium alloy munitions, or other indiscriminate weapon systems and, in particular the use of nuclear weapons, which may include B61-11s (tactical nuclear earth-penetrating weapons designed to destroy deep underground targets).[11]

4. The bombing of electricity supplies with consequent civilian casualties either related to those attacks or caused by the damage to plants reliant on electricity supplies, for example, water sanitation plants.

5. The bombing of works or installations containing dangerous forces, namely, dams, dykes and nuclear electrical generating stations.

This list of five summarises the specific concerns arising from the 1991 Gulf

War and the use of force in Kosovo. However it is without prejudice to our client's right to add to this list for any reason, for example, once the facts surrounding the use of force are known.

As far as weapons are concerned these are of particular concern to our clients particularly given the indiscriminate nature of weapon systems in the possession of both the US and the UK, and of those used in the 1991 Gulf War. As the International Court of Justice has noted in its Advisory Opinion on The Legality of The Threat or Use of Nuclear Weapons: "states do not have unlimited freedom of choice of means in the weapons they use." (Para 78). Thus our clients assert that the indiscriminate weapons we refer to above at 3 are prohibited by the rule of discrimination which the ICJ described in the Advisory Opinion on nuclear weapons as being an "intrasgressible rule." As the ICJ says in its Advisory Opinion on nuclear weapons: "States must never make civilians the object of attack and must consequently never use weapons that are incapable of distinguishing between civilian and military targets." (Para 78) The issue as to whether the UK has participated in the use of force against Iraq involving non-discriminatory weapon systems will assume critical importance in the tribunal we refer to above in the event of there being evidence of innocent civilian casualties due to attacks by indiscriminate weapon systems.

Relevant Provisions of International Criminal law

The following provisions of the Rome Statute creating the International Criminal Court (the ICC Statute) are relevant.

Article 7

Crimes against humanity

    1.   For the purpose of this Statute, 'crime against humanity' means any of the following acts when committed as part of a widespread or systematic attack directed against any civilian population, with knowledge of the attack:

        (a) Murder[12]

        (b) Extermination ....

        (k) Other inhumane acts of a similar character intentionally causing great suffering, or serious injury to the body or to mental or physical health.

    2.   For the purpose of paragraph 1:

        (a) 'Attack directed against any civilian population' means a course of conduct involving the multiple commission of acts referred to in paragraph 1 against any civilian population, pursuant to or in furtherance of a State or organisational policy to commit such attack;

(b) 'Extermination' includes the intentional infliction of conditions of life, inter alia, the deprivation of access to food and medicine, calculated to bring about the destruction of part of a population; ....

Article 8

War crimes

of such crimes.

2. For the purpose of this Statute, 'war crimes' means:

(a) Grave breaches of the Geneva Conventions of 12 August 1949, namely, any of the following acts against persons or property protected under the provisions of the relevant Geneva Convention:

(i) Wilful killing; ...

(iii) Wilfully causing great suffering, or serious injury to body or health;

(iv) Extensive destruction and appropriation of property, not justified by military necessity and carried out unlawfully and wantonly;

(b) Other serious violations of the laws and customs applicable in international law, namely any of the following acts:

(i) Intentionally directing attacks against the civilian population as such or against individual civilians not taking part in hostilities;

(ii) Intentionally directing attacks against individual civilian objects, that is, objects which are not military objectives;

Intentionally launching an attack in the knowledge that such attack will cause incidental loss of life or injury to civilians or damage to civilian objects or widespread, long-term and severe damage to the natural environment which would be clearly excessive in relation to the concrete and direct overall military advantage anticipated;

(v) Attacking or bombarding, by whatever means, towns, villages, dwellings or buildings which are undefended and which are not military objectives;

(ix) Intentionally directing attacks against buildings dedicated to religion, education, art, science, or charitable purposes, historic monuments, hospitals and places where the sick and wounded are collected, provided they are not military objectives;

(xii) Declaring that no quarter will be given

(xiii) Destroying or seizing the enemy's property unless such destruction or seizure be imperatively demanded by the necessities of war;

(xvii) Employing poison or poisoned weapons

(xviii)Employing asphyxiating, poisonous or other gases, and all analogous liquids, materials or devices;

(xxv) Intentionally using starvation of civilians as a method of warfare by depriving them of objects indispensable to their survival, including wilfully impeding relief supplies as provided for under the Geneva Conventions;

Article 15

Prosecutor

1. The Prosecutor may initiate investigations proprio motu on the basis of information on crimes within the jurisdiction of the court.

2. The Prosecutor shall analyse the seriousness of the information received. For this purpose, he or she may seek additional information from States, organs of the United Nations, intergovernmental or non-governmental organisations, or other reliable sources that he or she deems appropriate, and may receive written or oral testimony at the seat of the Court.

3. If the Prosecutor concludes that there is reasonable basis to proceed with an investigation, he or she shall submit to the Pre-Trial Chamber a request for authorisation of an investigation, together with any supporting material collected. Victims may make representations to the Pre-Trial Chamber, in accordance with the Rules of Procedure and Evidence.

4. If the Pre-Trial Chamber, upon examination of the request and the supporting material, considers that there is a reasonable basis to proceed with an investigation, and that the case appears to fall within the jurisdiction of the Court, it shall authorise the commencement of the investigation, without prejudice to subsequent determinations by the Court with regard to the jurisdiction and admissibility of a case.

5. The refusal of the Pre-Trial Chamber to authorise the investigation shall not preclude the presentation of a subsequent request by the Prosecutor based on new facts or evidence regarding the same situation.

6. If after the preliminary examination referred to in paragraphs 1 and 2,

the Prosecutor concludes that the information provided does not constitute a reasonable basis for an investigation, he or she shall inform those who provided the information. This shall not preclude the Prosecutor from considering further information submitted to him or her regarding the same situation in the light of new facts or evidence.

In terms of the specific concerns our clients have about modes of attack or weapons used itemised below at this stage we do not need to identify which specific provisions of Articles 7 and 8 (and the relevant Elements of Crime) cover the potential use of force against Iraq. For obvious reasons we cannot identify the relevant provisions prior to the facts emerging surrounding any use of force against Iraq. However the extracts from Articles 7 and 8 referred to above in our view cover the concerns outlined above from the 1991 Gulf War and the use of force in Kosovo. As you know it is our clients' concern now that these methods of attack and use of weapons will be repeated.

For the above mentioned crimes defined in Articles 7 and 8 we suggest that you read the elements of crime adopted by the Preparatory Commission for the International Criminal Court (PCNICC). These are self-explanatory and should make clear why it is our view that these are relevant in the above context. The crime defined by Article 8 (2)(b)(iv) if the ICC Statute is particularly relevant. It is noted that the actus reus of this offence is the launching of an attack to cause incidental loss of life or injury to civilians or damage to civilian objects or widespread, long-term, and severe damage to the natural environment in violation of the principles of necessity and proportionality.[13] The PCNICC have made clear that this crime "reflects the proportionality requirement inherent in determining the legality of any military activity undertaken in the context of an armed conflict" (document PCNICC/1999/WGEC/INF.2/ADD1, at 37-8). As it is our submission that Article 8(2)(b)(iv) is particularly relevant we think it helpful to draw your specific attention to the relevant Elements of Crime which read as follows:

"ARTICLE 8(2)(b)(iv)

War crime of excessive incidental death, injury or damage

Elements

1.   The perpetrator launched an attack.

2.   The attack was such that it would cause incidental death or injury to civilians or damage to civilian objects or widespread, long-term, and severe damage to the natural environment and that such death, injury, or damage would be of such an extent as to be clearly excessive in relation to the concrete and direct overall military advantage anticipated. 36

3.   The perpetrator knew that the attack would cause incidental death or injury to civilians or damage to civilian objects or widespread, long-term, an severe damage to the natural environment and that such death,

injury or damage would be of such an extent as to be clearly excessive in relation to the concrete and direct overall military advantage anticipated.37

4.   Conduct took place in the context of and was associated with an international armed conflict.

5.   The perpetrator was aware of factual circumstances that established the existence of an armed conflict.

(36). The expression "concrete and direct overall military advantage" refers to a military advantage that is foreseeable by the perpetrator at the relevant time. Such advantage may or may not be temporally or geographically related to the object of the attack. The fact that this crime admits the possibility of lawful incidental injury and collateral damage does not in any way justify any violation of the law applicable in armed conflict. It does not address justifications for war or other rules related to jus ad bellum. It reflects the proportionality requirement inherent in determining the legality of any military activity undertaken in the context of an armed conflict.

(37). As opposed to the general rule set forth in paragraph 4 of the General Introduction, this knowledge element requires that the perpetrator make the value judgement as described therein. An evaluation of that value judgement must be based on the requisite information available to the perpetrator at the time."

Kittichaisare notes as follows:

"In terms of the perpetrator's mens rea, the Elements depart from the general rule that it is not necessary for the perpetrator to have personally completed a particular value judgement. To be guilty of this war crime, the perpetrator must have known, in the sense of making the value judgement that the attack launched by him would cause incidental death or injury to civilians or damage to civilian objects or widespread, long-term and severe damage to the natural environment and that such death, injury or damage would be of such an extent as to be clearly excessive in relation to the concrete and direct overall military advantage anticipated. However, an evaluation of that value judgement must be based on the requisite information available to the perpetrator at the time.

It should be noted that there is no result requirement as part of the actus reus of this war crime. What is required is the act of launching the attack of the nature and with the perpetrator's state of mind as described above." (Kriangsak Kittichaisare, International Criminal Law, Oxford University Press, 2001, at 164).

The NGOs that we represent and the subsequent tribunal we refer to above will be examining the two elements of this crime with great care. In particular the state of mind of yourself and other senior members of the UK

Government will be judged in the light of the fact that this letter puts you on clear notice as to the requirements of IHL and the risk, that you may choose to ignore, of an investigation by the prosecutor if the use of force comes within the definitions of Articles 7 and 8 above.

Complicity

We now address the personal culpability of you as the UK's Secretary of State for Defence and other senior members of the UK Government in terms of complicity. In the 1991 Gulf War the US was the main participant but the UK provided active support and participated in some of the bombing raids. It might be thought that you and other members of the UK Government can escape responsibility for breaches of Articles 7 and 8 of the ICC Statute if the UK Government does no more than support a US led campaign. As we make clear below the ICC Statute and international criminal law establishes that in these circumstances you, and other senior members of the UK Government, may be held criminally liable for your participation in the commission of these offences.

Article 25 of the ICC Statute is relevant. It reads:

"Individual criminal responsibility

1. The Court shall have jurisdiction over natural persons pursuant to this Statute.

2. A person who commits a crime within the jurisdiction of the Court shall be individually responsible and liable for punishment in accordance with this Statute.

3. In accordance with this Statute, a person shall be criminally responsible and reliable for punishment for a crime within the jurisdiction of the Court if that person:

    (a) commits such a crime, whether as an individual, jointly with another or through another person, regardless of whether that other person is criminally responsible;

    (b) Orders, solicits or induces the commission of such a crime which in fact occurs or is attempted;

    (c) For the purpose of facilitating the commission of such a crime, aids, abets or otherwise assists in its commission or its attempted commission, including providing the means for its commission;

    (d) In any other way contributes to the commission or attempted commission of such a crime by a group of persons acting with a common purpose. Such contribution shall be intentional and shall either:

        (i) Be made with the aim of furthering the criminal activity or criminal purpose of the group, where such activity or purpose involves the commission of a crime within the jurisdiction of the Court; or

(ii) Be made in the knowledge of the intention of the group to commit the crime

....

Thus the ICC Statute recognises that in these circumstances you, and other members of the UK Government, may be an "accessory" or "secondary participant" in "complicity." Complicity is when two or more persons join together to play some part in the commission of a crime. Ordering, soliciting or inducing the commission of a crime as provided in Article 25 (3)(b) of the ICC Statute is no different from direct physical perpetration of the crime. As Lord Steyn put it in Pinochet, "there is no distinction between the man who strikes, and the man who orders another to strike." (R v Bow Street Metropolitan Stipendiary Magistrate, ex p Pinochet Ugarte [1998] 4 ALL ER 897, HL at 946).

The law of complicity is re-stated in the Ministries case that "he who participates [in a crime] or plays a consenting part therein" is guilty of a crime (US v Ernst von Weizsacker et al., TWC, 611, 470-1). In Tadic the International Criminal Tribunal for former Yugoslavia (ICTY) Appeals Chamber itself re-states the law as follows: "whoever contributes to the commission of crimes by the group of persons or some members of the group, in execution of a common purpose, may be held to be criminally liable, subject to certain conditions....." (Prosecutor v Dusko Tadic, case no. IT-94-1-A, ICTY APP.CH., 5 July 1999 at para 190.)

In the light of the above it is clear that the complicity of you, or other senior members of the UK Government, is as relevant for the purposes of potential breaches of Article 7 and 8 of the ICC Statute as if you were the main perpetrator. You should proceed accordingly.

Grave or Serious Breaches

You will be aware that Article 8 (2) of the ICC Statute deals with grave breaches of the 1949 Geneva Conventions of 12 August 1949. "Grave breaches" are serious war crimes that are subject to the universal jurisdiction of all states.[14] Moreover, if a state does not prosecute the offender it shall extradite him to any party to the respective Geneva Conventions that will prosecute and punish that person. Grave breaches must be committed against persons or property protected by any of the four Geneva Conventions of 1949, in particular civilians in the hands of a party to a conflict of which they are not nationals. Since the four Geneva Conventions of 1949 are a part of customary international law, so is the grave breach regime under these

Geneva Conventions. AP1 extends the definition of grave breaches. (See Articles 11, 44, 45, 73, 85(2) and (3)).

Article 8(2)(b) deals with other serious violations of the laws and customs applicable in international armed conflict. "Serious" means breach of a rule protecting important values, and the breach must involve "grave consequences" for the victim. All serious war crimes under AP1 and the Hague regulations are proscribed as war crimes under Article 8 (2)(b) of the ICC Statute.

Thus the concepts of "grave" and "serious" are relevant. We submit that in judging whether breaches are either "grave" or "serious" past breaches are relevant. Thus in deciding whether you, and other senior members of the UK Government, have been guilty of grave or serious breaches for the purposes of Article 8 we will invite the prosecutor, if in due course a report from the People's Tribunal referred to above is made, to take into account the UK Government's past misconduct during the 1991 Gulf War.

Command Responsibility

It is apposite, given your position within the Government, to address this question. Under the principle of command responsibility, a superior is criminally responsible for the acts committed by his subordinates if he knew or had reason to know that the subordinate was about to commit such acts or had done so and the superior failed to take the necessary and reasonable measures to prevent such acts or to punish the perpetrators thereof. This command responsibility emanates from a failure to act in breach of a clear, affirmative duty or moral obligation imposed by the law of war or by international law upon those in authority to act. When the superior acts positively by ordering, instigating, or planning criminal acts carried out by his subordinates, he incurs "direct" responsibility. However, if he fails to take measures to prevent or repress his subordinates' criminal act, his culpable omissions thereby incur "indirect" command responsibility. Where a superior fails to prevent or repress his subordinates' criminal acts he could be held liable for aiding and abetting or inciting the crimes if all the necessary elements for aiding and abetting or incitement, as the case may be, are present. (Prosecutor v Tihomir Blaskic, case no. IT-95-14-T, T.Ch..1 of the ICTY, 3 March 2000. Paras 337-9). This principle is also applicable to civilian, non-military commanders, who wield the requisite authority. International instruments and case law do not restrict this application to military commanders only but extend it to cover political leaders and other civilian superiors in positions of authority (Celebici, paras 356-63; Prosecutor v Alfred Musema, case no.ICTR-96-13-T, 27 Jan 2000, paras 136, 146-8). The crucial question is not the civilian or military status of the superior , but the degree of authority the superior exercises over his subordinates.

With the above principle of command responsibility in mind we consider it advisable that you copy this letter to those senior members of the UK Government who you know will be responsible for key decisions if the UK are to be involved with the use of force against Iraq.[15] Further, leaving aside the obvious requirement that you copy this letter to the senior members of the armed forces, we suggest that you copy this to those civilian superiors with the requisite degree of authority over their subordinates, who in accordance with the principle of command responsibility might be held liable if there are breaches of Article 7 and 8 of the ICC Statute. Finally we note that this principle has been transposed into UK law through Section 65 of the International Criminal Court Act 2001.

Your Evidence

If in due course it emerges that there is evidence of breaches of Articles 7 and 8 the tribunal we refer to above will sit in session to hear evidence from NGOs and others. Naturally you will be invited to submit your evidence to that tribunal on the issue of whether there have been breaches of Article 7 and 8. If in due course you decline to submit any evidence we will invite the prosecutor (if in due course a report from the tribunal is submitted to him), to draw such adverse inferences as may be appropriate. You are by this letter on notice of the intention to establish a People's Tribunal on this matter. We submit that if in due course it is your case that there have not been breaches of Articles 7 and 8 of the ICC Statute, you are now in a position where you know that your evidence on that point is highly relevant. Thus, if in due course you fail, or refuse, to produce evidence to show your innocence (or that of other members of the UK Government) of breaches of Articles 7 and 8 of the ICC Statute, in our view this will be highly admissible to show your guilt.

Conclusion

We suggest that you note carefully the contents of this letter and as we have suggested above copy it to all who might subsequently be held responsible for a breach of Articles 7 and 8 of the ICC Statute. You are on clear notice of the intention to present evidence to the prosecutor if it emerges that there have been breaches of Articles 7 and 8. We have made clear above the relationship between the Tribunal we describe and the prosecutor in the Hague using his Article 15 powers. You are required, if the UK participate in the use of armed force against Iraq, to ensure that the use of force does not breach Articles 7 and 8. A failure to ensure compliance will lead to the consequences set out in this letter.

Please acknowledge receipt of this letter within 14 days.

Yours faithfully
Public Interest Lawyers

FOOTNOTES

[1] We will provide a full list of these NGOs on request.

[2] We use the phrase "further force" deliberately as we note the continuing bombing raids to enforce the no-fly zones in Southern and Northern Iraq, that these have recently intensified, and that serious doubts exist among international lawyers as to their legality.

[3] We assume from recent press reports that in due course the UK will participate in a US led campaign against Iraq. We do not, of course accept that the use of force meets with the requirements of jus ad bellum or that all "peaceful means" to resolve the dispute have been exhausted (see Art. 33 of UN Charter).

[4] ICC-ASP/1/Res.1

[5] See Opinion of Professor Colin Warbrick, 30 October 2002, at www.matrixlaw.co.uk, and Opinion of Professor Vaughan Lowe of 19 December 2002 at http://www.bbc.co.uk/radio4/today/reports/ international/ iraq_hearing.shtml; Opinion of Rabinder Singh QC and Alison Macdonald, 10 September 2002; Opinion of Rabinder Singh QC and Charlotte Kilroy, 15 November 2002.

[6] In 1996 the UN Sub-Commision on the Promotion and Protection of Human Rights passed Resolution 96/16 which included weapons using depleted uranium as of "indiscriminate effect".

[7] Nuclear Posture Review report on the web at www.globalsecurity.org/ wmd/library/ policy/dod/ npr.htm

[8] Your evidence to the House of Commons Defence Committee 20 March 2002 records "....there are clearly some states who would be deterred by the fact that the United Kingdom possess nuclear weapons and has the willingness and ability to use them in appropriate circumstances. States of concern, I would be much less confident about, and Saddam Hussein has demonstrated in the past his willingness to use chemical weapons against his own people. In those kinds of states the wishes, needs and interests of citizens are clearly much less regarded and we cannot rule out the possibility that such states might be willing to sacrifice their own people in order to make that kind of gesture... they (states of concern) can be absolutely confident that in the right conditions we would be willing to use our nuclear weapons." (Paras 236-237).

On 24 March 2002 on the Jonathan Dimbleby programme on BBC you were asked whether nuclear use might be in response to non-nuclear weapons such as chemical or biological weapons and you replied: "Let me make it clear the long-standing British Government policy is that if our forces, if our people were threatened by weapons of mass destruction we would reserve the right to use appropriate proportionate responses which might....in extreme circumstances include the use of nuclear weapons. Later you were asked by the interviewer whether you would only use Britain's nuclear weapons system after an attack by Saddam Hussein using weapons of mass destruction and you replied: "Clearly if there were strong evidence of an imminent attack, if we knew that an attack was about to occur we could use our weapons to protect against it." (Transcript from the Jonathan Dimbleby programme 24 March 2002).

[9] ICJ Advisory Opinion, 8 July 1996, International Law Reports, vol. 110, pp.227-267.

[10] The International Court of Justice, in its Advisory Opinion on the Legality of the Threat or Use of Nuclear Weapons (8 July 1996) refer to fundamental rules of international law, such as the rule of discrimination, as being "intransgressible" rules: para. 78

[11] We make clear that it is the indiscriminate nature of these weapons systems, such as to breach "intransgressible" rules of IHL, that is relevant. It is not our clients' position that no particular weapons system, per se, is prohibited. In respect of Article 8 (2)(b)(xx) of the ICC Statute it is noted that the "comprehensive prohibition" and "annex to the ICC Statute" are not yet endorsed, and the Elements of Crime have not been drafted. However in respect of nuclear weapons, the threat or use of these must at all times (not withstanding the absence of a prohibition pursuant to article 8 (2)(b)(xx)) be consistent with the rules of proportionality and the "intransgressible" rules of IHL. As for cluster bombs we note that the chamber of the ICTY in the Martic rule 61 hearing stated "although there was not formal prohibition of the use of cluster bombs as such, the use of the Orkan rocket with a cluster bomb warhead in that case constituted evidence of the accused's intent to deliberately attack the civilian population" (Kittichaisaree, ibid, p.181).

[12] Kittichaisaree notes: "the actus reus of murder is the taking of the lives of persons taking no active part in hostilities in an internal armed conflict. The requisite mens rea is the intention to kill, or inflict serious injury in reckless disregard of human life. Recklessness means the taking of an excessive risk. ("Celebici" case, Case No. IT-96-21-T, ICTY T.Ch.ii quater, 16 Nov. 1998, paras 431,437-9) The specific elements of murder in this case are identical to murder as a crime against humanity, except for the context in which it takes place.

The Elements of Crime adopted by the PCNICC thus provide in this case that the perpetrator must have killed one or more persons who are either hors de combat, or were civilians, medical personnel, or religious personnel taking no active part in the hostilities, including those non-confessional, non-combatant military personnel carrying out a similar function. The perpetrator must have been aware of the factual circumstances that established this status of such person or persons." (ibid. p195)

[13] The International Court of Juctice's advisory opinion on the legality of the threat or use of nuclear weapons, 8 July 1996, at paragraph 30 states: "….states must take environmental considerations into account when assessing what is necessary and proportionate in the pursuit of legitimate military objectives. Respect for the environment is one of the elements that go to assessing whether an action is in conformity with the principles of necessity and proportionality."

[14] The concept of "Universal Jurisdiction" is important as it may be used in these circumstances by other states, who have ratified the Geneva Conventions, to demand that you, or other senior members of the UK Government, be extradited to stand trial in the requesting state.

[15] Other than the Prime Minister and the Secretary of State for Foreign and Commonwealth Affairs, whom we are formally serving (as we serve you) with this letter.

Editors' Note: There was no response to the letters to the Prime Minister and the Secretary of State for Defence apart from formal acknowledgements.

APPENDIX II
Some Security Council Resolutions cited in the Text
RESOLUTION 678 (1990)
Adopted by the Security Council at its 2963rd meeting
on 29 November 1990

The Security Council,

Recalling, and reaffirming its resolutions 660 (1990) of 2 August (1990), 661 (1990) of 6 August 1990, 662 (1990) of 9 August 1990, 664 (1990) of 18 August 1990, 665 (1990) of 25 August 1990, 666 (1990) of 13 September 1990, 667 (1990) of 16 September 1990, 669 (1990) of 24 September 1990, 670 (1990) of 25 September 1990, 674 (1990) of of 29 October 1990 and 677 (1990) of 28 November 1990.

Noting that, despite all efforts by the United Nations, Iraq refuses to comply with its obligation to implement resolution 660 (1990) and the above-mentioned subsequent relevant resolutions, in flagrant contempt of the Security Council,

Mindful of its duties and responsibilities under the Charter of the United Nations for the maintenance and preservation of internationalnd peace and security,

Determined to secure full compliance with its decisions,

Acting under Chapter VII of the Charter,

1. Demands that Iraq comply fully with resolution 660 (1990) and all subsequent relevant resolutions, and decides, while maintaining all its decisions, to allow Iraq one final opportunity, as a pause of goodwill, to do so;

2. Authorizes Member States co-operating with the Government of Kuwait, unless Iraq on or before 15 January 1991 fully implements, as set forth in paragraph 1 above, the foregoing resolutions, to use all necessary means to uphold and implement resolution 660 (1990) and all subsequent relevant resolutions and to restore international peace and security in the area;

3. Requests all States to provide appropriate support for the actions undertaken in pursuance of paragraph 2 of the present resolution;

4. Requests the States concerned to keep the Security Council regularly informed on the progress of actions undertaken pursuant to paragraphs 2 and 3 of the present resolution;

5. Decides to remain seized of the matter.

RESOLUTION 687 (1991)
Adopted by the Security Council at its 2981st meeting, on 3 April 1991

The Security Council,

Recalling its resolutions 660 (1990) of 2 August 1990, 661 (1990) of 6 August 1990, 662 (1990) of 9 August 1990, 664 (1990) of 18 August 1990, 665 (1990) of 25 August 1990, 666 (1990) of 13 September 1990, 667 (1990) of 16 September 1990, 669 (1990) of 24 September 1990, 670 (1990) of 25 September 1990, 674 (1990) of 29 October 1990, 677 (1990) of 28 November 1990, 678 (1990) of 29 November 1990 and 686 (1991) of 2 March 1991,

Welcoming the restoration to Kuwait of its sovereignty, independence and territorial integrity and the return of its legitimate Government,

Affirming the commitment of all Member States to the sovereignty, territorial integrity and political independence of Kuwait and Iraq, and noting the intention expressed by the Member States cooperating with Kuwait under paragraph 2 of resolution 678 (1990) to bring their military presence in Iraq to an end as soon as possible consistent with paragraph 8 of resolution 686 (1991),

Reaffirming the need to be assured of Iraq's peaceful intentions in the light of its unlawful invasion and occupation of Kuwait,

Taking note of the letter sent by the Minister for Foreign Affairs of Iraq on 27 February 1991 and those sent pursuant to resolution 686 (1991),

Noting that Iraq and Kuwait, as independent sovereign States, signed at Baghdad on 4 October 1963 "Agreed Minutes Between the State of Kuwait and the Republic of Iraq Regarding the Restoration of Friendly Relations, Recognition and Related Matters", thereby recognizing formally the boundary between Iraq and Kuwait and the allocation of islands, which were registered with the United Nations in accordance with Article 102 of the Charter of the United Nations and in which Iraq recognized the independence and complete sovereignty of the State of Kuwait within its borders as specified and accepted in the letter of the Prime Minister of Iraq dated 21 July 1932, and as accepted by the Ruler of Kuwait in his letter dated 10 August 1932,

Conscious of the need for demarcation of the said boundary,

Conscious also of the statements by Iraq threatening to use weapons in violation of its obligations under the Geneva Protocol for the Prohibition of the Use in War of Asphyxiating, Poisonous or Other Gases, and of Bacteriological Methods of Warfare, signed at Geneva on 17 June 1925, and of its prior use of chemical weapons and affirming that grave consequences would follow any further use by Iraq of such weapons,

Recalling that Iraq has subscribed to the Declaration adopted by all States participating in the Conference of States Parties to the 1925 Geneva Protocol and Other Interested States, held in Paris from 7 to 11 January 1989, establishing the objective of universal elimination of chemical and biological weapons,

Recalling also that Iraq has signed the Convention on the Prohibition of the Development, Production and Stockpiling of Bacteriological (Biological) and Toxin Weapons and on Their Destruction, of 10 April 1972,

Noting the importance of Iraq ratifying this Convention,

Noting moreover the importance of all States adhering to this Convention and encouraging its forthcoming Review Conference to reinforce the authority, efficiency and universal scope of the convention,

Stressing the importance of an early conclusion by the Conference on Disarmament of its work on a Convention on the Universal Prohibition of Chemical Weapons and of universal adherence thereto,

Aware of the use by Iraq of ballistic missiles in unprovoked attacks and therefore of the need to take specific measures in regard to such missiles located in Iraq,

Concerned by the reports in the hands of Member States that Iraq has attempted to acquire materials for a nuclear-weapons programme contrary to its obligations under the Treaty on the Non-Proliferation of Nuclear Weapons of 1 July 1968,

Recalling the objective of the establishment of a nuclear-weapons-free zone in the region of the Middle East,

Conscious of the threat that all weapons of mass destruction pose to peace and security in the area and of the need to work towards the establishment in the Middle East of a zone free of such weapons,

Conscious also of the objective of achieving balanced and comprehensive control of armaments in the region,

Conscious further of the importance of achieving the objectives noted above using all available means, including a dialogue among the States of the region,

Noting that resolution 686 (1991) marked the lifting of the measures imposed by resolution 661 (1990) in so far as they applied to Kuwait,

Noting that despite the progress being made in fulfilling the obligations of resolution 686 (1991), many Kuwaiti and third country nationals are still not accounted for and property remains unreturned,

Recalling the International Convention against the Taking of Hostages, opened for signature at New York on 18 December 1979, which categorizes all acts of taking hostages as manifestations of international terrorism,

Deploring threats made by Iraq during the recent conflict to make use of terrorism against targets outside Iraq and the taking of hostages by Iraq,

Taking note with grave concern of the reports of the Secretary-General of 20 March 1991 and 28 March 1991, and conscious of the necessity to meet urgently the humanitarian needs in Kuwait and Iraq,

Bearing in mind its objective of restoring international peace and security in the area as set out in recent resolutions of the Security Council,

Conscious of the need to take the following measures acting under Chapter VII of the Charter,

1. Affirms all thirteen resolutions noted above, except as expressly changed below to achieve the goals of this resolution, including a formal cease-fire;

A

2. Demands that Iraq and Kuwait respect the inviolability of the international boundary and the allocation of islands set out in the "Agreed Minutes Between the State of Kuwait and the Republic of Iraq Regarding the Restoration of Friendly Relations, Recognition and Related Matters", signed by them in the exercise of their sovereignty at Baghdad on 4 October 1963 and registered with the United Nations and published by the United Nations in document 7063, United Nations, Treaty Series, 1964;

3. Calls upon the Secretary-General to lend his assistance to make arrangements with Iraq and Kuwait to demarcate the boundary between Iraq and Kuwait, drawing on appropriate material, including the map transmitted by Security Council document S/22412 and to report back to the Security Council within one month;

4. Decides to guarantee the inviolability of the above-mentioned international boundary and to take as appropriate all necessary measures to that end in accordance with the Charter of the United Nations;

B

5. Requests the Secretary-General, after consulting with Iraq and Kuwait, to submit within three days to the Security Council for its approval a plan for the immediate deployment of a United Nations observer unit to monitor the Khor Abdullah and a demilitarized zone, which is hereby established, extending ten kilometres into Iraq and five kilometres into Kuwait from the boundary referred to in the "Agreed Minutes Between the State of Kuwait and the Republic of Iraq Regarding the Restoration of Friendly Relations, Recognition and Related Matters" of 4 October 1963; to deter violations of the boundary through its presence in and surveillance of the demilitarized zone; to observe any hostile or potentially hostile action mounted from the territory of one State to the other; and for the Secretary-General to report regularly to the Security Council on the operations of the unit, and immediately if there are serious violations of the zone or potential threats to peace;

6. Notes that as soon as the Secretary-General notifies the Security Council of the completion of the deployment of the United Nations observer unit, the conditions will be established for the Member States

cooperating with Kuwait in accordance with resolution 678 (1990) to bring their military presence in Iraq to an end consistent with resolution 686 (1991);

C

7. Invites Iraq to reaffirm unconditionally its obligations under the Geneva Protocol for the Prohibition of the Use in War of Asphyxiating, Poisonous or Other Gases, and of Bacteriological Methods of Warfare, signed at Geneva on 17 June 1925, and to ratify the Convention on the Prohibition of the Development, Production and Stockpiling of Bacteriological (Biological) and Toxin Weapons and on Their Destruction, of 10 April 1972;

8. Decides that Iraq shall unconditionally accept the destruction, removal, or rendering harmless, under international supervision, of:

(a) All chemical and biological weapons and all stocks of agents and all related subsystems and components and all research, development, support and manufacturing facilities;

(b) All ballistic missiles with a range greater than 150 kilometres and related major parts, and repair and production facilities;

9. Decides, for the implementation of paragraph 8 above, the following:

(a) Iraq shall submit to the Secretary-General, within fifteen days of the adoption of the present resolution, a declaration of the locations, amounts and types of all items specified in paragraph 8 and agree to urgent, on-site inspection as specified below;

(b) The Secretary-General, in consultation with the appropriate Governments and, where appropriate, with the Director-General of the World Health Organization, within forty-five days of the passage of the present resolution, shall develop, and submit to the Council for approval, a plan calling for the completion of the following acts within forty-five days of such approval:

(i) The forming of a Special Commission, which shall carry out immediate on-site inspection of Iraq's biological, chemical and missile capabilities, based on Iraq's declarations and the designation of any additional locations by the Special Commission itself;

(ii) The yielding by Iraq of possession to the Special Commission for destruction, removal or rendering harmless, taking into account the requirements of public safety, of all items specified under paragraph 8 (a) above, including items at the additional locations designated by the Special Commission under paragraph 9 (b) (i) above and the destruction by Iraq, under the supervision of the Special Commission,of all its missile capabilities, including launchers, as specified under paragraph 8 (b) above

  (iii) The provision by the Special Commission of the assistance and cooperation to the Director-General of the International Atomic Energy Agency required in paragraphs 12 and 13 below;

10. Decides that Iraq shall unconditionally undertake not to use, develop, construct or acquire any of the items specified in paragraphs 8 and 9 above and requests the Secretary-General, in consultation with the Special Commission, to develop a plan for the future ongoing monitoring and verification of Iraq's compliance with this paragraph, to be submitted to the Security Council for approval within one hundred and twenty days of the passage of this resolution;

11. Invites Iraq to reaffirm unconditionally its obligations under the Treaty on the Non-Proliferation of Nuclear Weapons of 1 July 1968;

12. Decides that Iraq shall unconditionally agree not to acquire or develop nuclear weapons or nuclear-weapons-usable material or any subsystems or components or any research, development, support or manufacturing facilities related to the above; to submit to the Secretary-General and the Director-General of the International Atomic Energy Agency within fifteen days of the adoption of the present resolution a declaration of the locations, amounts, and types of all items specified above; to place all of its nuclear-weapons-usable materials under the exclusive control, for custody and removal, of the International Atomic Energy Agency, with the assistance and cooperation of the Special Commission as provided for in the plan of the Secretary-General discussed in paragraph 9 (b) above; to accept, in accordance with the arrangements provided for in paragraph 13 below, urgent on-site inspection and the destruction, removal or rendering harmless as appropriate of all items specified above; and to accept the plan discussed in paragraph 13 below for the future ongoing monitoring and verification of its compliance with these undertakings;

13. Requests the Director-General of the International Atomic Energy Agency, through the Secretary-General, with the assistance and cooperation of the Special Commission as provided for in the plan of the Secretary-General in paragraph 9 (b) above, to carry out immediate on-site inspection of Iraq's nuclear capabilities based on Iraq's declarations and the designation of any additional locations by the Special Commission; to develop a plan for submission to the Security Council within forty-five days calling for the destruction, removal, or rendering harmless as appropriate of all items listed in paragraph 12 above; to carry out the plan within forty-five days following approval

by the Security Council; and to develop a plan, taking into account the rights and obligations of Iraq under the Treaty on the Non-Proliferation of Nuclear Weapons of 1 July 1968, for the future ongoing monitoring and verification of Iraq's compliance with paragraph 12 above, including an inventory of all nuclear material in Iraq subject to the Agency's verification and inspections to confirm that Agency safeguards cover all relevant nuclear activities in Iraq, to be submitted to the Security Council for approval within one hundred and twenty days of the passage of the present resolution;

14. Takes note that the actions to be taken by Iraq in paragraphs 8, 9, 10, 11, 12 and 13 of the present resolution represent steps towards the goal of establishing in the Middle East a zone free from weapons of mass destruction and all missiles for their delivery and the objective of a global ban on chemical weapons;

D

15. Requests the Secretary-General to report to the Security Council on the steps taken to facilitate the return of all Kuwaiti property seized by Iraq, including a list of any property that Kuwait claims has not been returned or which has not been returned intact;

E

16. Reaffirms that Iraq, without prejudice to the debts and obligations of Iraq arising prior to 2 August 1990, which will be addressed through the normal mechanisms, is liable under international law for any direct loss, damage, including environmental damage and the depletion of natural resources, or injury to foreign Governments, nationals and corporations, as a result of Iraq's unlawful invasion and occupation of Kuwait;

17. Decides that all Iraqi statements made since 2 August 1990 repudiating its foreign debt are null and void, and demands that Iraq adhere scrupulously to all of its obligations concerning servicing and repayment of its foreign debt;

18. Decides also to create a fund to pay compensation for claims that fall within paragraph 16 above and to establish a Commission that will administer the fund;

19. Directs the Secretary-General to develop and present to the Security Council for decision, no later than thirty days following the adoption of the present resolution, recommendations for the fund to meet the requirement for the payment of claims established in accordance with paragraph 18 above and for a programme to implement the decisions in paragraphs 16, 17 and 18 above, including: administration of the fund; mechanisms for determining the appropriate level of Iraq's contribution to the fund based on a percentage of the value of the exports of petroleum and petroleum products from Iraq not to exceed a figure to be

suggested to the Council by the Secretary-General, taking into account the requirements of the people of Iraq, Iraq's payment capacity as assessed in conjunction with the international financial institutions taking into consideration external debt service, and the needs of the Iraqi economy; arrangements for ensuring that payments are made to the fund; the process by which funds will be allocated and claims paid; appropriate procedures for evaluating losses, listing claims and verifying their validity and resolving disputed claims in respect of Iraq's liability as specified in paragraph 16 above; and the composition of the Commission designated above;

F

20. Decides, effective immediately, that the prohibitions against the sale or supply to Iraq of commodities or products, other than medicine and health supplies, and prohibitions against financial transactions related thereto contained in resolution 661 (1990) shall not apply to foodstuffs notified to the Security Council Committee established by resolution 661 (1990) concerning the situation between Iraq and Kuwait or, with the approval of that Committee, under the simplified and accelerated "no-objection" procedure, to materials and supplies for essential civilian needs as identified in the report of the Secretary-General dated 20 March 1991, and in any further findings of humanitarian need by the Committee;

21. Decides that the Security Council shall review the provisions of paragraph 20 above every sixty days in the light of the policies and practices of the Government of Iraq, including the implementation of all relevant resolutions of the Security Council, for the purpose of determining whether to reduce or lift the prohibitions referred to therein;

22. Decides that upon the approval by the Security Council of the programme called for in paragraph 19 above and upon Council agreement that Iraq has completed all actions contemplated in paragraphs 8, 9, 10, 11, 12 and 13 above, the prohibitions against the import of commodities and products originating in Iraq and the prohibitions against financial transactions related thereto contained in resolution 661 (1990) shall have no further force or effect;

23. Decides that, pending action by the Security Council under paragraph 22 above, the Security Council Committee established by resolution 661 (1990) shall be empowered to approve, when required to assure adequate financial resources on the part of Iraq to carry out the activities under paragraph 20 above, exceptions to the prohibition against the import of commodities and products originating in Iraq;

24. Decides that, in accordance with resolution 661 (1990) and subsequent related resolutions and until a further decision is taken by the Security

Council, all States shall continue to prevent the sale or supply, or the promotion or facilitation of such sale or supply, to Iraq by their nationals, or from their territories or using their flag vessels or aircraft, of:

(a) Arms and related materiel of all types, specifically including the sale or transfer through other means of all forms of conventional military equipment, including for paramilitary forces, and spare parts and components and their means of production, for such equipment;

(b) Items specified and defined in paragraphs 8 and 12 above not otherwise covered above;

(c) Technology under licensing or other transfer arrangements used in the production, utilization or stockpiling of items specified in subparagraphs (a) and (b) above;

(d) Personnel or materials for training or technical support services relating to the design, development, manufacture, use, maintenance or support of items specified in subparagraphs (a) and (b) above;

25. Calls upon all States and international organizations to act strictly in accordance with paragraph 24 above, notwithstanding the existence of any contracts, agreements, licences or any other arrangements;

26. Requests the Secretary-General, in consultation with appropriate Governments, to develop within sixty days, for the approval of the Security Council, guidelines to facilitate full international implementation of paragraphs 24 and 25 above and paragraph 27 below, and to make them available to all States and to establish a procedure for updating these guidelines periodically;

27. Calls upon all States to maintain such national controls and procedures and to take such other actions consistent with the guidelines to be established by the Security Council under paragraph 26 above as may be necessary to ensure compliance with the terms of paragraph 24 above, and calls upon international organizations to take all appropriate steps to assist in ensuring such full compliance;

28. Agrees to review its decisions in paragraphs 22, 23, 24 and 25 above, except for the items specified and defined in paragraphs 8 and 12 above, on a regular basis and in any case one hundred and twenty days following passage of the present resolution, taking into account Iraq's compliance with the resolution and general progress towards the control of armaments in the region;

29. Decides that all States, including Iraq, shall take the necessary measures to ensure that no claim shall lie at the instance of the Government of Iraq, or of any person or body in Iraq, or of any person claiming through

or for the benefit of any such person or body, in connection with any contract or other transaction where its performance was affected by reason of the measures taken by the Security Council in resolution 661 (1990) and related resolutions;

G

30. Decides that, in furtherance of its commitment to facilitate the repatriation of all Kuwaiti and third country nationals, Iraq shall extend all necessary cooperation to the International Committee of the Red Cross, providing lists of such persons, facilitating the access of the International Committee of the Red Cross to all such persons wherever located or detained and facilitating the search by the International Committee of the Red Cross for those Kuwaiti and third country nationals still unaccounted for;

31. Invites the International Committee of the Red Cross to keep the Secretary-General apprised as appropriate of all activities undertaken in connection with facilitating the repatriation or return of all Kuwaiti and third country nationals or their remains present in Iraq on or after 2 August 1990;

H

32. Requires Iraq to inform the Security Council that it will not commit or support any act of international terrorism or allow any organization directed towards commission of such acts to operate within its territory and to condemn unequivocally and renounce all acts, methods and practices of terrorism;

I

33. Declares that, upon official notification by Iraq to the Secretary-General and to the Security Council of its acceptance of the provisions above, a formal cease-fire is effective between Iraq and Kuwait and the Member States cooperating with Kuwait in accordance with resolution 678 (1990);

34. Decides to remain seized of the matter and to take such further steps as may be required for the implementation of the present resolution and to secure peace and security in the area.

RESOLUTION 1441 (2002)
Adopted by the Security Council at its 4644th meeting, on 8 November 2002

The Security Council,

Recalling all its previous relevant resolutions, in particular its resolutions 661 (1990) of 6 August 1990, 678 (1990) of 29 November 1990, 686 (1991) of 2 March 1991, 687 (1991) of 3 April 1991, 688 (1991) of 5 April 1991, 707 (1991) of 15 August 1991, 715 (1991) of 11 October 1991, 986 (1995) of 14 April 1995, and 1284 (1999) of 17 December 1999, and all the relevant statements of its President,

Recalling also its resolution 1382 (2001) of 29 November 2001 and its intention to implement it fully,

Recognizing the threat Iraq's non-compliance with Council resolutions and proliferation of weapons of mass destruction and long-range missiles poses to international peace and security,

Recalling that its resolution 678 (1990) authorized Member States to use all necessary means to uphold and implement its resolution 660 (1990) of 2 August 1990 and all relevant resolutions subsequent to resolution 660 (1990) and to restore international peace and security in the area,

Further recalling that its resolution 687 (1991) imposed obligations on Iraq as a necessary step for achievement of its stated objective of restoring international peace and security in the area,

Deploring the fact that Iraq has not provided an accurate, full, final, and complete disclosure, as required by resolution 687 (1991), of all aspects of its programmes to develop weapons of mass destruction and ballistic missiles with a range greater than one hundred and fifty kilometres, and of all holdings of such weapons, their components and production facilities and locations, as well as all other nuclear programmes, including any which it claims are for purposes not related to nuclear-weapons-usable material,

Deploring further that Iraq repeatedly obstructed immediate, unconditional, and unrestricted access to sites designated by the United Nations Special Commission (UNSCOM) and the International Atomic Energy Agency (IAEA), failed to cooperate fully and unconditionally with UNSCOM and IAEA weapons inspectors, as required by resolution 687 (1991), and ultimately ceased all cooperation with UNSCOM and the IAEA in 1998,

Deploring the absence, since December 1998, in Iraq of international monitoring, inspection, and verification, as required by relevant resolutions, of weapons of mass destruction and ballistic missiles, in spite of the Council's repeated demands that Iraq provide immediate, unconditional, and unrestricted access to the United Nations Monitoring, Verification and

Inspection Commission (UNMOVIC), established in resolution 1284 (1999) as the successor organization to UNSCOM, and the IAEA, and regretting the consequent prolonging of the crisis in the region and the suffering of the Iraqi people,

Deploring also that the Government of Iraq has failed to comply with its commitments pursuant to resolution 687 (1991) with regard to terrorism, pursuant to resolution 688 (1991) to end repression of its civilian population and to provide access by international humanitarian organizations to all those in need of assistance in Iraq, and pursuant to resolutions 686 (1991), 687 (1991), and 1284 (1999) to return or cooperate in accounting for Kuwaiti and third country nationals wrongfully detained by Iraq, or to return Kuwaiti property wrongfully seized by Iraq,

Recalling that in its resolution 687 (1991) the Council declared that a ceasefire would be based on acceptance by Iraq of the provisions of that resolution, including the obligations on Iraq contained therein,

Determined to ensure full and immediate compliance by Iraq without conditions or restrictions with its obligations under resolution 687 (1991) and other relevant resolutions and recalling that the resolutions of the Council constitute the governing standard of Iraqi compliance,

Recalling that the effective operation of UNMOVIC, as the successor organization to the Special Commission, and the IAEA is essential for the implementation of resolution 687 (1991) and other relevant resolutions,

Noting that the letter dated 16 September 2002 from the Minister for Foreign Affairs of Iraq addressed to the Secretary-General is a necessary first step toward rectifying Iraq's continued failure to comply with relevant Council resolutions,

Noting further the letter dated 8 October 2002 from the Executive Chairman of UNMOVIC and the Director-General of the IAEA to General Al-Saadi of the Government of Iraq laying out the practical arrangements, as a follow-up to their meeting in Vienna, that are prerequisites for the resumption of inspections in Iraq by UNMOVIC and the IAEA, and expressing the gravest concern at the continued failure by the Government of Iraq to provide confirmation of the arrangements as laid out in that letter,

Reaffirming the commitment of all Member States to the sovereignty and territorial integrity of Iraq, Kuwait, and the neighbouring States,

Commending the Secretary-General and members of the League of Arab States and its Secretary-General for their efforts in this regard,

Determined to secure full compliance with its decisions, Acting under Chapter VII of the Charter of the United Nations,

278

1. Decides that Iraq has been and remains in material breach of its obligations under relevant resolutions, including resolution 687 (1991), in particular through Iraq's failure to cooperate with United Nations inspectors and the IAEA, and to complete the actions required under paragraphs 8 to 13 of resolution 687 (1991);

2. Decides, while acknowledging paragraph 1 above, to afford Iraq, by this resolution, a final opportunity to comply with its disarmament obligations under relevant resolutions of the Council; and accordingly decides to set up an enhanced inspection regime with the aim of bringing to full and verified completion the disarmament process established by resolution 687 (1991) and subsequent resolutions of the Council;

3. Decides that, in order to begin to comply with its disarmament obligations, in addition to submitting the required biannual declarations, the Government of Iraq shall provide to UNMOVIC, the IAEA, and the Council, not later than 30 days from the date of this resolution, a currently accurate, full, and complete declaration of all aspects of its programmes to develop chemical, biological, and nuclear weapons, ballistic missiles, and other delivery systems such as unmanned aerial vehicles and dispersal systems designed for use on aircraft, including any holdings and precise locations of such weapons, components, sub-components, stocks of agents, and related material and equipment, the locations and work of its research, development and production facilities, as well as all other chemical, biological, and nuclear programmes, including any which it claims are for purposes not related to weapon production or material;

4. Decides that false statements or omissions in the declarations submitted by Iraq pursuant to this resolution and failure by Iraq at any time to comply with, and cooperate fully in the implementation of, this resolution shall constitute a further material breach of Iraq's obligations and will be reported to the Council for assessment in accordance with paragraphs 11 and 12 below;

5. Decides that Iraq shall provide UNMOVIC and the IAEA immediate, unimpeded, unconditional, and unrestricted access to any and all, including underground, areas, facilities, buildings, equipment, records, and means of transport which they wish to inspect, as well as immediate, unimpeded, unrestricted, and private access to all officials and other persons whom UNMOVIC or the IAEA wish to interview in the mode or location of UNMOVIC's or the IAEA's choice pursuant to any aspect of their mandates; further decides that UNMOVIC and the IAEA may at their discretion conduct interviews inside or outside of Iraq, may facilitate the travel of those interviewed and family members outside of Iraq, and that, at the sole discretion of UNMOVIC and the

IAEA, such interviews may occur without the presence of observers from the Iraqi Government; and instructs UNMOVIC and requests the IAEA to resume inspections no later than 45 days following adoption of this resolution and to update the Council 60 days thereafter;

6. Endorses the 8 October 2002 letter from the Executive Chairman of UNMOVIC and the Director-General of the IAEA to General Al-Saadi of the Government of Iraq, which is annexed hereto, and decides that the contents of the letter shall be binding upon Iraq;

7. Decides further that, in view of the prolonged interruption by Iraq of the presence of UNMOVIC and the IAEA and in order for them to accomplish the tasks set forth in this resolution and all previous relevant resolutions and notwithstanding prior understandings, the Council hereby establishes the following revised or additional authorities, which shall be binding upon Iraq, to facilitate their work in Iraq:

– UNMOVIC and the IAEA shall determine the composition of their inspection teams and ensure that these teams are composed of the most qualified and experienced experts available;

– All UNMOVIC and IAEA personnel shall enjoy the privileges and immunities, corresponding to those of experts on mission, provided in the Convention on Privileges and Immunities of the United Nations and the Agreement on the Privileges and Immunities of the IAEA;

– UNMOVIC and the IAEA shall have unrestricted rights of entry into and out of Iraq, the right to free, unrestricted, and immediate movement to and from inspection sites, and the right to inspect any sites and buildings, including immediate, unimpeded, unconditional, and unrestricted access to Presidential Sites equal to that at other sites, notwithstanding the provisions of resolution 1154 (1998) of 2 March 1998;

– UNMOVIC and the IAEA shall have the right to be provided by Iraq the names of all personnel currently and formerly associated with Iraq's chemical, biological, nuclear, and ballistic missile programmes and the associated research, development, and production facilities;

– Security of UNMOVIC and IAEA facilities shall be ensured by sufficient United Nations security guards;

– UNMOVIC and the IAEA shall have the right to declare, for the purposes of freezing a site to be inspected, exclusion zones, including surrounding areas and transit corridors, in which Iraq will suspend ground and aerial movement so that nothing is changed in or taken out of a site being inspected;

– UNMOVIC and the IAEA shall have the free and unrestricted use and landing of fixed- and rotary-winged aircraft, including manned and unmanned reconnaissance vehicles;

- UNMOVIC and the IAEA shall have the right at their sole discretion verifiably to remove, destroy, or render harmless all prohibited weapons, subsystems, components, records, materials, and other related items, and the right to impound or close any facilities or equipment for the production thereof; and

- UNMOVIC and the IAEA shall have the right to free import and use of equipment or materials for inspections and to seize and export any equipment, materials, or documents taken during inspections, without search of UNMOVIC or IAEA personnel or official or personal baggage;

8. Decides further that Iraq shall not take or threaten hostile acts directed against any representative or personnel of the United Nations or the IAEA or of any Member State taking action to uphold any Council resolution;

9. Requests the Secretary-General immediately to notify Iraq of this resolution, which is binding on Iraq; demands that Iraq confirm within seven days of that notification its intention to comply fully with this resolution; and demands further that Iraq cooperate immediately, unconditionally, and actively with UNMOVIC and the IAEA;

10. Requests all Member States to give full support to UNMOVIC and the IAEA in the discharge of their mandates, including by providing any information related to prohibited programmes or other aspects of their mandates, including on Iraqi attempts since 1998 to acquire prohibited items, and by recommending sites to be inspected, persons to be interviewed, conditions of such interviews, and data to be collected, the results of which shall be reported to the Council by UNMOVIC and the IAEA;

11. Directs the Executive Chairman of UNMOVIC and the Director-General of the IAEA to report immediately to the Council any interference by Iraq with inspection activities, as well as any failure by Iraq to comply with its disarmament obligations, including its obligations regarding inspections under this resolution;

12. Decides to convene immediately upon receipt of a report in accordance with paragraphs 4 or 11 above, in order to consider the situation and the need for full compliance with all of the relevant Council resolutions in order to secure international peace and security;

13. Recalls, in that context, that the Council has repeatedly warned Iraq that it will face serious consequences as a result of its continued violations of its obligations;

14. Decides to remain seized of the matter.

BIBLIOGRAPHY

Books cited

The British Yearbook of International Law 1998

Christine Gray, *International Law and the Use of Force*, Oxford 2000

Antonio Cassesse, *International Law*, Oxford 2001

Yoram Dinstein, *War Aggression and Self-Defence*, 3rd Edn, 2001, Chs 6-9

Kriangsak Kittichaisare, *International Criminal Law*, OUP 2001

Ingrid Detter, *The Law of War*, 2nd Edn Cambridge University Press, 2000

Deiter Fleck, *The Handbook of Humanitarian Law in Armed Conflicts*, 2000

Clive Lewis, *Judicial Remedies in Public Law*, 2nd Ed 2000.

Max Planck Yearbook of United Nations Law, Eds Frowein & Wolfrum, 1998

The United Nations and the Development of Collective Security, Oppenheim's International Law 9th Edn 1991, ed R.Jennings and A. Watts

Danesh Saroshi, *The United Nations and the Development of Collective Security*, Oxford 1999,

Bruno Simma, Ed., *The Charter of the United Nations*, 2nd Ed., 2002.

The United Nations and the Iraq-Kuwait Conflict, UN Blue Book Series Vol IX, 1990-1996 (1996).

Zamir & Woolf, *The Declaratory Judgement*, 3rd Edn, 2002.Danesh Saroshi,

Journal articles

Constantine Antonopolos, 'The Unilateral Use of Force by States After the end of the Cold War' *JACL* 1999 117, p155.

Neils Blokker, 'Is the Authorisation authorised? Powers and Practice of the UN Security Council to authorise the Use of Force by "Coalitions of the Able and Willing"' *EJIL* 2000 11, p541.

Michael Byers, 'Terrorism, the Use of Force and International Law after 11 September', *ICLQ*,

(51 *ICLQ* 401).

O'Connell, 'Evidence of Terror', *Jnl of Conflict and Security Law*, 7, Issue 1, April 2002: pp19-36

O'Connell, 'The Legality of the 1993 US Missile Strike on Iraq and the right of Self-Defence in International Law' 45 *ICLQ*, 162 (1996).

Thomas Franck, 'Legal Authority for the possible use of force against Iraq', *ASIL* Proceedings 1998, UN Document S/PV, 4644,8.11.2002.

Christine Gray, 'After the Ceasefire: Iraq, the Security Council and the Use of Force', *BYIL* 1994 135, p162.

Christine Gray, 'From Unity to Polarisation: International Law and the Use of force against Iraq', *EJIL* 2002 131, p22.

'International Law in a Changing Legal System' *CLJ* 1999 78 p.94. (U of Cambridge Rede Lecture Oct 1998).

Jules Lobel and Michael Ratner, 'Bypassing the Security Council, Ambiguous Authorisations to use force, Cease-fires and the Iraqi Inspection Regime', 1999 *AJIL* 124, p127.

M.Wood, The Interpretation of Security Council resolutions' *Max Plank Yearbook of United Nations Law 2, 73.*

Web Sites

World Court Project UK	www.gn.apc.org/wcp
Peacerights	www.peacerights.com
Matrix Chambers	www.matrixlaw.co.uk
Human Rights Watch	www.hrw.org/
Campaign for Nuclear Disarmament	www.cnduk.org/
Public Interest Lawyers	www.publicinterestlawyers.co.uk/
Legal Action Against War	www.laaw.org/

SOME ABBREVIATIONS USED IN THE TEXT

AC	Appeal Cases
AJIL	American Journal of International Law
ASIL	American Society of International Law
BYIL	British Yearbook of International Law
CCSU	Council of Civil Service Unions
CLJ	Cambridge Law Journal
CPAG	Child Poverty Action Group
EuLR	European Law Reports
EWCA	England and Wales Court of Appeal
FLR	Family Law Reports
ICLQ	International and Comparative Law Quarterly
ICTR	International Criminal Tribunal for Rwanda
ICTY	International Criminal Tribunal for former Yugoslavia
JACL	Journal of Armed Conflict Law
PNICC	Preparatory Commission for the International Criminal Court
QB	Queen's Bench
SIAC	Special Immigration Appeals Commission
UKHL	United Kingdom House of Lords
WLR	Weekly Law Reports

The Legal Inquiry was launched in August 2002 by:

Jenny Bailey	Brighton Quaker Peace and Social Witness
George Farebrother	World Court Project UK
Nicola Freedman	Public Interest Lawyers
Rob Grant	Birmingham Stop the War Coalition
Nick Kollerstrom	Institute for Law and Peace
Mark Levene	Department of History, Southampton University
Juliet McBride	Nukewatch UK
Di McDonald	Nuclear Information Service
Glen Rangwala	Newnham College, Cambridge
Phil Shiner	Public Interest Lawyers and Peacerights
Chris Spain	Brighton Quaker Peace and Social Witness
James Thring	Legal Action Against War
Andrew Williams	School of Law, University of Warwick, and Peacerights

Editors

George Farebrother: 67 Summerheath Rd, Hailsham, Sussex, BN27 3DR, 01323 844 269, geowcpuk@gn.apc.org

Nick Kollerstrom: 9Primrose Gardens, London NW3 4UJ 020 7 722 8196, nk@astro3.demon.co.uk

This edition was partially financed by the Institute for Law and Peace from the Ted Dunn Memorial Fund.

INDEX

THE CASE AGAINST WAR

*"The Case Against War" is an excellent collection of the material which
establishes beyond doubt that the war against Iraq was unlawful.
It should be in every library*

MARK LITTMAN QC

*'The calm logic and rigour of legal reasoning of the highest calibre is
brought to bear in presenting the case for and against the legality at
international law of the impending intervention, purportedly in
support of the authority of the UN*

LORD R.K.MURRAY, FORMER LORD ADVOCATE OF SCOTLAND

*I think that there is an ever-increasing need for the public to be reminded of
the legal principles underlying any decision concerning the use of power to
wage war in the context of the UN Charter when politicians consistently
mislead us on the legal basis and justification for the war in Iraq.*

MIKE MANSFIELD QC

*"We're being told a lot about the doctrine of pre-emptive strikes...
Given that our Defence Secretary Geoff Hoon explicitly threatened
to use 'our' nuclear weapons system, Trident, against the Iraqi civilians
in the Defence Committee of the House of Commons on 20 March
would it not be essential in a democracy, given the fundamental commitment
we have to the rule of law.... for a UK citizen to challenge that decision if it
was in breach of international humanitarian law?
As a lawyer, I say it is."*

PHIL SHINER, PEACERIGHTS SOLICITOR
'THE FUTURE OF DEMOCRACY' IMPERIAL COLLEGE,
NOVEMBER 2, 2002.

*"In my view it is unthinkable that the national courts would entertain a
challenge to a Government decision to declare war or to authorise the use of
armed force against a third country".*

MR JUSTICE RICHARDS IN CND'S HIGH COURT CASE,
DECEMBER 2002